POWER GRAB

Also by Jason Chaffetz

The Deep State

POWER GRAB

THE LIBERAL SCHEME TO UNDERMINE TRUMP, THE GOP, AND OUR REPUBLIC

JASON CHAFFETZ

BROADSIDE BOOKS

An Imprint of HarperCollins*Publishers*

HarperCollins books may be purchased for educational, business, or sales promotional use. For information, please email the Special Markets Department at SPsales@harpercollins.com.

Broadside Books™ and the Broadside logo are trademarks of HarperCollins Publishers.

Library of Congress Cataloging-in-Publication Data has been applied for.

ISBN 978-0-06-294442-9

19 20 21 22 23   LSC   10 9 8 7 6 5 4 3 2 1

"Seek first to understand, then to be understood."

—STEPHEN R. COVEY

"First you win the argument, then you win the votes."

—PRIME MINISTER MARGARET THATCHER

Dedicated to those who want to be part of the solution, not part of the problem.

"I think we're a superior branch, quite frankly."

—NANCY PELOSI

CONTENTS

POWER GRAB

INTRODUCTION: THE LAST TOWN HALL

The opening line of a call to action on a *Daily Kos* message board said it all: "How is it that Trump is not being investigated for treason?" wrote the author, who posted under the name Archprogressive. Just three weeks after Donald Trump's shocking presidential victory over Hillary Clinton, the Russia collusion narrative was already in full swing.

The soon-to-be president's alleged treasonous crimes had quickly become an article of faith among true leftist believers. In this post, Archprogressive laid out the case: Donald Trump "had a computer that communicated only with a Russian bank." The Russian government had "hacked at least two election databases"— a claim that implied votes had been changed. The allegations suggested Trump had "borrowed money from the Russians."

Then came the call to action. The call had already gone viral by this point, having been repeated by countless activists, non-profits, pundits, and celebrities in the progressive universe. "If everyone opposing Trump's takeover of our government calls the local office of their Senators & Congress person as well as President Obama every day," wrote Archprogressive, "and demand that Trump be investigated for the treasonous act of colluding with the Russians to influence the presidential election, we might be able to stop Trump from getting into office."

That was a tall order. But progressives pursued it with alacrity.

Without a shred of evidence, many of those theories would be easily debunked. But in the weeks between the election and the inauguration, speculation ran wild. The desperate frenzy to stop Donald Trump from even being sworn in called for congressional intervention. That intervention, so the theory went, would have to come from the committee I chaired.

As a result, many of the calls to action included the number of the House Committee on Oversight and Government Reform as well as those of my D.C. and Utah congressional offices. The calls overwhelmed every office and every voice mail box for many weeks. At one point, someone even posted to Reddit the direct line of the House Oversight Committee staff.

It was in this environment that I decided to host a town hall in my deep Red Utah congressional district. I love doing town hall meetings. They give me an opportunity to explain the backstory that constituents don't always get to hear. I love the dialogue, the differences of opinion, the aha moments when constituents learn something they didn't know before.

Although there have often been wide differences of opinion at these events, they remained productive and respectful. Prior to what would be my last town hall, my biggest such event was an August 2010 event attended by more than one thousand people concerned about the very predictable (and ultimately accurate) projected shortcomings of the so-called Affordable Care Act. Although people on both sides of the issue were angry, we managed to maintain a civil, productive discussion. I think we had a local police officer or two on hand to provide security. But never at any time did I feel I was putting constituents in physical danger by inviting them to a public town hall. That would all change with the progressive backlash to the election of President Donald Trump.

Given the heartburn from so many on the left over the election of President Trump, I opted to schedule the town hall in the most moderate area of my district—a city nestled along Salt Lake County's majestic Wasatch mountains and the last stop before ascending the canyons that contain the Greatest Snow on Earth. Cottonwood Heights, Utah, was more than happy to host. Little did it know this town hall would not be the event any of us were expecting.

When we booked this routine event, we expected heated debate. But we had no way of knowing that national opposition groups would see it as a chance for televised performance theater. Within hours of our announcing the date, unusual things began to happen.

Our offices and the Cottonwood Heights city offices began receiving phone calls from people requesting information about the town hall. But unlike past town halls, many of the callers were irate—and many seemed to be reading from the same script. Cottonwood Heights police chief Robbie Russo remembers, "The city was barraged with phone calls. Social media that we monitor as a common practice blew up. It was inciting people to attend from outside the city, which is never a good indicator that it's going to be a peaceful event."

Indeed, announcements began circulating throughout the metro area, within the state and beyond, in left-leaning Facebook groups, on Twitter, and in mass emails from activist organizations. The event was announced several weeks early, which gave opposition groups lots of time to organize, book flights, and engage a full media blitz.

In our congressional offices, we noticed many of the rude calls we received originated from area codes outside of Utah. The vast majority of calls—both local and long distance—all asked a similar question: "Will you be checking ID at the door?" It didn't take long to figure out why. The callers wanted to make sure they wouldn't be turned away for not residing in the district. Like most representatives, I did not check IDs and didn't care if people outside of my district wanted to attend my town halls. We welcomed all comers, and I tried to be just as responsive to visitors.

Recognizing that this town hall would likely attract more people than our usual one hundred to two hundred constituents, we quickly moved the venue from the Cottonwood Heights City Hall to the Brighton High School auditorium across the street, where we knew we could seat up to one thousand people. Even that venue would prove to be too small, but for the safety of everyone involved, we were advised not to go any larger.

At that point, we still had no clear picture of the extent of the other side's coordination. But we did catch wind of a few ominous developments.

Not long after the calls began, we were given a screenshot of a Facebook group called Utah Indivisible, in which plans were being finalized for disruptive behavior at our town hall. They even had a training manual (produced by national, nonlocal groups) providing a how-to primer for disrupting and derailing town halls. They called it "Indivisible: A Practical Guide for Resisting the Trump Agenda." The plans were very detailed. Fortunately for us, they were also very public.

The Security Challenge

You're going to get death threats. If you serve in the United States Congress and you do anything at all controversial, someone somewhere will get angry and become unhinged. You have to take it seriously, but unfortunately, threats are not all that unusual. I once had a man leave me a voice mail suggesting he would find me and string me up on a light post. Another tweeted that he would shoot me in the head and yet another would slit my throat. Some threats were hand delivered. Some targeted my wife or my children. Direct threats were unusual but not unexpected.

This was different. We were not dealing with a few isolated

cases of mental instability. We needed to be prepared to respond to real constituents with genuine fears and concerns. Against all odds, Donald Trump had just been inaugurated as the forty-fifth president of the United States. Despondent Hillary Clinton voters were still, two months later, trying to process the results of an election for which they had been wholly unprepared. They sincerely believed America had made a terrible mistake.

In their minds, nothing less than our democracy was at stake. At this point, many of them saw Donald Trump as a modern-day iteration of Adolf Hitler, intent on plundering the Treasury, selling us out to the Russians, and reenergizing the Ku Klux Klan. Elected officials, activist groups, celebrities, and media pundits had been ratcheting up the hysteria for months.

In what they rationalize as a noble effort to save democracy, any means justify those ends. The only problem with this story is practically everything about it.

Fortunately, opposition organizers tipped their hand early enough for a savvy local chief of police and his extraordinarily professional team to have a few surprises in store for the would-be anarchists descending on Cottonwood Heights.

Now aware that scheming was under way to disrupt the event, the Cottonwood Heights Police Department (CHPD) went to work. They obtained a copy of the Indivisible Guide so they could be prepared for the planned disruptions. Working with my security team, they performed threat assessments, did a site survey of the venue, and put contingency plans in place. I credit them with the fact that we saw no violence that night.

I won't lie—the conclusions of the initial threat assessment were disconcerting. But police assured us that the department had the training and personnel to control access to the venue, to calm the crowd, and to get me out safely when the event concluded. They were right.

"This one felt like a legitimate threat," said Detective Brent Jex, a West Jordan City police officer who headed my private security team and warned my wife to stay away from the event. "Let's be honest," Jex said. "Sometimes security stuff is window dressing—the appearance of security versus the actual need. When it came to this one, I knew early on it was something that Julie Chaffetz shouldn't attend. From a security standpoint, we didn't want her there. Our hands were going to be full enough protecting Jason."

Since this was not the first time left-wing groups had used the Indivisible Guide to disrupt a town hall, Chief Russo called around to police departments in other states to find out what tactics to expect. One department told him their biggest mistake at an event the previous week was opting to have too visual a SWAT team presence, which only provoked the crowd.

Instead, Chief Russo wisely planned to deploy a mixture of uniformed and plainclothes officers to keep the police presence from feeling overwhelming, even though some thirty officers would work the event with more available if needed.

"We did not have a visual presence," Russo said. "We had snipers out there. We had all the tools. But we didn't make it obvious." Russo had even arranged with the Salt Lake County sheriff's office to have transport in place (but not visible) in case mass arrests became necessary. They ran bomb dogs through the venue before seating anyone and kept dogs nearby in case they were needed. To take such precautions for a simple town hall was unprecedented and something none of us wished to see.

On the day of the event, we learned national news crews planned to be on-site. That should have been the first hint that something didn't add up. I was one of 435 members of Congress. I had just won my reelection with a convincing victory. My Democrat opponent had momentarily caught fire among social media progressives sufficient to raise a quick half-million online campaign dollars, which constituted her fifteen minutes of fame.

After her fifteen minutes were over, I won with 73 percent in a "contested" race. Why would national and cable news show up at my humble little town hall? What made cable assignment editors think this particular event would be sufficiently newsworthy to scramble camera crews all the way out in Utah?

With a 7:00 start time, most of my constituents expected to be able to show up at 6:30 or 6:45—as at town halls past. But this time was different. We received a report from the high school that people were hanging around in the parking lot and trying to get into the school during the lunch hour—while school was still in session! Some were upset that neither the school nor the police would allow them to choose a seat in the auditorium hours ahead of the event. By 5:30, the line wound around the building, taking on the aspect of a somewhat malevolent festival.

We later learned that the opposition groups had instructed their people to show up at least two hours early. That tactic successfully crowded out genuine constituents unaware that the seats would all be filled by those in line two hours or more ahead of time. It was an effective way to silence opposing views without having to shout them down. It worked. The auditorium was packed with hard-left progressives, many from outside my district, while constituents not aligned with progressive groups were left outside at the back of the line.

What was the point of crowding out opposing voices? Presumably, they were there because they thought we had elected a fascist tyrant who would threaten their rights and suppress their speech. Yet here they were, conspiring to pack the venue with a united voice of opposition. Did they believe I would be hoodwinked into believing my district had taken a hard-left turn overnight?

As the opposition groups arrived at the venue, the CHPD began to execute their carefully developed plans. Officers began cordially greeting early arrivals and quickly ascertained that many were not local residents. "We made it a point to walk through the crowd and shake people's hands, introducing ourselves," Russo explained. "I talked to them, introduced myself. I asked each of them where they were from. And they would tell me. They weren't locals. I remember some from Washington State, Portland, lots of different places."

The interactions seemed to follow a pattern. They would ask if police were IDing people before they could go in and if anyone would be stopped. My staff and the police officers all reported talking to people who had come from Colorado, Arizona, Nevada, California, and one group reportedly saying they had flown in from New York. Even the ones who were from Utah often reported coming from areas I did not represent. Liberal bastions outside my district, such as the ski resort community of Park City and deep Blue Salt Lake City, were reportedly well represented that night.

As planned, the officers simply welcomed people and let them know police were available if they needed anything. They were friendly, welcoming, and nonconfrontational. They educated people about what was acceptable behavior and what would not be tolerated. I believe the professional and friendly demeanor of the CHPD was disarming and was instrumental in diffusing the worst of the tension that night.

At one point, a uniformed officer reported seeing a group in black bandannas openly carrying weapons. They were not local, according to Russo. Utah is an open-carry state, so there was nothing illegal in simply possessing weapons. Police did not approach them.

All in all, the crowd outside, while disappointed not to have been admitted, was better behaved than the cohort inside the venue.

Inside, as the meeting began, things were less settled. We kicked things off in the usual manner but to a much different response. As instructed by organizers, the audience attempted to shout me down on every question. Thanks to the manual, we knew ahead of time how the organizers had instructed attendees to take control of the meeting and prevent me from answering questions, to disrupt the dialogue and incite an incident.

Everything about the opposition was calculated. They were specifically instructed to spread out among the seats to create the illusion of consensus. The Indivisible Guide reads, "Do not all sit together. Sit by yourself or in groups of 2, and spread out throughout the room. This will help reinforce the impression of broad consensus." They even orchestrated the applause. The guide reads, "After one member of your group asks a question, everyone should applaud to show that the feeling is shared throughout the audience. Whenever someone from your group gets the mic, they should note that they're building on the previous questions— amplifying the fact that you're part of a broad group."

Who were they trying to deceive with this performance? These strategies are designed to create an illusion of unanimity. Who were they trying to persuade? The audience was filled with like-minded people. The crowd would have been content to drown me out all night. I was not their target audience. So, who was?

The Indivisible Guide offers this advice: record everything. ". . . unfavorable exchanges caught on video can be devastating for MoCs [Members of Congress]. These clips can be shared through social media and picked up by local and national media."

There is the answer. The whole thing was intended to be political theater for a national news audience. It was a show—a highly choreographed, carefully orchestrated, nationally directed pageant for coastal elites to feast upon, comfort for the broken souls of the progressive left.

Both in and outside the venue, people were supporting extreme left-wing positions that actual Utah 3rd Congressional District voters resoundingly rejected by large majorities. For example, the most vociferous, visceral reaction of the night came when I said Mike Pence was a good person. This audience exploded with catcalls and jeers.

Who were these people? Even allowing for the fact that this town hall was in a more moderate area of my district, the unified trigger response to the mention of the vice president's name was notable. The voters of my district may have had some concerns about Donald Trump, but they love Mike Pence. This crowd was triggered by him.

According to the guide, questions were scripted, with each supporter choosing from the same list of questions provided by organizers. Attendees were encouraged to "Look friendly or neutral so that staffers will call on you." Then, "Don't give up the mic until you're satisfied with the answer," because staffers might try to "limit your ability to follow up" by taking the mic back. The guide tells them to hold firm "because no staffer in their right mind wants to look like they're physically intimidating a constituent, so they will back off."

The guide further instructs, "If they object, then say politely but loudly: 'I'm not finished. The Congressman/woman is dodging my question. Why are you trying to stop me from following up?'" We had done enough research to know what this advice looked like in practice. They wouldn't just use the microphone for follow-up questions. They would use it to wrest control of the meeting and essentially hijack the event, hoping it would descend into chaos. Any answer to a question that was not the progressive answer would be rejected and would trigger a follow-up with an allegation of dodging the question. Fortunately, we were prepared for that. All this instruction on how to dominate the microphone and use it to disrupt and intimidate would turn out to be wasted effort.

Had the crowd been actual constituents who had attended our past town halls, they would have known this tactic was a dead end. I've never set up more than one microphone at a town hall meeting, and that one was for me. I always take a lot of questions but insist that the audience allow questions to be heard without a mic. I'm very aware that people come to hear me explain why I voted the way I did. They don't come to listen to someone "ask questions" that sound a lot more like a Senate filibuster or a courtroom interrogation.

My constituents have never appreciated the person who tried to take over the meeting. So, I have always called on people myself, had them ask their questions without a mic, then repeated their questions for the broader audience if the volume was a problem.

The protestors, having never been to our town halls, did not expect to be unamplified. It messed up their chi, so to speak. They complained bitterly during and after the town hall, angry that their plans had been thwarted. They could cry foul all they wanted; it was the right decision. Maintaining control of the microphone allowed me to turn down the temperature when the crowd got aggressive, ensuring the safety and security of everyone there. I hate to think what might have happened had things gotten any more heated than they already were.

Who Will Resist the Resistance?

Why are they destroying the town hall as an American institution? To save democracy, of course! It is the story of the post-2016 political left. As the succeeding chapters will demonstrate, political theater has become a substitute for public policy.

This is a book about what happens when one political party decides that to save democracy they must subvert it. To protect free speech, they must silence it. To fend off fascism, they must practice it. To promote good public policy, they must resist it. In the end, it appears that to uphold the rule of law, some felt they must violate it.

Throughout this book, we'll explore two emerging patterns in American politics. The first is the left's deliberate substitution of political theater in place of any real policy agenda. The second and more disturbing pattern is the use of authoritarian tactics to defeat perceived authoritarianism. We will look at which side poses the *real* authoritarian threat. We consistently get this conflict wrong. We misunderstand what politicians are doing, and the media misinterprets the reasons they're doing it. The hysteria sweeping the left is shaping our country in ways we've failed to appreciate, and with results that may matter more to our future than anything President Trump has accomplished.

The resistance talks so much about saving democracy that they've obscured the extent to which they threaten it. Sure, they sought to overturn a free and fair election, but it wasn't clear at first that they didn't intend to stop there. They want to manipulate our election process to permanently tilt the playing field in their favor. All in the name of protecting freedom and fairness, naturally.

In the chapters that follow, I'll show why we're still not taking this threat seriously enough. The Democrats are playing a high-stakes game, gambling with the most prosperous economy and the most stable government in the history of the world. For what? Power.

I would argue we don't see the approaching crisis clearly enough. Should we lose our prized institutions, we may never see them restored. Seemingly small procedural changes could have far-reaching repercussions in the life of every American. Show trials, ballot fraud, quiet rule changes, political donation laundering—the list of outrages is long and growing longer. But the main puzzle remains: why do the Democrats think they are the good guys here?

The Escape

Back at the town hall, the tension was peaking. "It was definitely a powder keg just waiting for one little spark," Jex said, adding, "Honestly, the spark was almost there. Had it gone on another ten–fifteen minutes, it would have erupted."

We had known ahead of time that my exit from the event might prove challenging. We were prepared. Even during the program, my security detail was on high alert at all times. I stood alone on the front of a stage, backed by curtains. On either side, hidden from view, two beefy, athletic off-duty cops (who are my friends) stood like guard dogs at the ready on both sides. A third officer mostly waited directly behind me, hidden by the curtains. Had someone rushed the stage, the reaction would have been swift and physical. Though unarmed, the assailant would have been quickly subdued, and I'd have been whisked out the back. I hoped nothing like that would happen, but we were ready if something did.

That still left the matter of leaving the venue. A group at another event had mobbed a congressman's car as he exited the hall. In that case, the car had been some distance away, forcing the congressman to run the gauntlet on foot through a crowd of rowdy protestors. "There's no winning on that," Russo said, so an evasion plan took shape.

Chief Russo happened to drive the same model vehicle as I did. So, the chief parked his unit at the top of the school's driveway with officers standing around it as if securing the area. During the event, they kept checking the car, walking around it, making their presence obvious. They even stuck an American flag in the windshield.

Sure enough, the protestors surrounded the chief's car as the event concluded, hoping to corner me on my way out. Jex was there. "A group started to mobilize at the west end of the building," he remembers. "This was the same group that one of the CHPD uniformed officers reported brandishing guns earlier in the night. They were organizing a search for Jason's car. They were masked—bandannaed up."

"Operation Decoy" worked to plan. Drawing the menacing group's attention to Chief Russo's car created a window of opportunity for my exit from the venue. I won't reveal the exact plan that got me safely out, but I do recall a few harrowing Crazy Ivans (high-speed U-turns) at the hands of Mike Fullwood, an off-duty officer who also worked private security for me at the event.

Jex, who has done security for at least a dozen other town halls, remembers this one feeling different. "There wasn't that constituent feel," he said. "All the other events that Jason did, there was definitely a different feel based on how the constituents talked and interacted. In the past, even the people who were not fans of Jason, who asked critical questions, were not like this. It was a different mentality."

I share all that to fully illustrate the sea change in the public conduct we all witnessed that night. There was a malevolence, a barely subdued violence that dominated the night's events. It was like nothing we had seen before in Utah, certainly where a congressional town hall—one of the oldest customs of our representative republic—was concerned.

I don't think they got what they were after at my town hall, at least not if one cable news reporter I spoke with can be believed. But they had MSNBC, CNN, and other national outlets on hand just in case.

This opposition was far from organic. This was a reality show organized by groups outside my district, scripted and promoted like the professional public relations campaign it was, specifically designed to disappear the conservative supermajority in Utah's 3rd Congressional District for the benefit of cable TV news audiences.

What did the national media think was going to happen? I can't say for sure, but given my conversation with the cable news reporter, it's fair to say the event was less explosive than promised. As loud and unruly as it may have been, that town hall did not deliver all that the outside instigators had implied.

They were looking for violence and chaos. Great staff preparation; an excellent display of community policing, crowd control, and crisis deescalation; and some terrific on-the-fly tactical execution kept it from going where anarchist forces wanted to go.

My office had been contacted ahead of the town hall by a national cable news reporter who wanted to ensure she could get an on-camera interview with me at the event. To be as open and transparent as possible, I insisted on speaking with her myself earlier in the day to prepare for the interview.

I asked her, "Why are you here?" I was fascinated that she and others would come. I reminded her that I'm a Republican in Utah who won with 73 percent of the vote. It was January—we were less than thirty days into my new term. Why were they here? She admitted that they were told there was going to be a riot, perhaps a fire, and that this was something that they would want to be covering as a network.

Incredulous, I asked her, "Did you feel any duty or obligation to communicate that with law enforcement?" People were potentially going to be in harm's way. "Did you tell our campaign? Law enforcement?" I asked. Sheepishly she admitted they had not. We later confirmed with Chief Russo that none of the media outlets covering the event that night had contacted him to warn of the potential for violence. They all just kept quiet and showed up hoping for a figurative train wreck. It was justified as long as they got some good footage.

I told her, "You really need to think about who told you this." She told me the network had had conversations with some people in San Francisco about what would happen at a town hall in Utah. News outlets expected something violent to happen—and they were there to capitalize on the mayhem. That's what brought them there.

"You were getting used," I told her. "This was a setup." I appreciated her candor. She ended up not asking me to go on camera that night.

Now, there was no fire, no riot. There were no guns discharged, despite reports of people brandishing weapons. But given the tenor of the crowd, I credit the Cottonwood Heights Police Department and my team for maintaining the degree of order that prevailed. Their preemptive planning prevented the type of violence television crews had been warned to expect. But for the outstanding efforts of seasoned law enforcement professionals, the event might have ended very differently.

As far as Indivisible Utah was concerned, the event was a huge success. They got their national footage of a large crowd shouting down a congressman. But what price did they pay for that footage?

All across the country, elected officials began thinking twice about hosting town hall meetings. What representatives want to put their staff or their constituents at risk of physical harm? What community wants to pay overtime for three dozen or five dozen police officers to keep the peace at such an event? Certainly, there are still members of Congress doing town hall meetings—especially freshmen and those who serve on committees that pose no threat to the Democratic agenda.

The radicals target selectively. Here in Utah, my successor has hosted a number of town hall meetings without incident. But he is a freshman in a safe seat. Next door, in the 4th Congressional District, Representative Mia Love was perpetually targeted for harassment by Indivisible groups who saw her as vulnerable and who resented the threat she posed to the Democratic iconography of identity politics. Leftist nonprofits would spend heavily to unseat her in the next election. They would succeed by the narrowest of margins.

I didn't see then what I see so clearly now—not right away. That first town hall in the wake of a presidential election no one saw coming was just an opening salvo.

What happened that night was my first glimpse of the Democrats' bold new battle plan to deceive, intimidate, and overpower their opposition. I didn't grasp then the significance of what we were seeing—or what it portended. But I do now.

This made the Tea Party wave of 2010 look like, well, a tea party.

It was the opening skirmish of a battle in which Democrats would reveal their new willingness to gladly sacrifice the core institutions that made America great in exchange for absolute power. From the moment Donald Trump was elected, nothing would be so sacred to Democrats that it could not be repurposed or renounced in the single-minded pursuit of leftist dominance in every quarter. One of the first casualties, after the truth, would be the traditional town hall. But the quest for power in 2020 will see a long list of institutions politicized, weaponized, or otherwise sacrificed in a progressive power grab.

CHAPTER 1

MONETIZING ANGER

Nonprofits called it the Trump Bump. As a wave of televised despair and indignation overwhelmed Blue America on election night 2016, the unexpected electoral upset unleashed a powerful green wave of rage donations. In their anguish and despondency, progressive voters opened their checkbooks. But it wasn't just political campaigns on the receiving end of the cash flow. It was progressive nonprofit groups as well. The biggest bumps went to the 501(c)(4) advocacy nonprofits. Named for the section in the IRS code that defines them, 501(c)(4)s have some latitude to engage in political activities (provided that engagement is limited and nonpartisan). By contrast, 501(c)(3) charities, which we'll scrutinize in the next chapter, ostensibly have minimal ability to engage in politics.

Planned Parenthood received 80,000 donations in the first three days after the election. The American Civil Liberties Union (ACLU) reported receiving $7 million from 120 donors in the five days following Donald Trump's victory. By contrast, the *New*

York Times reported, the five days following President Obama's reelection brought in just $28,000 from 354 donors to the ACLU. Around the same time that I was holding my last town hall in late January 2017, the ACLU reported receiving $24 million in donations over a single weekend due to the release of the Trump administration's travel ban policy.

Nonprofit news outlets on the left also saw the bump. Pro Publica, best remembered by conservatives for publishing confidential tax information about conservative nonprofits requesting tax-exempt status in 2013, was among these. Pro Publica raised more money in the days following the Trump election—$750,000—than it raised in all of 2015. Inside Philanthropy reported similar large fund-raising bumps for the Center for Public Integrity, the Marshall Project, and NPR affiliates like WNYC.

This phenomenon dubbed "rage donating" lit up the nonprofit sector in the days and weeks following Hillary Clinton's epic election loss. It would continue to varying degrees throughout the Trump presidency, ultimately enabling Democrats to take back the House in the 2018 midterm elections.

Nonprofits Take Center Stage

The growing significance of the nonprofit sector in our political and electoral landscape will potentially have far-reaching implications for future elections. Well-meaning campaign finance reforms that require donor disclosure, cap campaign donations, prohibit foreign financing, and preclude the use of government resources for partisan activity may appear successful on the surface. But much of the activity that is now illegal in the campaign world has shifted to the nonprofit world. While this is true for both parties, the effect is far more pronounced on the left.

In the progressive-dominated nonprofit sector, partisan political activity is helping swing the results of elections using the very methods Congress has criminalized on the campaign side. With no limits on donations, no disclosure of who is donating, no means of discerning whether foreign governments are participating, and with minimal oversight, a growing list of political nonprofit advocacy groups operate freely and openly in the partisan political space.

The last two election cycles have shown that the impact of non-profit engagement in our political process has been profound. And it is growing, fueled by the tsunami of rage donations that have energized Democratic campaigns in the wake of the Trump presidency.

The same kind of energy might have propelled more significant fund-raising gains on the right in the heady days of the 2009 Tea Party movement had conservatives been able to access the kind of nonprofit infrastructure available to progressives. But many of the groups purporting to lead the Tea Party movement were formed after the fact and missed the big opportunities of the nascent movement's early days. They were not established nonprofits with large endowment funds, high name recognition, or extensive databases of supporters and volunteers. Furthermore, as Tea Party groups began cropping up around the country from 2009 to 2012, many had difficulty getting up and running in the face of unexplained IRS delays approving their applications for nonprofit status.

By contrast, the Trump Bump came at a time when the nonprofit world was already dominated by established left-leaning organizations, many of which control multimillion-dollar endowments, enjoy steady revenue from government contracts, and have a long history of political activism.

Rage donating has been good for nonprofit advocacy groups under both the Obama and the Trump administrations, benefiting groups across the political spectrum, though disproportionately favoring progressives. In my experience, the phenomenon also has a downside that sometimes had a counterproductive influence on our work in Congress.

Motivated by a pattern of rage-driven fund-raising hauls, political advocacy groups on the right and left had more incentive to drive that rage than to calm it. Efforts to shame anyone found working across the aisle resulted in greater polarization in Congress. Any attempt at bipartisanship or compromise spawned a fund-raising campaign or what was called a key vote—a vote that would appear on an end-of-year scorecard marketed to voters as a means to judge lawmaker performance. This was good news for partisans and purists, but in a form of government that depends on finding common ground to pass legislation, it intensified the gridlock in Congress.

The success of rage donating also gave rise to another problem: scams and scavengers on both the left and the right. I remember clearly the frustration of my colleague Representative Trey Gowdy, Republican of South Carolina, whose image was used repeatedly in fund-raising pitches during the height of his work on the Select Committee on Benghazi, which was investigating the September 11, 2012, terrorist attack on an American diplomatic facility in Libya. Ads would appear telling viewers to "help Trey Gowdy" by donating money. But none of that money ever actually went to Representative Gowdy's campaign or any campaign that we knew of. Every time he turned around there was a new ad on the internet. His campaign never got a dime of it. He felt terrible that there were people all across the country sending in money and we had no idea where it was actually going.

Despite the downside of nonprofit political engagement, the practice is likely here to stay. Monetizing political anger may have become too lucrative for politicians to give up. Whether we like it or not, the practice of politicizing nonprofit entities is now a driving force in American politics. But it is one that potentially poses an existential threat to the Republican Party.

An Uneven Playing Field

While American voters may be aware of nonprofit engagement in elections, they may not realize just how much that engagement favors progressive candidates and causes.

During my work on the House Oversight Committee, I had an opportunity to take a meeting with someone who had done a deep dive into the public filings of certain nonprofit charities.

"There's something really fishy about the way these charities are raising money," the woman told me, pulling out graph after graph of fund-raising numbers for some of America's biggest non-profits. A veteran of many nonprofit audits herself, the woman had approached my office in 2016 with information she wanted the House Oversight Committee to look into. "If I were working for the IRS, I would be auditing every one of these," she said, pointing to a list of large, high-profile charities. The one thing these charities all had in common? They were all associated with progressive politics.

This wasn't the first time I had been shown evidence of the Democrats' success in using nonprofits as political weapons. The seeds of this practice—acorns as it were—were first planted in my mind back in 2009.

I was a freshman member of the House Oversight Committee at that time, but we had jurisdiction of the upcoming census. Democrats had controlled the House, the Senate, and the presidency in the years leading up to the census, which meant they got to dictate the terms under which it would take place.

In an effort to find 1.4 million temporary workers to conduct the census, the government partnered with hundreds of nonprofit organizations to help count a U.S. population in excess of 300 million people. Among these groups was the Association of Community Organizations for Reform Now (ACORN), which was a collection of local charity organizations operating under a national umbrella.

Ostensibly, ACORN was created to advocate for low-income families. But by the time the group engaged with the census, it already had a long history of fraudulent voter registration efforts dating back to 1998 in Arkansas, Missouri, and Pennsylvania. In 2007, Washington State filed felony charges on a number of ACORN employees for falsely submitting in excess of seventeen hundred fraudulent voter registrations there. The organization also had a history of wage violations. On top of that, ACORN had covered up a $1 million embezzlement scandal by the brother of one of its founders.

In spite of all that history, the left-leaning ACORN had received $48 million in federal grants and contracts between 2005 and 2009, according to a Government Accountability Office (GAO) audit. That same audit found that "of 22 investigations and cases of election and voter registration fraud and wage violations involving ACORN or potentially related organizations from fiscal years 2005 through 2009, most were closed without prosecution. One of the eight cases and investigations identified by the Department of Justice resulted in guilty pleas by eight defendants to voter registration fraud and seven were closed without action due to insufficient, or a lack of, evidence."

None of that stopped the U.S. Census Bureau in early 2009 from partnering with ACORN to send workers door-to-door counting every person in the country. These would be from the same pool of workers accused of submitting false voter registrations in the names of Mickey Mouse and Donald Duck in previous election cycles. I and many of my colleagues on the committee expressed serious concerns about the group's history of fraud allegations and its well-documented partisan agenda.

Ultimately, the public outcry stemming from an undercover video operation exposing ACORN's deceptive practices helped scuttle the partnership with the census. But this was just the beginning of a growing strategy to use voter registration as a pretext for nonprofits to engage in political activities intended to impact election outcomes to favor Democrats.

Flash forward to 2016. I was chair of the House Oversight Committee, and once again I was being shown evidence of partisan activity by Democratic-aligned nonprofits that claimed to be nonpartisan. The woman who brought me this information, which I'll cover in the next chapter, had serious concerns about the overwhelming influence of partisan Democrats she was seeing throughout the whole nonprofit sector.

Of course, the groups on her list weren't the groups the IRS had been interested in auditing up to that point. These groups all leaned left. But as we all remember, the nonprofit groups garnering all the IRS attention beginning in 2013 were the ones on a BOLO (Be On the Lookout) list containing words like "tea party," "patriot," and "9/12 project" in their names. Democratic allies in the news media faithfully reported at the time that progressive groups were also flagged for review, but a subsequent audit by the Treasury Inspector General for Tax Administration (TIGTA) dispelled the notion that the targeting was bipartisan.

The fear exhibited by Democrats and their IRS allies during the 2013 targeting scandal seemed like an overreaction at the time. Why did they see conservative-leaning nonprofits as such a threat?

After digging into some of the publicly available nonprofit filings, I now wonder if the apparent overreaction by the IRS was a classic case of projection. With a career community organizer at the helm of the executive branch—one who had worked with ACORN himself in 1992—Obama's IRS may have been fearful that Republicans would figure out how to do what Democrats were already doing. A review of nonprofit filings since 2013, which we'll scrutinize in a moment, will show the type of partisan activity senior IRS officials may have been overlooking on the left in their zeal to pursue conservative advocacy groups. Data from progressive groups during the exact time period of the Tea Party scrutiny is difficult to analyze given that disclosure laws only require tax filings to be publicly available for three years.

Today ACORN's work is continued by an army of progressive volunteers who use voter registration drives as a pretext for helping progressive candidates win.

While the left-leaning bias of America's largest advocacy nonprofits will come as no surprise to conservatives, the extent to which some are engaged in partisan political activities is greatly underestimated.

No comparable infrastructure exists on the right, partly because of the dominance of Democrats in an industry dependent on big government spending. After learning more about how Democrats are using nonprofits, I decided to compare the public tax filings of the largest conservative groups with the numbers I was seeing on the left. I found that the scale of conservative nonprofits is dwarfed by the scale of progressive ones.

The patterns we see on the left are not repeated on the right. Besides, to duplicate the tactics we're seeing from the left, conservatives would need to create more of their own nonprofits— something a politically weaponized Obama-era IRS worked hard to prevent. Even many of the conservative nonprofits that sought 501(c)(4) status after 2010 and won an apology from the Justice Department for the scandal have since been targeted for audits. Judicial Watch reports that in February 2014, then-chairman of the House Ways and Means Committee Dave Camp, Republican of Michigan, testified about improper IRS targeting of existing conservative groups:

> Additionally, we now know that the IRS targeted not only right-leaning applicants, but also right-leaning groups that were already operating as 501(c)(4)s. At Washington, DC's direction, dozens of groups operating as 501(c)(4)s were flagged for IRS surveillance, including monitoring of the groups' activities, websites and any other publicly available information. Of these

groups, 83 percent were right-leaning. And of the groups the IRS selected for audit, 100 percent were right-leaning.

Through a Freedom of Information Act request, Judicial Watch was able to uncover emails and other documents confirming that the IRS not only used donor disclosures to identify targets, but chose those targets based on their politics. Judicial Watch uncovered snarky messages about the U.S. Chamber of Commerce, special interest in Karl Rove's Crossroads GPS nonprofit, and acknowledgments that interest in the issue on Capitol Hill was related to the upcoming elections.

Social Welfare as a Pretext for Partisan Politics

The proliferation of social welfare and advocacy nonprofits capitalizing on rage donations has polarized our politics in new ways. These groups were ideally suited to operate in this role, because our largest and most successful charitable nonprofits have already been functioning as fronts for political fund-raising. Using their venerable histories of social welfare work, they are able to trade on their credibility as nonprofits to generate donations that are ostensibly intended for nonprofit work, but that may actually be converted to partisan political campaign activity.

For some of America's most successful nonprofits, their original purpose has become little more than a side hustle. Their real purpose is now to fund and promote progressive politics.

Nowhere is this problem more apparent than at the Southern Poverty Law Center (SPLC), ostensibly operating to fight intolerance. The group is known for its hate map that in 2018 identified 1,020 organizations provocatively labeled by SPLC as hate groups. The term is designed to inflame passions and open wallets—the real purpose of the SPLC. But the group's targets are frequently not purveyors of hate, but purveyors of ideas SPLC cannot tolerate.

In 2010, SPLC labeled the Christian group Family Research Council as a hate group. The justification? The group "hates" the LGBT community because they object to policies supported by that community, such as hate crime laws, gay marriage, and gay scout leaders. SPLC claims Family Research Council has embraced "junk science" to raise concerns about LGBT parenting. Instead of taking issue with that "junk science" in the marketplace of ideas, SPLC simply labels these organizations with a debate-killing epithet.

Soon after Family Research Council appeared on the hate list, the organization was the target of a politically motivated shooting in 2012. Telling a security guard at the organization's Virginia headquarters that he disagreed with the group's politics, a twenty-eight-year-old gay rights volunteer carrying a 9 mm handgun and fifteen Chick-fil-A sandwiches opened fire. The shooter later told investigators he planned to shoot as many people as possible and then smear the Chick-fil-A sandwiches in their faces as a political statement.

Conservative backlash to SPLC following the attack received muted media coverage of the "conservatives pounce" variety, suggesting there was no way to know for sure whether SPLC's hate designation motivated the shooter. The shooter himself laid those concerns to rest in subsequent interviews with federal investigators. In video obtained from the FBI by Family Research Council, the shooter can be heard saying, "Southern Poverty Law lists anti-gay groups. I found them online, did a little research, went to the website, stuff like that."

Even as SPLC points the finger at the tiniest organizations on the right, major violent movements like Antifa on the left get a pass. The group has lobbed bricks and glass bottles at police, thrown Molotov cocktails and smashed windows on the University of California, Berkeley campus, slashed tires of right-wing activists, and doxxed 1,595 U.S. Immigration and Customs Enforcement (ICE) officers by publishing their names and photographs. Despite

Antifa's pattern of violence, SPLC president Richard Cohen told Congress, "Antifa is not a group that vilifies people on the basis of race, ethnicity, religion and the like." He told the *Washington Free Beacon* in 2017, "There might be forms of hate out there that you may consider hateful, but it's not the type of hate we follow." We all know what type of "hate" they follow.

What's not hateful to the SPLC? Apparently when the governor of Virginia, a Democrat, appears in a yearbook photo allegedly either wearing blackface or dressed as a Ku Klux Klansman, that incident merits no response from the fighters of hate at SPLC. When it comes to hate on the left, SPLC's approach is to see no evil, hear no evil.

In the fight against hate and intolerance on the right, SPLC deploys both. The results are nothing if not profitable. The organization sits on a $471 million endowment. In 2017, thanks in part to the anger resulting from the violent riots in Charlottesville, Virginia, SPLC raised $132 million.

Public reporting indicates SPLC has moved $121 million to offshore accounts. The reports don't indicate how the offshore dollars are invested, but in its 2015 business tax filings, Southern Poverty Law Center reported having bank accounts in the Cayman Islands, Bermuda, and the British Virgin Islands. The Cayman Islands is a well-known tax haven. An investigation by the *Washington Free Beacon* uncovered tax forms showing transfers to Cayman Islands bank accounts and foreign partnerships totaling millions of dollars.

With its vaunted history of winning lawsuits against the Ku Klux Klan and the Aryan Nation, the organization attracts idealists. But the firing of cofounder Morris Dees in early 2019 amid allegations of sexual harassment, gender discrimination, and racism exposed the internal contradictions of an organization infected with the very intolerance it is paid to fight.

SPLC bills itself as "dedicated to fighting hate and bigotry and to seeking justice for the most vulnerable members of our society."

In reality, former SPLC employee and writer Bob Moser said, it was hard for employees not to "feel like we'd become pawns in what was, in many respects, a highly profitable scam."

The posh Alabama headquarters (snarkily referred to by employees as "the Poverty Palace") is focused on fund-raising programs, not civil rights lawsuits. Karl Zinmeister of Philanthropy Roundtable reports that SPLC has never spent more than 31 percent of its donations on fighting hate and intolerance. In some years, he reports, that number has dropped to as little as 18 percent, far less than the fund-raising budget.

> *Its two largest expenses are propaganda operations: creating its annual lists of "haters" and "extremists," and running a big effort that pushes "tolerance education" through more than 400,000 public-school teachers. And the single biggest effort undertaken by the SPLC? Fundraising. On the organization's 2015 IRS 990 form it declared $10 million of direct fundraising expenses, far more than it has ever spent on legal services.*

The bad publicity following the firing of Morris Dees resulted in the resignation of SPLC president Richard Cohen as the group faces perhaps the worst public relations disaster in its history. To help navigate the problem, the Daily Wire reports they've hired the former chief of staff to First Lady Michelle Obama, Tina Tchen. She will lead an internal investigation into alleged racial and gender bias.

You may have heard of Tchen. She played a role in getting hate crime charges against actor Jussie Smollett dropped. A grand jury had indicted the actor from the television series *Empire* with sixteen counts of disorderly conduct after police found evidence he had falsely reported a hate crime. The actor had alleged an attack in January 2019 in which he claimed he was assaulted by two men who put a noose around his neck, doused him in chemicals, and said, "This is MAGA country." The allegations described precisely the type of crime that fills SPLC coffers with donations from angry progressives.

In a text message to Cook County state's attorney Kim Foxx, Tchen wrote, "I wanted to give you a call on behalf of Jussie Smollett and family who I know. They have concerns about the investigation." Foxx emailed back saying, "Spoke to the Superintendent [Eddie] Johnson" and "convinced him to reach out to FBI to ask that they take over the investigation." Presumably Tchen's intervention helped Foxx connect with a member of Smollett's family. In subsequent texts between that family member and Foxx, Foxx reassured the family member, writing, "Spoke to the superintendent earlier, he made the ask. Trying to figure out logistics. I'll keep you posted." To which Smollett's undisclosed relative replied, "Omg this would be a huge victory." Foxx responded that she would "make no guarantees, but I'm trying."

Just one month after his arrest, the charges against Smollett for faking a hate crime were mysteriously dropped. There would be no prosecution. The case was closed. The record was sealed. Smollett did not even have to take responsibility for a hate crime hoax that targeted Trump supporters and undermined the credibility of other hate crimes going forward.

You know which nonprofit should be really upset about this? That's right. The Southern Poverty Law Center. Instead, they decided Tina Tchen was the person they should rely on to get to the bottom of their own racism and bigotry. Obviously, they are very serious about that. The extent to which these nonprofit charities are tied together with progressive politics and politicians is laid bare.

Though SPLC is an extreme example of a nonprofit that has completely subjugated its charitable mission to the demands of its political and fund-raising work, we'll see in the next chapter that SPLC is not alone in weaponizing its charitable work for political purposes.

Following the Rules

To understand how nonprofits can be weaponized, you first have to understand a few key facts about the framework of rules that govern them. Because they operate under a different set of rules than political campaigns, they have become the key conduit for the so-called dark money that flows into political Super PACs. But before we get to that, let's zoom out and look at the bigger picture.

The ability to operate tax free is an advantage that comes with a price. These organizations must actually do charitable work. They can't just be fronts for business or politics.

There are more than 1.6 million nonprofits approved for tax-exempt status in the United States. They fall under twenty-seven different classifications, encompassing everything from religious groups to trade unions. For our purposes, we are focused on two of the most common: the 501(c)3 charitable organization and the 501(c)(4) advocacy organization. Both types of nonprofit are required to file an IRS Form 990 each year showing revenues and expenses, which is the only way we're able to ferret out the political activities.

The most common and most sought-after classification is the 501(c)(3). Donations made to a 501(c)(3) are tax deductible, but these organizations must adhere to rigid restrictions on political activity or risk losing their own tax-exempt status. They may lobby legislative bodies on specific pieces of legislation that impact them, but even then they have to report that activity and demonstrate that it stays below a very low threshold governed by statute. With that one exception, they simply cannot engage in political or campaign-related activity directly or indirectly.

My research indicates some of them have found a way around

that prohibition. What would be the incentive to use charitable nonprofits to influence elections?

For one thing, the restrictions on donors are much looser than they would be on campaign donations or even the kind of advocacy group donations we've discussed thus far. Charities can take money from sources political groups cannot—corporations, citizens of other countries, foreign governments. The tax advantages for donors make 501(c)(3) charities a much more attractive option than an advocacy nonprofit. Amounts donated to charities can be written off on taxes. For another thing, large and venerable American charities maintain massive endowment funds that generate an income of their own. This would make them a perfect political dark money vehicle—if only the law allowed it. It unequivocally does not. Don't forget that charities are not required to report who gives them money. They shouldn't be. But that lack of disclosure makes them a tempting target for those looking to bypass campaign finance regulations.

Advocacy organizations, on the other hand, have a little bit more political latitude. There are more than 80,000 such organizations approved by the IRS. They are classified as 501(c)(4) groups and are subject to very different rules than charities. They still operate with tax-exempt status like charities, but they cannot offer a tax deduction to donors like a charity could. They also have no restrictions on who can donate or how much, nor are they required to disclose their donors.

They are allowed to engage politically under very specific conditions. A 501(c)(4) may participate in politics, provided politics is not the primary purpose of the group. That means they must spend less than 50 percent of their revenues on politics. When you hear the term "dark money groups" it is usually a reference to 501(c)(4) nonprofits that are doing some political work and do not have to disclose their donors.

Advocacy groups classified as 501(c)(4) have traditionally been required to disclose their donors to the IRS, although not to the public. But in July 2018, Treasury secretary Steven Mnuchin removed that disclosure requirement both for 501(c)(4) social welfare organizations and for 501(c)(6) labor unions amid evidence that the IRS was using those reports to target organizations based on the identity of specific (conservative) donors.

By contrast, the world of campaign finance is subject to very different and more complicated rules. Candidates for federal office have the most restrictions. They must strictly adhere to limits on who can donate (no corporate donations, no foreign governments, etc.) and how much they can give. In 2018, an individual donor was limited to giving $2,800 per election, although primary and general elections count as two separate elections. Parties and political action committees (PACs) are also strictly regulated, although the contribution limits are higher. For example, in 2018 an individual could give $5,000 per year to a PAC, $10,000 to a state or local party committee, $35,500 to a national party committee, and $106,500 to the national party.

Less restrictive are the regulations on independent expenditures—essentially free speech campaigns (you probably know them as Super PACs). Since the Supreme Court's *Citizens United* decision overturned restrictions on independent expenditures from corporations and labor unions in 2010, more and more political spending has been routed through Super PACs. Typically, conservative Super PACs have outraised liberal ones in the dark money spending race. These groups can accept unlimited contributions from any nonforeign source for political use, provided they do not coordinate with specific candidates and campaigns. They must disclose those donations—eventually. But donors wishing to remain anonymous may simply donate to a 501(c)(4), which does not disclose the names. Then the Super PAC lists only the name of the 501(c)(4) on its disclosure. This is known as dark money because the money cannot be traced back to its original source.

The Problem with Donor Disclosure

The solution seems easy. Just require nonprofits to disclose their donors. Problem solved.

It's not that easy. All politics aside, people would be less likely to donate to charity if they knew their donation would trigger calls and targeting from every other charity that sees their name on a donor list.

There are numerous other legitimate reasons American citizens or corporations may not want to make donations public, not the least of which is the threat of retaliation, intimidation, or boycotts. In 2015, watchdog group Judicial Watch released documents showing the IRS itself had used donor lists to select audit targets. The *Wall Street Journal*'s Kimberley Strassel wrote a book thoroughly detailing the many ways public disclosures have been used—particularly on the left—to intimidate. In *The Intimidation Factor*, she explained how campaign finance disclosure laws have been successfully used to persecute private individuals who supported specific candidates.

I take the position that "dark money"—ominous though it sounds—is still constitutionally protected free speech. Our First Amendment rights do not end when we reach a certain income level. Furthermore, no donors should have to risk their livelihood in order to influence a political issue. In this country, you can donate anonymously to political causes and still be completely within the law. Democrats are doing it. Republicans are doing it. It is neither illegal nor immoral.

In one of many real-life demonstrations of why nonprofits oppose disclosure laws, the Obama campaign in 2012 waged an intimidation campaign against donors to the Republican nominee, Mitt Romney. A campaign-sponsored website, keepinggophonest .com, called out eight Romney donors by name and followed up with tweets disparaging those individuals. Democrat-friendly media followed up with profile pieces that intensified the trolling and harassment. The onslaught targeted not just the individual donors, but their businesses, and by extension, their families and employees. How could such tactics not have a chilling effect on free speech?

Disclosure laws for nonprofits would eliminate dark money in American elections, but at a cost of compromising our First Amendment right to free speech. That price is too high.

The Changing Nonprofit Landscape

Americans gave $410 billion to charity in 2017. That represented a 5.2 percent increase in charitable giving over the previous year. The sector is the third-largest workforce in the United States, behind only retail and manufacturing in the number of people it employs, according to the Johns Hopkins Center for Civil Society Studies. In twenty-four states and the District of Columbia, nonprofit jobs even outnumber manufacturing jobs.

Charitable donations are a huge part of who we are as a nation. But the nonprofit charity sector is also becoming a huge part of who Democrats are. The sector has become so politicized that conservatives in the industry tell me they have to hide their politics or risk being ostracized. I've heard anecdotal stories of how uncomfortable they feel at ostensibly apolitical conferences when speakers routinely use their time to bash the president or the Republican Party.

What I have learned since that first meeting in my office about nonprofits is terrifying. It raises important questions that can probably only be answered by IRS audits, which seldom seem to target left-leaning groups.

Increasingly, traditional 501(c)(3) charitable organizations are becoming fronts for partisan political campaigning. When they leverage the power of their charitable assets, nationwide infrastructure, and grassroots networks obtained through decades of legitimate charitable work to engage in partisan political activity, that is deceptive, wrong, and potentially illegal.

Over the last decade, some of America's legacy nonprofits have figured out how to convert their vast fund-raising and grassroots apparatus into political weapons of war. They have pioneered new methods of fund-raising that may enable them to bypass campaign finance limits and disclosure and potentially access huge charitable reserves. They devised strategies to get out the vote, a nonpartisan activity, that would get out only the Democratic vote. Even as Democrats in Congress point to conservative Super PACS and run bills to "end corruption," you'll notice that little in their proposals will endanger their political support from the nonprofit sector.

Charity as a Means to a Political End

The focus on diverting charitable donations away from social welfare and using them instead to facilitate political power grabs reflects classic liberal thinking. Liberals believe government is the answer to every social ill. That perspective renders charities superfluous—entities to be used as nothing more than means to a political end.

Attitudes toward philanthropy reveal a deep chasm between left and right. A recent county-by-county study of charitable giving found a correlation between partisan affiliation and charitable giving. The *New York Times* reported the study's conclusion that "the more Republican a county was, the more its residents report charitable contributions." Conversely, Democratic-leaning counties tend to give less to charity, but support much higher taxes to fund a government safety net.

This contrast between voluntary and involuntary giving, between freedom and force, can also be seen among presidential hopefuls. Tax returns released by 2020 Democratic hopefuls reflect high incomes, relatively small charitable contributions, and an agenda of higher taxes.

Front-runner Bernie Sanders in 2016 made over $1 million, but gave just 1 percent (just over $10,000) to charity. With an eye to another presidential run, Sanders tripled his charitable giving in 2017 and 2018 to 3 percent and 3.4 percent respectively. Beto O'Rourke gave just three-tenths of a percent of his income to charity that same year, a figure that was fairly consistent throughout the ten years of returns released by O'Rourke. Kamala Harris gave just 1.4 percent to charity in 2017. Kirsten Gillibrand and Amy Klobuchar each donated less than 2 percent in 2018. The 2020 candidate with the largest charitable contributions was Cory Booker at 15 percent.

On the Republican side, President Trump's decision to withhold his personal tax returns makes any assessment of his charitable giving claims incomplete. We do, however, know he gives away his full presidential salary each quarter to charitable endeavors run by federal agencies. Those range from Science, Technology, Engineering, and Math (STEM) camps for children to military cemeteries to the National Institute on Alcohol Abuse and Alcoholism.

Republican 2012 presidential nominee Mitt Romney is perhaps the poster child for philanthropic giving, reportedly donating 29.4 percent of his income to charity in 2011, the year before he became the Republican nominee for president. This was despite a clumsy attempt by Democrat Senate majority leader Harry Reid to tar Romney as a tax cheat from the Senate floor. That allegation was proven to be a lie, but as usual, the correction didn't get anywhere near the traction of the original allegation.

That same year, President Obama gave a healthy 21.8 percent to charity, but Vice President Joe Biden reported donating just 1.5 percent of his income. Biden's numbers were even more anemic pre-2008, when the Obama campaign released past tax returns of its vice presidential nominee showing total charitable donations of just $3,690 over ten years.

These numbers reflect profound philosophical differences in the perceived role of charitable institutions in American life. Republicans treat charities as an indispensable part of the social safety net to which Americans have an individual responsibility to voluntarily contribute. At best, Democrats see them as an extension of government, to be dependent on government and politicians for ongoing funding. At worst, they treat charities as pass-through entities from which political donations can be laundered.

Progressive ideology already dominates the 501(c)(4) nonprofit sector. Right-leaning charities exist, but in quantity and size they are dwarfed by left-leaning ones. If Democrats can co-opt the charity nonprofit sector for political purposes, they can gain access to immense reserves. Instead of having to build a whole new political apparatus, they would be able to leverage the existing staff, buildings, donor lists, and credibility of powerful nonprofit organizations to act as virtual subsidiaries of the Democratic National Committee.

With anger over the 2016 election result driving donations, one might expect to see those contributions isolated to 501(c)(4) groups that have more flexibility to engage in elections. But that hasn't been the case. The supposedly apolitical charity arms of progressive nonprofits also benefited from the spike in donations. Why would charitable nonprofits, legally prohibited from engaging in politics, benefit from the Trump Bump? I did a deep dive into their IRS tax filings to look for the answer. What I found is far more disturbing than anything the IRS hoped to find in its audits of conservative nonprofits.

CHAPTER 2

THE WEAPONIZATION OF PUBLIC CHARITIES

We expect nonprofit 501(c)(4) advocacy groups to engage in politics. But we see charities as nonpolitical. The 501(c)(3) charities legally have very little latitude to engage in partisan politics. But because the assets and income they control are so much more substantial than those of advocacy groups, the temptation to repurpose them for political use is real. Weaponizing 501(c)(3) charities for political purposes is not easy. But where there is a will, there is a way.

It's important to understand the enormity of the resources some of these charities control. Let's start by looking at the Planned Parenthood Federation, a 501(c)(3) charitable organization.

In their 2016 Form 990 return, the Planned Parenthood Federation had assets totaling more than $446 million—almost half a billion dollars. We looked at a cross section of thirty-four independent U.S. Planned Parenthood organizations, including the Federation, and calculated combined total assets of $1,726,804,908 (yes, $1.7 billion) at the end of 2016. In most cases, this reflected large increases across-the-board in donations during the 2016 election cycle. This was not even the full complement of Planned Parenthood organizations—just a cross section.

The Federation's endowment funds were valued at almost $88 million in 2013 and had grown to over $157 million in their 2016 financial report—an incredible rate of growth. Keep in mind that the Federation does not supply direct services to the public. That is done by the various Planned Parenthood organizations throughout the country, each with its respective revenue and budgets. The Planned Parenthood Federation is a coordinating and advocacy body.

Even this is not the complete picture. Planned Parenthood has international organizations that are directly related to its Federation in the United States. It has forged relationships with UNESCO and UNFPA, the former referring twenty times to Planned Parenthood as a source for sex education and abortion in its revised "Comprehensive Sexuality Standards" (February 2018). It is also in partnership with more than one hundred organizations across Africa and Latin America.

In its 2016 IRS report, International Planned Parenthood Foundation/Western Hemisphere Region stated that it worked with fifty partner organizations in forty countries. It described "averting two million unintended pregnancies" and working with partners to facilitate nineteen country-level policy changes.

At CSW62 (Commission on the Status of Women, 2018), African country delegates described how sexual reproductive health services now received more funding in Africa than those providing for fresh water, education, or economic development. That's a shocking statistic, but it got hardly any play in the U.S. media. Funding for sexual reproductive health services has increased 1,923 percent between 1993 and 2012.

They are experiencing pushback from traditionalist countries such as Burkina Faso, which described how they resented having funding for humanitarian purposes tied to whether they would create abortion clinics. The work of Planned Parenthood Global and other similar organizations was described by them as ideological colonization. This Western institution has swept into Africa, looking to decrease the African population rather than offer life-supporting services and education. Imperialism is alive and well on the left.

Among all of these organizations, Planned Parenthood controls vast amounts of wealth. Of course, they cannot simply use these resources to buy elections. That would be illegal. That's where Grassroots Campaigns Inc. comes in.

Grassroots Campaigns Inc.

One of the most influential groups you've probably never heard of is a for-profit organization founded in 2003 "with the goal of building support for progressive candidates, parties and causes through engaging everyday people in political action." As a for-profit entity, they have no restrictions on political activity. They count as one of their clients Planned Parenthood's 501(c)(3) charity.

They credit themselves with some of America's biggest political success stories. After its first year, Grassroots Campaigns had staff in more than forty cities canvassing on behalf of the Democratic National Committee. According to its website:

In October of 2004, Grassroots Campaigns joined forces with MoveOn.org in order to identify and activate Democratic voters. During this campaign, we recruited a volunteer force of almost 50,000 people and worked in 17 of the most highly contested

swing states. Following the election, we helped launch a nation-
wide project called Operation Democracy through which we
organized grassroots activists to end Republican control of
Congress. Operation Democracy laid the groundwork for the
2006 Call for Change Campaign in which we ran massive volun-
teer phone banks that turned out infrequent Democratic voters
in over 50 congressional districts. Our hard work paid off that
November when we successfully took back Congress.

For 2008, the organization's website claims credit for helping organize 7,480 house parties where volunteers made 2.14
million calls and recruited over 90,000 volunteers for Obama
in swing states. Additionally, they report registering more than
230,000 new voters in thirteen battleground states, an effort
that they say helped to win many states and turned North
Carolina Blue for the first time since Jimmy Carter's election
in 1976.

With each election cycle, the claims grow bigger. In 2012, they
targeted the western swing states of Nevada and Colorado and
ran get-out-the-vote (GOTV) efforts in ten states. In 2014 they
knocked on more than 200,000 doors in states with key Senate
races with a commitment to "mobilizing the grassroots base of
the progressive movement."

This is an explicitly political organization.

So what service do they provide to 501(c)(3) charities? According to the 990 forms of three major nonprofits, Grassroots Campaigns has earned more than $69 million over the six-year period
for which data is available, from just three charities: Planned
Parenthood, the Southern Poverty Law Center, and the Nature
Conservancy. Not just the advocacy arm of these organizations,
but the charity arm. A visit to the Grassroots Campaigns website
shows a much longer client list. On the clients page, we see some
familiar names:

CURRENT AND FORMER CLIENTS OF GRASSROOTS CAMPAIGNS INC.

America Votes
American Civil Liberties Union
Amnesty International USA
CA League of Conservation Voters
Center for American Progress
Colorado State Democratic Party
College Matters
Common Cause
Conservation Law Foundation
D.C. Public Schools
DCCC [Democratic Congressional Campaign Committee]
Democratic National Committee
Doctors Without Borders
Equality California
Equality Maine
Everytown for Gun Safety
Freedom to Marry
League of Conservation Voters
Media Matters
MoveOn.org Political Action
Nevada State Democratic Party
Obama for America
Oxfam America
Pennsylvania Coordinated Campaign
People for the American Way
Plan International USA
Planned Parenthood of NYC
Repower America
Respect ABQ Women
Sierra Club
Southern Poverty Law Center

Media Fund
Nature Conservancy
UNICEF
VoteVets.org Political Action
WA State Coordinated Campaign
WETA

What kind of work do these nonprofits need from a political canvassing organization? Some of it is consulting. It's unclear what consulting a for-profit political canvassing organization provides to 501(c)(3) charities. But much of the work Grassroots Campaigns is paid to do is what they're calling fund-raising. It involves hiring entry-level staff to knock on doors or man tables at public events asking people to donate to the nonprofit.

If Grassroots Campaigns fund-raisers are working for Planned Parenthood, they show up at the door in a Planned Parenthood T-shirt asking you to donate to Planned Parenthood. You might naturally assume that the money you contribute will be used to do the work of the organization to which you donated—funding abortions, for example. You would be wrong about that. Because at the end of the day, Grassroots Campaigns is paid significantly more money than it raises for its nonprofit clients.

Ultimately, that donation results in a net loss to the charity, not a net gain. It's right there in the 990 forms filed with the IRS. That means your donation is funding Grassroots Campaigns, not Planned Parenthood, the Southern Poverty Law Center, the Nature Conservancy, or any other client engaged in this sleight of hand.

Planned Parenthood Federation has been engaged in this scheme since 2009. Notably, only the charity side of Planned Parenthood engages with Grassroots Campaigns, Inc. Though the social welfare, or 501(c)(4), entities also do fund-raising, they don't use this particular company. Why? Could it be that they don't actually hire Grassroots Campaigns for the fund-raising? Is it just a scheme to direct charity funds to partisan political activities?

PLANNED PARENTHOOD FEDERATION LOSSES
TO GRASSROOTS CAMPAIGNS, INC.

	Amount Fund-Raised	Amount Charged by Grassroots	Loss by PPF
2016	$2,686,919.00	$4,599,074.00	$(1,912,155.00)
2015	$1,954,196.00	$3,400,000.00	$(1,445,804.00)
2014	$909,925.00	$2,273,485.00	$(1,363,560.00)
2013	$1,049,817.00	$2,261,872.00	$(1,212,055.00)
2012	$1,849,612.00	$3,493,461.00	$(1,643,849.00)
2011	$1,569,663.00	$3,776,470.00	$(2,206,807.00)
2010	$902,515.00	$2,420,841.00	$(1,518,326.00)
2009	$97,079.00	$370,874.00	$(273,795.00)
	$11,019,726.00	$22,596,077.00	$(11,576,351.00)

Source: 990 tax filings

Let's take a look at the success of Grassroots Campaigns Inc. in fund-raising for Planned Parenthood Federation. The chart above shows Grassroots Campaigns hasn't come close to raising the amount of money Planned Parenthood is paying them. In fact, in the eight years for which I was able to see records, Planned Parenthood's 501(c)(3) charity has paid out more than $11.5 million to the canvassing organization above and beyond the amounts they have received for fund-raising.

To a nonprofit auditor, these numbers would make no sense. In the real world, if a nonprofit pays a fund-raiser, that fund-raiser had better raise at least enough to cover the cost of the contract. In the real world, if a fund-raiser costs more than the amount raised, the nonprofit would hire someone else the following year. But Planned Parenthood doesn't. Note that the amounts fund-raised by Grassroots Campaigns each year (column two) are consistently exceeded by the amounts charged for fund-raising (column three). Normally, after a single year of failing to raise the amount of the fee, we would expect a nonprofit to fire the fund-raiser and hire someone who can raise at least as much as he or she is paid. But Planned Parenthood doesn't. They have continued to use Grassroots Campaigns each year since 2009. The last column shows the loss incurred each year—the difference between what was paid and what was raised. In addition to the money Grassroots Campaigns was paid for fundraising, they were also paid for consulting.

While most nonprofits of its size do their fund-raising in-house, the Planned Parenthood Federation has consistently rehired Grassroots Campaigns for both consultancy and fund-raising services over the most recent six-year reporting period, paying out a total of $38 million (including consulting) and raising less than $6 million during that time.

The for-profit organization Grassroots Campaigns is making millions of dollars each year from the contract with Planned Parenthood alone. Where is that money going? Well, let's revisit their website and look at what Grassroots Campaigns says it does.

"In addition to running ongoing small-donor fund-raising canvasses throughout the U.S., Grassroots Campaigns also has more than a decade of experience running cutting-edge voter contact, volunteer organizing, and grassroots advocacy campaigns on behalf of progressive political groups and candidates. The services we provide include:

- Fundraising
- Paid Voter Contact and GOTV
- Volunteer Voter Contact and GOTV
- Voter Registration
- Volunteer Recruitment and Organizing
- Advocacy
- Phone Services
- Training"

What happens to your donation when Grassroots Campaigns knocks on your door? We've already established it isn't going back to the nonprofit organization—they're paying more for the fund-raising service than the donations given. It appears to be used, directly or indirectly, to fund these other services—services that the nonprofit itself, particularly the charity arm, cannot legally fund.

As a for-profit organization, Grassroots Campaigns doesn't have to report how this money—the money that came from a 501(c)(3) charity—is used. This would be an easy way to access those deep reserves for political purposes. Is that why those reserves seem to increase so dramatically after an organization pays Grassroots Campaigns for "consulting" services? Is Grassroots helping get the word out to donors that political donations to the nonprofit charity will not only be tax deductible, but will also be used to help fund the resistance? That's a question that deserves much greater scrutiny.

Southern Poverty Law Center

Planned Parenthood Federation is just one of many clients of Grassroots Campaigns, although it is perhaps the largest. Another large client is the troubled but prosperous Southern Poverty Law Center.

According to the 990s filed with the IRS for the period between 2010 and 2017, the pattern we saw at Planned Parenthood held true for Southern Poverty Law Center. Once again, Grassroots Campaigns collected significantly more than it raised, taking in nearly $12 million over eight years, and raising just over $4 million.

Like Planned Parenthood, Southern Poverty Law Center grew considerably during the years for which we found public data—in both its revenue and its reserves. The amounts are staggering.

SOUTHERN POVERTY LAW CENTER LOSSES
TO GRASSROOTS CAMPAIGNS, INC.

	Amount Fund-Raised	Amount Charged by Grassroots	Loss by SPLC
2017	$317,336.00	$1,028,324.00	$(710,988.00)
2016	$787,881.00	$2,530,660.00	$(1,742,779.00)
2015	$623,596.00	$1,811.174.00	$(1,187,578.00)
2014	$757,182.00	$2,028,857.00	$(1,271,675.00)
2013	$581,478.00	$1,712,158.00	$(1,130,680.00)
2012	$770,211.00	$1,926,976.00	$(1,156,765.00)
2011	$731,694.00	$1,601,380.00	$(869,686.00)
2010	$142.899.00	$355,113.00	$(212,214.00)
	$4,394,941.00	$11,966,318.00	$(7,571,377.00)

Source: 990 tax filings

Numbers released in March 2019 indicate that the organization's total assets now top half a billion dollars. Of those assets, some $121 million is held in offshore accounts. Assets have doubled since 2011, when SPLC reported $256 million and an increase of $41 million in the twelve-month period since the previous filing. Total revenues in 2018 were $121 million. On top of that $518 million in assets, the organization reported an endowment fund, which was valued at a healthy $281 million in 2011 and is now worth $471 million as of 2018.

For each of the six years of reports we studied, Southern Poverty Law Center has engaged the services of Grassroots Campaigns both as consultants and as fund-raisers.

And still, remarkably, whatever Grassroots Campaigns may have been telling donors, Southern Poverty Law Center did not *actually* receive any funds directly from Grassroots Campaigns. The IRS asks nonprofits to report whether funds raised remained in the control of the fund-raiser or whether the organization had control. Each year,

Grassroots Campaigns was described as maintaining control over contributions, unlike other fund-raisers used during this same time.

Even as SPLC's 501(c)(3) is paying Grassroots Campaigns for so-called fund-raising services, the group has joined the trend of forming a 501(c)(4) entity to engage in political campaigns. SPLC claims its Action Fund focuses on "critical ballot initiatives" and "legislative battles at every level of government."

I can tell you what that looks like in my state. In 2018, progressive groups funded ballot initiatives to impose policies that could not pass in Utah's conservative state legislature. With marijuana legalization, Medicaid expansion, and redistricting reform on the ballot, and with large infusions of cash and volunteers from outside the state, Democrats managed to spike turnout among progressives and political agnostics, resulting in big wins for their party. Already these groups have a carbon tax ballot initiative on tap to help spike turnout among their voters in 2020. Such efforts can potentially benefit Democrat candidates up and down the ballot. All of this is being done with the help of deep-pocketed nonprofits that pay no taxes, do little real charity work, send their money offshore, and in many cases allow rich donors to write off the contributions to offset high tax bills. Taxpayers quite literally subsidize the work of the Democratic Party.

What is Grassroots Campaigns doing with the millions they are being paid? Again, the clues are on their website. They do political canvassing. One page explains "Why we canvass." In their own words, they do it to build organizations: "Canvassing builds lists of new members and supporters. These lists of supporters are an invaluable resource for Progressive groups." They do it to "deepen Democratic participation," to "win elections," and to "train activists." That's all very legal, but if the point is to help win elections, then it's not the kind of activity a 501(c)(3) can legally engage in.

According to their website, Grassroots "collectively knocked on over 1.3 million doors to get out the vote in 2016. Our work was concentrated in a few key swing states and important Senate battlegrounds."

Notice where they worked in the presidential election year of 2016:

TOTALS BY STATE

	Shifts	Knocks	Contacts
Totals	19,783	1,334,941	288,859
Ohio	1,028	72,593	16,764
Pennsylvania	4,739	332,179	85,226
Florida	6,606	436,853	84,638
Missouri	374	27,408	6,397
Nevada	986	64,838	14,913
Connecticut	388	22,172	5,224
Colorado	5,237	346,282	70,781
North Carolina	425	32,076	4,916

Source: grassrootscampaignsinc.tumblr.com

American Civil Liberties Union (ACLU)

With the information about these three nonprofits in hand, my team and I decided to compare them to numbers for another left-leaning nonprofit—the ACLU. The ACLU operates both types of nonprofits at every level. In other words, the national and affiliate organizations all have a charitable 501(c)(3)—usually with significant reserves—and a separate 501(c)(4) for political activism.

The trend toward operating two separate entities allows nonprofits to have their cake and eat it, too. It's all completely legal, but it most certainly blurs the lines between charity and political activism. Given the ability of nonprofits to work within both sets of rules, there is no excuse for engaging the charitable entity in partisan political activities. That's what the social welfare nonprofit side is doing.

Of course, the ACLU is adamant that the organization is nonpartisan, writing in a 2016 Medium op-ed: "The ACLU is a staunchly non-partisan organization. For 96 years, we have fought to defend the rights enshrined in our Constitution. We have never opposed or supported any candidate for office. And we are not starting now."

When you visit the ACLU website, the first thing you see is a large image of Donald Trump with the words, "THE FIGHT IS STILL ON" and a red box that says, "Give Monthly." A pop-up appears that reads, "SEE YOU IN COURT, PRESIDENT TRUMP. We're fighting to protect democracy and we need your support" followed by the big red "Donate Now" button. Certainly this is an organization that is raising money off of opposition to President Trump rather than support for its core mission of protecting civil liberties. Is the ACLU's top priority to defend our constitutional rights or to be a front for the Democrat Party? They might tell you both are priorities. But what happens when their two priorities conflict with each other?

That question was answered during the 2018 confirmation hearings for Supreme Court justice Brett Kavanaugh. On the one hand, the ACLU had a history of fighting for due process and the presumption of innocence, which Kavanaugh had obviously been denied. These constitutional rights clearly applied to Kavanaugh, who was the target of uncorroborated allegations that failed to meet even the lowest evidentiary standard. On the other hand, Kavanaugh was a Republican and the ACLU is aligned with Democrats. Having to choose between their stated mission and their political objective, the ACLU jettisoned the mission.

They didn't just stand back and refuse to take a side, either. They proactively undermined their organization's core principles, bragging in a news release about a $1 million multistate ad buy against Kavanaugh. Not just against Kavanaugh—but essentially against his right to due process and to the presumption of innocence. They wrote, "The ad buy is part of a larger advocacy effort that will engage the ACLU's over 1.8 million members in actions that include phone banks, online petitions, congressional office visits, and a national day of action in partnership with other organizations."

The outrageous ads they ran actually compared Kavanaugh to high-profile accused sexual assaulters Bill Cosby and Harvey Weinstein—against whom there was corroborated evidence as well as due process. They were the kind of ads that can get you condemned by the ACLU.

As Scott Bledsoe deftly explained in an October 2018 *Federalist* piece, "The ACLU is less interested in ensuring a fair process—and more keen on joining in the liberal firing squad against a judge who will solidify a conservative majority on the Supreme Court. It is no secret that the ACLU has a liberal bias, but their recent attack efforts against Kavanaugh show that they are willing to put partisanship above their core principles of defending civil liberties and due process."

Normally a nonprofit would be loath to take a position that might offend the donor base who presumably joined the organization to promote its mission. Why didn't the ACLU worry about that? Is the ACLU's donor base really filled with civil libertarians? That brings us back to Grassroots Campaigns.

There is no indication that the ACLU uses Grassroots Campaigns for fund-raising purposes like some of the other nonprofits we looked at. But it did hire them for consultancy services totaling more than $10 million from 2014 to 2016. It gave more than twice the consulting fee to Grassroots Campaigns than to the next consultancy service listed in their 990 report.

Like the other left-leaning charities who use consulting services from Grassroots Campaigns, ACLU has seen huge influxes of revenue during the time they've received these services. In these same reports for these years, the ACLU has gone from $10 million in debt in 2013 to $118 million in net assets in the 2016 report, three years later. Most of this increase occurred in the year 2016. The ACLU reports that most of its funding comes from membership dues.

Who are these members? Are they people who genuinely care about civil liberties? Go back and look at ACLU.org. Their target audience is obvious—and it's not necessarily civil libertarians. When the numbers are released for 2018, it will be interesting to note the impact of the Kavanaugh position on the ACLU's fundraising. If civil libertarians are funding the ACLU, we should see a significant drop in support post-Kavanaugh.

Describing the Kavanaugh hit job as "the final nail in the ACLU's coffin," famed civil libertarian and longtime ACLU supporter Alan Dershowitz lamented the loss of America's premier defender of civil rights. Writing for the *Hill*, Dershowitz said:

> [T]he core mission of the ACLU—and its financial priority—is to promote its left-wing agenda in litigation, in public commentary and, now, in elections. If you want to know the reason for this shift, just follow the money. ACLU contributors, including some of its most generous contributors, are strong anti-Trump zealots who believe that the end (getting rid of Trump) justifies any means (including denying Trump and his associates core civil liberties and due process).

More recently, Dershowitz criticized the ACLU for failing to speak out on a judge-imposed gag order against Trump confidant Roger Stone. Partisan interests seem to be the driving force for the organization. Has civil liberties become nothing more than a side hustle for the ACLU?

Other Fund-Raisers

Grassroots Campaigns is not the only political group in this category. It's not even the only such group owned by Colorado's Douglas Phelps. Phelps has built a network of nonprofit organizations, each with the stated mission of furthering progressive causes. His biography says his organizations seek "a coordinated strategic approach to getting things done." Coordinated is right. It seems many of the progressive groups are tied together.

Among Phelps's organizations are Telefund, Public Interest Network, the National Association of Organizations with Public Interest, US PIRG, the Fund for the Public Interest, and Environment America. Phelps remains the president or chairperson of each of them. In particular, Telefund is known for aggressive telemarketing tactics. Once someone donates to one of these charities, they can expect to be called by many more— often looking for ongoing monthly contributions.

Former president Barack Obama got some of his community organizing experience at one of these groups. He referred to his time employed by US PIRG in the year following his graduation, saying, "I used to be a PIRG guy. You guys trained me well."

Most of Phelps's nonprofit organizations are 501(c)4 advocacy organizations rather than 501(c)3 charity organizations. A review of public disclosures shows a close connection between these organizations. The 990 form for Environment America showed that it gave the Public Interest Network control over the selection of its board in 2016. Donations have been made between these organizations as well.

There is also an investment vehicle for the Public Interest Network called 1543 LLC, in which Environment America invested and which comes under the direction of Douglas Phelps and the Public Interest Network. Other related parties to this group of nonprofits are the Clinton Foundation, the Sierra Club, the Center for American Progress, and the Democratic National Committee. Joe Biden was reported as having a fund-raiser at the home of Douglas Phelps in the 2014 election.

The political infrastructure of the Democratic Party is inextricably linked to the infrastructure of America's nonprofit sector.

An Analysis of Conservative Nonprofits

After learning what was happening on the left, I was curious to see whether the same patterns could be found on the right. *Forbes* magazine's William P. Barrett compiles an annual list of America's top charities. The most recent list, published in December 2018, includes several of Grassroots Campaigns' clients. The ACLU comes in at #50. The Planned Parenthood Federation is #27 and the Nature Conservancy is #20.

Perhaps the most well-known and liberal-maligned conservative nonprofit—the National Rifle Association (NRA)—does not appear anywhere on the list. For all the fearmongering from the left about the power of the NRA, it doesn't even approach the size of the Clinton Foundation (#69) or the Barack Obama Foundation (#63). The NRA's 2016 reserves of $75 million were dwarfed by the Clinton Foundation's $326 million, although the NRA's revenues were higher in the year of Hillary Clinton's infamous defeat.

The only charities on the *Forbes* list remotely tied to conservative political views might be the handful of religious ones—none of which engage in politics.

There are, of course, conservative nonprofits. They may not approach the size and scale of their reflections on the left, but they do exist.

As we began delving through the 990 forms of a cross section of some of America's most influential conservative groups, the first difference we noted was the revenues and assets. Whereas politically oriented nonprofits on the left were seeing significant growth in those categories over time, conservative nonprofits looked more like the rest of the nonprofit sector with very modest gains.

Over on the left, the Planned Parenthood Federation's endowment funds had grown from $88 million in 2013 to $157 million in 2016. The Nature Conservancy went from having $5.7 billion in assets in 2013 to $6.2 billion in 2016. The Nature Conservancy's endowment fund grew from $993 million to $1.2 billion over that three-year period. Same story for the Southern Poverty Law Center, whose endowment fund was $281 million in 2013 and grew to $470 million by 2019.

How do those numbers compare to conservative nonprofits? Let's start with the venerable NRA, which has both a 501(c)(3) charity organization as well as a 501(c)(4) advocacy arm. In the 2016 Form 990, the foundation had $366 million in revenue, up a little from the $336 million they saw in 2015 and the $310 million in 2014. Net assets during those three years declined, primarily because of increased spending. These are healthy numbers, but the growth rates don't match those of the left-leaning 501(c)(3) charities. Despite NRA's huge membership and long history, its revenue numbers are dwarfed by those in the top one hundred charities. Similarly, the Gun Owners of America saw insignificant increases in revenues over the three years reported—from $1.9 million in 2013 to $2.2 million three years later with minimal reserves.

Numbers USA, which considers itself a bipartisan group that works to decrease immigration, raised $7.4 million in 2016 with net assets of $10 million. Those are healthy numbers, but they are dwarfed by the left-wing nonprofits. The even smaller Eagle Forum is an influential family-run nonprofit with limited revenue. Total income dropped from just over $1 million in 2015 to $275,661 in 2016. Expenses have outspent revenue by $1.5 million during the 2015–16 cycle, with total assets at the time of $4.6 million. Similarly, the Center for Immigration Studies is a 501(c)3 organization. It had revenues of $2,772,885 in 2014 with net assets of $3,000,323. In 2015 it had revenues of $2,907,224 with net assets of $3,267,051. In 2016, it had revenues of $2,902,940 with net assets of $3,425,201. It's certainly not having the exponential growth of its left-leaning counterparts but still is in a healthy position.

The National Organization for Marriage had steady revenues at $1.3 million during the three years reported, but saw an operating loss in 2014. Focus on the Family, another well-known conservative nonprofit, has no public reporting since 2014. At that time, it had revenues of $86 million, or $2 million less than it raised the previous year. Net assets for 2013 and 2014 were $52 million and $51 million respectively. The National Right to Life Committee raised about $5 million in 2014 and 2015, but only about $3 million in 2016. The Family Research Council had a mixed bag with revenues of $15 million in 2014, $12 million in 2015, and $16 million in 2016.

The one anomaly in my admittedly limited cross section of conservative nonprofits was Judicial Watch, a 501(c)(3) that has had some real success using Freedom of Information Act (FOIA) requests to force government transparency. There is no evidence Judicial Watch is engaged in the scheme to overpay fund-raisers who then turn around and do political canvassing. I only found this pattern on the left. But Judicial Watch does benefit from the same pattern of increasing donations that left-leaning groups are experiencing.

Judicial Watch revenues in 2013 were $20 million. In 2014 the revenues significantly increased to almost $30 million; they increased again in 2015 to $37 million and went up even more dramatically in the last reported filing, to $45 million in 2016. Those numbers are nowhere close to ACLU or Planned Parenthood numbers, but they do reflect the same types of revenue increases as other political nonprofits. That could be a result of their proximity to political donors. But it may simply be a result of their unmitigated and high-profile success in obtaining substantive evidence withheld from Congress.

Another pattern that didn't repeat within conservative nonprofits was the net loss to fund-raising consultants. That pattern seems to be unique to clients of Grassroots Campaigns.

The NRA paid for a number of fund-raising consultants in 2016 for which they received no funding, but they also did not raise any funds that were retained by the consultants. The fund-raisers that they did use, Allegiance and InfoCision, both produced profits for the NRA from their fund-raising, the former for a flat fee and producing excellent results. For example, in 2016 the NRA paid Allegiance $480,000 and Allegiance raised a net profit to NRA of $42,551,885. That's the year Planned Parenthood raised $2.6 million from the $4.6 million they paid the fund-raiser, for a net loss of $1.9 million. According to the 990s, the NRA routinely distributes money to other organizations of all sizes and types. In 2016 they reported $47 million in expenses. Of these expenses, grants made to organizations (and some individuals) totaled $33,793,429, or 72 percent of their revenue.

Many of the conservative nonprofits we analyzed didn't even use outside fund-raisers. National Organization for Marriage, Gun Owners of America, Center for Immigration Studies, Eagle Forum— none of them reported payments to a fund-raiser. Of those that did, the fund-raiser consistently raised at least enough to break even.

As for Judicial Watch, they did use outside fund-raisers. They paid one group $4.8 million for production of fund-raising packages and used another for administration of fund-raising lists. For actual fund-raising, they used the same organization as Family Watch, Center for Immigration Services, and Right to Life: MDS Communications Corporation. The fund-raising was not lucrative, but it never ran negative.

Planned Parenthood's use of outside fund-raisers is a bit of an anomaly among nonprofits of similar size. My review of the 990 forms for similarly sized nonprofits with no connection to politics showed they tend to do their fund-raising in-house. While it appears most nonprofits struggle to find outside fund-raisers who can raise significantly more than they cost, only clients of Grassroots Campaigns seem to be dramatically overpaying for fund-raising and allowing the fund-raiser to control the money raised.

Corrupting Our Nonprofit Institutions

The information we glean from public filings of nonprofit entities certainly raises some questions.

For example, is the 501(c)(3) charity fund-raising activity only happening in politically competitive states and districts? When those volunteers knock on a door for fund-raising purposes, are they also canvassing? Are they gathering information to be used for political purposes at the same time they are supposedly raising funds? When they promise these people their donations will go to a charity, but then don't actually net any funds for that charity, is that fraudulent?

What about the massive reserves charities are stockpiling—how much of that money have they been able to indirectly funnel to their political activities? Is the dramatic increase in reserves of politicized charities over the last few years related to the fact that donors can now use charities as political vehicles? Is that conversion part of the consulting service that Grassroots Campaigns provides? Is this a new way for Democrats to signal virtue—as they funnel dark money into charities while pretending to eschew dark money from Super PACs?

Those questions raise even more questions. Does the IRS have the necessary tools and data to figure any of this out? If so, are they even willing to do so? Are there any enterprising journalists brave enough to take on the pillars of the nonprofit community to investigate? And what is the opportunity cost of all of this political activity? Are charities even focused on the social welfare priorities upon which they were founded? Does the use of both a 501(c)(3) and a 501(c)(4) within the same organization ultimately politicize the whole endeavor? How far does the politicization extend? Are organizations with no explicit political bias somehow engaging in a clandestine way?

Domestic Spending as a Conduit to Nonprofits

These questions shed new light on the federal budget battles of the last ten years. The Democratic push for more domestic spending actually results in more spending on nonprofits. In fiscal year 2018, the federal government allocated $59 billion for nonprofit contracts and grants, according to USAspending.gov. Does any of that money directly or indirectly fund political activities?

I remember when Republicans gained control of the House of Representatives after the 2010 midterms and made a concerted effort to cut federal spending. Democrats had been increasing domestic spending, which includes heavy spending on government grants and contracts to nonprofit organizations, for years. Having been demoted from Speaker to House minority leader, Pelosi went to the mat to protect domestic spending.

Because we had not yet won back control of the Senate and did not have support for Republican budgets there, we kept funding the government with continuing resolutions. These just extended the inflated funding levels previously set by Democrats. In 2011, Republicans used the debt ceiling vote as leverage to pass the Budget Control Act, which ultimately imposed automatic spending cuts. I didn't vote for sequestration—I think tailored budget cuts are preferable to across-the-board cuts—but more important, I worried about defense spending.

We were engaged in two foreign wars and President Obama wanted to cut defense spending by $100 billion a year annually. It had a huge impact on military readiness. Republicans were fighting to restore the massive cuts in military spending, with tens of billions of dollars needed to rebuild military infrastructure and modernize our weapons. Democrats were reluctant to increase military spending, but seemingly went along as long as there was an equivalent increase in domestic spending, from which the many grants and contracts to nonprofit entities flow.

We had a strong and legitimate rationale for funding the military. Democrats had no corresponding rationale for increasing domestic spending. Pelosi even went so far as to tell CNN's State of the Union, "The cupboard is bare. There's no more cuts to make. It's really important that people understand that."

Hogwash. They just want more government. We were already spending at the time more than $1 trillion a year on more than eighty federal welfare programs, according to a December 2012 Senate Budget Committee report. The people living at or below the poverty level already qualify for these programs.

Bypassing Congress to Fund Nonprofit Allies

The cuts to domestic spending during those years may have given rise to what the *Wall Street Journal* called "one of the Obama Administration's worst practices"—the misuse of settlement slush funds. Unbeknownst to Congress, the Eric Holder–led Justice Department initiated a program in which federal prosecutors could require big companies to settle federal fines by giving money to nonprofit organizations. These mandatory settlements often involved large financial institutions giving money to politically favored causes completely unrelated to their industry.

According to internal Justice Department documents exposed by former Judiciary Committee chairman Bob Goodlatte, government officials were directly involved in choosing which organizations would receive settlement money, and even intervened at times to prevent money from going to politically disfavored nonprofits.

In what Goodlatte called a "smoking gun" email, one senior Justice Department official appeared to intervene in a settlement with Citigroup, expressing concerns that a conservative group might be a beneficiary. The email provides proof of political bias. In it, the senior official outlines political objections to a proposed settlement agreement. "Concerns include: a) not allowing Citi to pick a statewide intermediary like the Pacific Legal Foundation (does conservative property-rights legal services)." Writing under the title of "Acting Senior Counselor for Access to Justice," the official added that "we are more likely to get the right result from a state bar association affiliated entity." The right result? Exactly what results are DOJ officials hoping to receive from nonprofit entities?

The DOJ apparently directed nearly $1 billion to handpicked nonprofits during a two-year period, according to a subsequent probe by the House Judiciary and House Finance Committees. The probe also turned up documents suggesting that outside groups began to lobby the DOJ to be included in these settlement agreements. One document recorded a meeting in which an outside group urged the DOJ to make donations "mandatory in all future settlements" of mortgage-lending cases.

When Trump attorney general Jeff Sessions closed the DOJ's Access to Justice (A2J) office and ended the settlement slush funds in 2017, congressional Democrats and outside groups bemoaned the closure of a program "dedicated to making legal aid accessible to all."

Goodlatte responded in a *Hill* op-ed correcting the misinformation:

Due to an investigation by the House and Senate Judiciary committees, it was discovered that the A2J office was responsible for a terrible abuse of power. In just two years, the Justice Department—thanks to suggestions from A2J—directed nearly a billion dollars in settlement funds away from victims and gave them to their preferred third-party organizations instead. These settlements provisions were designed to funnel money to political allies. The Spending Power is one of Congress's most effective tools in reining in the Executive Branch and ensures that elected officials are accountable for how taxpayer money is spent. Sadly, unelected A2J officials, working with then–Assistant Attorney

General Tony West, circumvented this Constitutional requirement by forcing settling defendants to donate money to third-party groups chosen by DOJ. In some cases, DOJ used settlements to reinstate funding to groups that Congress had specifically cut.

Money that should have gone to the federal Treasury to be appropriated by Congress was instead diverted to Democratic allies. In reversing the program, Sessions issued a memo that read "When the federal government settles a case against a corporate wrongdoer, any settlement funds should go first to the victims and then to the American people—not to bankroll third-party special interest groups or the political friends of whoever is in power. Unfortunately, in recent years the Department of Justice has sometimes required or encouraged defendants to make these payments to third parties as a condition of settlement. With this directive, we are ending this practice and ensuring that settlement funds are only used to compensate victims, redress harm, and punish and deter unlawful conduct."

The House Judiciary Committee, under its new chairman Jerry Nadler, Democrat of New York, is determined to reinstate the settlement slush funds. In a fact sheet on the committee's website, committee Democrats argue that "a broad coalition of public-interest organizations oppose the bill." Among those public interest organizations? US PIRG—a sister organization to Grassroots Campaigns Inc.—and a host of left-leaning non-profits that would no doubt hope to be future recipients of settlement fund largesse.

Trump Changes Everything

The story told by the 990 forms of progressive nonprofits is incomplete. Only three years of data is available at any one time. We only had data through 2016 at the time this book went to press.

We can see the trend that began in 2013, but much of this story remains to be written.

The end of 2016 marked the beginning of what these progressive groups consider to be an existential threat—the presidency of Donald Trump. What might they be willing to do in the face of an election result they believe to have been illegitimate? What role did nonprofits play in the 2018 midterms? What are they doing in the run-up to 2020? We don't have 990 forms to answer those questions yet, but we will continue to see the work of nonprofits show up as we explore the progressive response to the Trump presidency.

One thing is clear: the nonprofit sector seems to have become weaponized in the service of one political party. We can predict where this trend will take us. More anger will be needed to drive more donations. More polarization will be required to drive that anger. More resistance in an attempt to attract more votes, all in the pursuit of more power. Should this effort prove successful, conservatives will need every constitutional tool at our disposal to protect the institutions we revere. Fortunately, we have a Constitution equal to the task.

But make no mistake, our Constitution is under attack. Democratic hysteria is reaching a fever pitch.

CHAPTER 3

THE REAL AUTHORITARIANS

Fascist. That is a word we have heard over and over again from terrified liberals who believed the 2016 election signaled the end of American life as we know it. The presidency of Donald Trump made Blue America apoplectic with rage and fear. Over-the-top reactions have flourished everywhere on social media and in news reports since the moment he became the Republican nominee. The forces opposing President Trump were looking to reverse what they saw as the disastrous outcome of the 2016 presidential election.

In the months between the election and the inauguration, while I was still serving as the chairman of the House Oversight Committee, some groups (probably nonprofit advocacy groups) saw that committee as one tool to make it happen. They promptly messaged their grass roots to call and demand investigations of the president-elect.

I don't know that firsthand—I just know that when you get hundreds of phone calls all using the exact same words in the exact same order to demand the exact same thing, there's probably an advocacy group involved somewhere. I had the authority to investigate the president-elect in the aftermath of Hillary Clinton's catastrophic defeat. Reporters who had ignored our substantive investigations of the Obama administration for years suddenly came out of the woodwork to inquire about even the most farfetched or benign allegations against Donald Trump.

The calls pouring in from the public included dire warnings about the "authoritarian" or "fascist" America had just elected. Over and over again those two words came up—authoritarian, fascist. Believing those words were accurate, Democrats demanded Congress intervene to prevent this man from being sworn in as president.

They weren't accurate. A common definition of an authoritarian is someone who enforces strict obedience to authority at the expense of personal freedom. That's a serious charge. The definition of fascism is more flexible, but the textbook definition of fascism is a system characterized by the following: centralization of authority, dictatorship, stringent socioeconomic controls, suppression of the opposition through terror and censorship, and typically a policy of belligerent nationalism and racism.

It's hard to see how a philosophy of smaller government, deregulation, federalism, and tax cuts can be depicted as aligning with a fascist agenda. Many of the allegations against President Trump hinged on the nationalism component of the definition. Because Trump had an America-first agenda and campaigned on border security, that allegedly made him a racist xenophobe.

What did Blue America most fear a President Donald Trump would do? Believe it or not, the most common warnings from callers to my office predicted that he would curtail the freedoms of LGBTQ people and people of color. The callers we heard from were also certain he would use the power of government to take out his political enemies (particularly Hillary Clinton), feather his own nest, destroy our free press, crash our economy, and take us into needless wars.

To date, none of that has happened. The predictions were not even remotely close to the truth. Though President Trump undeniably makes comments that are construed by leftists as nationalistic (as when he prioritizes illegal immigration and putting America first), those comments align with the views of many past presidents from both parties. He has not in fact governed like a fascist at all. In fact, President Trump has done more or less the exact opposite of most of the things fearmongers told us we should be worried about.

Whatever a person may think of Donald Trump's personality, weighing his results against the presumed agenda of a fascist dictator reveals few similarities. Law-abiding Americans have not had their freedom curtailed under this president. To the contrary, the forces of oppressive government have been lightened. On the other hand, Democrats have promoted an agenda heavy on force, willingly exacting a price in personal freedom.

As for the LGTBQ community, their freedoms remain intact under a Trump presidency. Some LGBTQ activist groups would certainly prefer someone who, like President Obama, puts more restrictions on the freedom of those who disagree with them. They would like more Obama-era restrictions on vulnerable women who don't want to be forced to share public bathrooms with transgender women. They would prefer restrictions against health-care workers with a religious objection to performing sex reassignment surgery. But those policies do not restrict freedom of LGBTQ people—they protect the freedoms of others. Furthermore, we have to acknowledge the work of this administration to decriminalize homosexuality in seventy-one countries. The U.S. ambassador to Germany, Richard Grenell, the highest-ranking openly gay official in the history of Republican administrations, leads the global effort.

Much to the chagrin of some Republicans, Trump hasn't reflexively targeted and jailed his political adversaries, even when his administration could have justifiably done so. Nor has he pardoned political allies who have been charged with criminal offenses. He didn't use his authority to put a stop to the special counsel investigation, instead providing extensive access to privileged documents needed to reach an accurate conclusion. It's possible we will yet see prosecutions and pardons, but given the level of evidence coming forward regarding the origins of the Russia collusion hoax, Foreign Intelligence Surveillance Act (FISA) abuse, and disparate treatment of Clinton operatives and Trump operatives by the Justice Department, those investigations are warranted.

Far from feathering his own nest, President Trump has donated his salary each quarter, taking just one dollar a year in pay. He may be seeing an uptick in the number of people who patronize businesses that bear his name, much as President Obama saw an uptick in sales of his books during his administration. But there is no evidence to suggest Donald Trump has cashed in on his presidency.

Where is this fascism we were told to expect? If we use freedom and force as our metric, whose freedom has been restricted by this presidency? Perhaps drug cartels, human traffickers, and coyotes could make such an argument. But their increasing presence in this country impinges on the freedoms of every American. Too many of the people crossing our borders illegally have criminal histories or are engaged in criminal enterprises. Settling criminals in our communities does not make us more free.

The media continues to gleefully bash the man and his administration without restraint, so it's difficult to make a case for suppression of speech unless you consider Trump's insults and name-calling a serious threat to the First Amendment. Some people do. But where have those threats been followed up by any actual restriction of freedom or imposition of force?

There are disturbing threats to free speech in this country, but they are not coming from President Trump. They are being imposed by college faculties, social media giants, internet browsers, and activist mobs. They are even embedded in House-sponsored legislation promoted by Democratic House Speaker Nancy Pelosi.

We are enjoying the strongest economy in decades, complete with record low unemployment and strong wage growth. Progressives may argue that presidents don't get credit for good economies, but these are the same people who warned that Trump would be the one to crash the economy if we allowed him to be sworn in.

Perhaps the most obvious contrast between the predictions about a Trump presidency and the reality of it is in foreign policy. This president is extracting us from war zones, not entering them. Far from instigating new wars, Trump is preparing to exit Syria and Afghanistan, going to great lengths to facilitate peace with longtime enemy North Korea, and cutting off the Obama administration's financial support of Iranian terror operations. Arguably there is potential for U.S. military involvement in Venezuela, but the administration's support of grassroots regime change efforts in that country have thus far yielded more successes and fewer risks than President Obama's failed Arab Spring strategy. That disastrous policy destabilized Libya, Egypt, Yemen, Syria, and Bahrain.

I suppose one could argue that President Trump is taking advantage of centralized power—but he does so in the same way that President Obama did before him. And unlike the Obama administration, this administration has also restrained the power of the federal government through massive deregulation, federal income tax cuts, and policies empowering states. For example, President Obama's Affordable Care Act used force to require states to expand Medicaid while giving them no flexibility to defend their budgets against proliferating health-care populations and costs. Fortunately a Supreme Court ruling restored freedom to states to opt out of the program. Recently the Trump administration approved a waiver for my state that will enable Utah to provide expanded health-care coverage and still maintain control of costs. Honoring the freedom of states to innovate and the flexibility to revise federal programs is not fascism. It is not force. It is an expansion of freedom that enables states to experiment with real solutions without risking their ability to educate their kids, invest in infrastructure, or provide other programs and services.

President Trump's emphasis on border security has also been used to paint him as a fascist. His policies have been interpreted by leftists as some kind of nationalist bigotry, but the policies he has espoused would have had the full support of Democrats just ten years ago. No one thought them fascist back then, because these policies hardly fit the textbook definition of an authoritarian or fascist regime.

So where did people get the idea that President Trump was going to be a fascist authoritarian? Let's look back at what we were all reading about in 2016.

Is Donald Trump a Fascist? An Expert Weighs In, *Slate*, 2/10/2016
Donald Trump's Authoritarian Fantasies, *Reason*, 2/29/16
Trump's Totalitarian Instincts, *RedState*, 2/27/16
George Clooney: Donald Trump is a "Fascist," *Variety*, 3/3/16
Trump: The authoritarian's candidate of choice, *Washington Post*, 3/4/16
Trump: The American Fascist, BillMoyers.com, 3/11/2016
Trump's not Hitler, he's Mussolini, *Salon*, 3/12/16
The rise of American authoritarianism, *Vox*, 3/1/16
Is Donald Trump actually a fascist? *Toronto Star*, 4/3/16
Donald Trump and the Authoritarian Temptation, *The Atlantic*, 5/3/16
Here's How Donald Trump's Authoritarianism Would Actually Work, *New York Magazine*, 5/13/16
Eclectic Extremist: Donald Trump's distinctly American authoritarianism draws equally from the wacko right and wacko left, *Slate*, 5/13/16

This is how fascism comes to America, *Washington Post*, 5/18/16

I asked 5 fascism experts whether Donald Trump is a fascist. Here's what they said, *Vox*, 5/19/16

Rise of Donald Trump Tracks Growing Debate over Global Fascism, *New York Times*, 5/28/16

Yes, a Trump Presidency Would Bring Fascism to America, *Forbes*, 5/31/16

Fascism is rising in the U.S. and Europe—and Donald Trump is the face of this disturbing new reality, *Salon*, 6/12/16

Is Donald Trump an Actual Fascist? *Vanity Fair*, 6/14/2016

The F-Word: Donald Trump and concerns about fascism, *National Review*, 6/20/16

Is Donald Trump a Fascist? *Newsweek*, 7/07/15

What Would Trump Fascism Look Like? Ten Traits, *Daily Kos*, 7/10/16

An American Authoritarian, *The Atlantic*, 8/10/2016

Is Donald Trump a fascist? *The New Republic*, 9/30/16

Is Trump an Ur-Fascist? *The Atlantic*, 10/5/2016

Trump is America's Franco: How Fascism Finds a Foothold in Democratic Nations, *Paste Magazine*, 10/11/16

How Fascist is Donald Trump? There's actually a formula for that, *Washington Post*, 10/21/16

A Scholar of Fascism Sees a Lot That's Familiar with Trump, *The New Yorker*, 11/04/2016

Is Donald Trump a Fascist? *Financial Times*, 11/5/2016

Donald Trump Is Already Acting Like an Authoritarian, *The New Republic*, 11/14/16

Donald Trump is actually a fascist, *Washington Post*, 12/9/16

Is Donald Trump a Threat to Democracy? *New York Times*, 12/16/16

Donald Trump: Strong Leader or Dangerous Authoritarian? NPR, 12/16/16

Those are just from the election year. That list reads like one big Democrat PR campaign. And maybe it was.

To be fair, some of these pieces are opinion submissions. Several of them conclude that Trump is not a fascist, albeit with subheadlines like these from *The New Republic*: "His 'movement' lacks the revolutionary élan of classical fascism, but the repercussions for American democracy are still frightening." Or this one: "Just days since the election, the worst fears about him are coming true." Incidentally, this notion that the worst fears about Donald Trump ever came true is patently absurd. It hardly seems possible given the tone and tenor of the fearmongering in the articles on this list.

Of course, as the articles published in 2016 demonstrate, we don't necessarily agree on exactly what fascism means. As author Jonah Goldberg deftly explained in his 2008 book *Liberal Fascism*, "even though scholars admit that the nature of fascism is vague, complicated, and open to wildly divergent interpretations, many modern liberals and leftists act as if they know exactly what fascism is. What's more, they see it everywhere—except when they look in the mirror."

Ruling with Force

To the extent that elements of fascist philosophy have emerged, they have come from the left. Freedom and fascism are not compatible. When you implement policies that expand freedom, force contracts. When you expand force, freedom is suppressed. And the left is all about suppressing freedom.

That's not to say that I equate progressive politics with fascism, socialism, or any other ism. I think such labels degrade our political discourse and leave us with no language to describe the real thing when it emerges. However, I find it ironic that those scaremongering about right-wing fascism are actually themselves promoting policies that employ more force and less freedom.

The many articles published in 2016 were right about the growing threat of fascist tendencies (not to be confused with outright fascism). They just misdiagnosed the source of those problems. In Democrats' zeal to stop the perceived authoritarian tendencies of Donald Trump, they have doubled down on deploying the very authoritarian strategies they claimed to be trying to prevent.

Political neophyte Alexandria Ocasio-Cortez has proposed a Green New Deal that openly seeks to phase out cars, air travel, hamburgers, and access to affordable power. Is there any possibility that this agenda can be implemented without a massive show of force? To make it a reality, government will have to take on new responsibilities—enforcing new restrictions on how we can travel, what we can eat, and what we can sell. Americans will have to accept dramatic price increases in energy, goods, food, and transportation. What are the chances they will do so willingly?

Nearly every declared Democratic presidential hopeful initially praised this specific proposal and continues to support its broad framework. Not one Democratic senator was willing to vote against it when Majority Leader Mitch McConnell put it to a vote. Instead they all voted "present" in the hope of avoiding going on the record.

There are plenty of other examples of force-deploying policies from the left. Presidential hopeful Kamala Harris has released a comprehensive immigration plan that would prevent the deportation of over 6 million illegal border crossers. The proposal bypasses Congress completely. Her unconstitutional solution calls for a presidential expansion of DACA (Deferred Action for Childhood Arrivals) that would eliminate any requirement for Dreamers to apply for legal status by the age of thirty-one, would raise to seventeen the age at which qualifying applicants could have been brought to the United States as children, and would give Dreamers green cards. All without any input from the lawmaking branch of government.

Bernie Sanders is supporting a Medicare-for-all scheme that would make private health insurance illegal and centralize the power over every American's health in the federal bureaucracy. The House version of the bill has 107 cosponsors—half of the Democratic caucus. The bill replaces what's left of the free market in health care (such as it is) with policies that restrict freedom and expand force. Your freedom to choose a private or employer-sponsored health plan will be taken away. In its typical one-size-fits-all fashion, the government will dictate your health plan, your doctor, your hospital, and your ability to get approved for a procedure. Government will set the prices for drugs, surgeries, and preventive care. This represents a massive expansion of government force with no means for anyone to opt out of the program. This policy encompasses the key components of fascism: centralization of authority and stringent socioeconomic controls.

Free speech in particular has been under attack from the left. By labeling traditionally mainstream Christian beliefs as racist, homophobic, or bigoted, they seek to marginalize people of faith. Left-leaning progressive nonprofits like the Southern Poverty Law Center clamor to dox organizations that engage in speech they don't like. Progressives at the IRS targeted nonprofit groups based on their political leanings. Progressive students at college campuses clamor to exclude or disrupt conservative speakers, abridging the freedom of others on campus who wish to hear them. When was the last time we saw conservatives shut down a progressive speaker on a college campus?

One particularly ironic example is happening in my own state, where progressive groups have demanded that a conference scheduled at Utah's Brigham Young University in 2023 be moved because of the university's morality standards. The Classical Association of the Middle West and South (CAMWS), an academic organization for scholars of ancient Greece and Rome, initially stood firm against the heavy pressure from progressives. But the group eventually caved, ironically invoking the group's policies on inclusivity and diversity to justify excluding a university with a divergent view. These are the tactics of authoritarians.

The first bill introduced by Democrats in the 116th Congress also contains a raft of provisions limiting free speech. As my friend and colleague Senator Mike Lee often explains, Democrats believe anyone is free to publish opinions about political campaigns, but only if they don't actually own the printing press.

Some in the media have taken to attacking what they call "bothsidesism"—which *New York Times* columnist Paul Krugman describes as the "almost pathological determination to portray politicians and their programs as being equally good or equally bad, no matter how ludicrous that pretense becomes." Krugman believes some opinions (apparently, even mainstream conservative ones) are so beyond the pale that good journalists have a duty to shun them. Yes, fascist threads run deep in the fabric of the American left.

One need look no further than the confirmation hearings of Justice Kavanaugh to find fascism gone mainstream in America. They built upon some of the very same tactics I saw deployed at my last town hall. They were not interested in truth. They were interested in narrative. It didn't matter what was real, only what could be projected. We saw key players dispense with the battle of ideas, again relying on debate-killing epithets to destroy the opposition at any cost. Truth became collateral damage.

We saw the divide-and-conquer tactics of identity politics in which men were pitted against women and stereotypes were taken as gospel truth. We witnessed the deployment of nonprofit networks to help stage the show. But most disturbing was the willingness to sacrifice long-standing institutional norms—the presumption of innocence, due process, and the very confirmation process itself—to protect political power. None of that is compatible with freedom. It's far more compatible with fascism.

Again, I'm hesitant to call it fascism, because I think we have been far too careless in our use of that term. We should be reticent to use the word casually. Shame on the Democrats and their media allies for devaluing a term that should be reserved for extreme totalitarian regimes. When such radical terms are employed in the service of petty political battles, we are left with no language sufficiently strong to describe legitimate threats to our republic.

Nonetheless, if President Trump can be called a fascist for prioritizing border security or objecting too strongly to biased news coverage, then those same standards easily convict Trump's opposition. Are there threads of fascism in American politics?

The government has indeed targeted, framed, and in some cases prosecuted political enemies—but they were not the enemies of Donald Trump. Thus far they have been the enemies of the left, ranging from conservative nonprofits to Trump appointees to the president himself.

The Democratic House under Speaker Pelosi looks to double down on this tactic going into 2020 with an avalanche of new congressional investigations designed to serve as opposition research rather than actual oversight.

Furthermore, we are seeing proposals to curtail freedoms guaranteed in the Bill of Rights—but again, those proposals are coming from Democrats in Congress, not from the Trump administration. An in-depth look at the priority bills filed by Democrats in the 116th Congress shows an alarming attempt to fundamentally transform American institutions and forever alter our constitutional checks on centralized power.

In the political realm, we are seeing Democrats attempt to achieve through legislation what cannot be done at the ballot box, with proposals for vast new federal authority over state and local elections and campaign finance rules carefully crafted to do exactly the opposite of what they purport to do.

We are seeing a weaponization of national consensus on issues like fascism and racism. But perhaps most alarming is what we are not seeing. The weaponization of traditionally apolitical entities, particularly in the nonprofit sector, is invisible to most Americans. But the nefarious practice of using nonprofit charities as fronts for political organizations represents a chilling new battleground in the quest for political power.

What happens to people who express unpopular opinions in a fascist state? They get suppressed. Leftists once again turn to their time-honored tactic of suppressing debate with anger-inducing labels. Hate speech is the one they use to justify retaliation against ideas they wish to suppress. Where are we seeing suppression of political views in America today? The threat to free speech actually comes from the likes of left-leaning cultural, educational, and media sectors. Technology giants like Twitter, Facebook, YouTube, Google, and even PayPal have gotten into the censorship game—where errors or overreach almost inevitably fall to the benefit of leftist speech.

Tucker Carlson called out PayPal in a February 2019 broadcast, pointing out that the online payment platform, upon which many rely for income, has taken to banning users whose speech the left-leaning company dislikes. He explained:

> *Last year, PayPal banned Alex Jones from using the platform for saying things they didn't like. They have also banned anti-Muslim activist Laura Loomer, the publication VDARE, and a number of other people and organizations whose speech they believe should be silenced.*
>
> *[PayPal CEO Dan] Schulman admitted that his company takes guidance on who to ban from the Southern Poverty Law Center—that's an entirely fraudulent organization that works as an arm of the Democratic National Committee. According to Schulman, "The line between free speech and hate, nobody teaches it to you in college. Nobody defined it in the law." Well, that is ridiculous. It is very much defined in the law and has been for 50 years. In 1969, the Supreme Court conclusively decided that hate speech does not exist. But it doesn't matter to Schulman or any of his allies on the left. To them, the First Amendment is merely a legal obstacle. It's something to subvert rather than celebrate.*

Granted, fascist elements can be found in the extreme movements of both right and left. The likes of Alex Jones and open white supremacists like VDARE are certainly beyond the pale. We are fortunate to live in a society in which we are free to reject such rhetoric. But when the left, using the SPLC as a metric, gets to decide what constitutes extreme speech, even the most mainstream conservative outlets can become a target.

There are plenty of fascist policies coming from outside the Trump administration. Trump may occasionally talk the authoritarian talk, but it's the left that walks the authoritarian walk.

Branding Trump as a fascist is not about fascism. It's about grabbing power. Even the Democrats' most loyal allies in the press know it. *Salon* cynically warned, "Branding Trumpism Fascist has the political benefit of mobilizing disparate forces in the fight against him just like the antifascist coalition of World War II led to unprecedented alliances between ideologically disparate forces (the Soviet-American alliance being the primary example). In the American context, seeing Trump as a 2016 reincarnation of Mussolini can unite Democrats, Republicans, independents, Naderites, neo-cons, constitutionalists, and others, into a broad anti-Fascist coalition which would bring Trump down and save our democracy."

Of course, Democrats aren't so much focused on saving democracy as they are on saving their own power. They will pay any price—scratch that—they will ask you to pay any price to make that happen.

Case in point: President Trump's declaration of a national emergency to provide funding for a border wall. Former secretary of state Madeleine Albright called President Trump's use of that authority an example of "fascist" behavior. Prior to the House vote on the resolution blocking the emergency declaration, Nancy Pelosi said, "Perhaps it's time for our country to have a civics lesson. Our founders rejected the idea of a monarch." That's all well and good, except for one problem: Pelosi doesn't believe in rejecting a powerful executive and neither do her Democrat colleagues in Congress, who uniformly cheered President Obama's use of pen and phone to avoid traditional checks and balances by the legislative branch.

The dead giveaway can be found in the resolution blocking Trump's national emergency. It blocks the president's ability to reprogram authorized funds in this specific case. It does nothing to rein in future presidents—a move for which there would be strong bipartisan support.

This is about blocking this president, this time. The last thing Nancy Pelosi wants is to rein in the executive authority upon which Democrat presidents have relied to bypass legislative checks and balances.

The casualty in all of this is foundational institutions that have been key to the success of the world's most successful economy. Many of the articles warning of Trump's fascism warned of potential damage to our democratic institutions. But a more careful look at institutions from the Electoral College to the First Amendment and from the Supreme Court to the Department of Justice shows the real damage is coming not from President Trump's allies but from his political enemies. Much of it begins in Congress.

CHAPTER 4

CREATING FALSE NARRATIVES

Two years after her devastating defeat at the hands of Donald Trump, Hillary Clinton stood before a Selma, Alabama, crowd and attempted to explain why she isn't the president of the United States. She offered one simple reason. "I was the first person who ran for president without the protection of the Voting Rights Act and I will tell you, it makes a really big difference," Clinton said.

We have heard Clinton offer a bevy of reasons for her loss, but this was a new one. Affecting her best southern accent, Clinton clumsily attempted to construct a narrative that would conform to the formula her party had successfully used for years. It is a formula that weaponizes public consensus—in this case the consensus against racism—and attempts to cast political opponents as coming down on the wrong side of that consensus.

She explained that people she referred to as opponents of the half-century-old law had "found a receptive Supreme Court" that "gutted the Voting Rights Act." She then proceeded to spin a narrative that attributed her electoral defeat to voters in Wisconsin who she says were turned away from the polls "because of the color of their skin, because of their age, because of whatever excuse could be made up to stop a fellow American citizen from voting."

There was a problem with this narrative. It just flat out was not true. The Supreme Court decision to which Clinton was referring, *Shelby Co. Ala. v. Holder*, applied only to nine states, mostly in the Deep South. It did not apply to Wisconsin. Even *Salon*, one of the premier outlets for Democratic Party propaganda, called Clinton out. Their story cited legal experts who explained that the key states in Clinton's loss (Ohio, Wisconsin, Michigan, Pennsylvania) were not even covered by the part of the Voting Rights Act the Court had struck down. Eventually the *Washington Post* fact-checker gave Clinton four Pinocchios for her claim.

Besides being factually inaccurate on the legal details, Clinton's narrative was clearly hyperbolic. The effects of the Supreme Court decision were not broad enough to have the impact she described. Such a notion may resonate with progressive voters in America's Blue cities whose exposure to conservative voters is limited to stereotypes. But for your average American voter who is not racist, the argument that Clinton lost because of racist voter suppression is an outrage. The claim is a way to quickly shut down debate and win the argument without actually having to take a position against election security.

We shouldn't be surprised to see Clinton attach herself to this narrative. We have seen not-so-subtle foreshadowing that this narrative will play a huge role in the 2020 election cycle.

Why else would Democrats choose a failed gubernatorial candidate to offer the party's rebuttal to the State of the Union address? Georgia Democrat Stacey Abrams blames her 54,000-vote loss on voter list maintenance or—as she calls it—voter suppression. The fact that her opponent, as secretary of state, removed voters who had died, moved, become inactive (usually because they died or moved), or used names that did not match their government ID is being characterized as an act of racism and suppression. Trotting out Abrams on the national stage was one signal that Democrats will ramp up this narrative for 2020.

In the world of political narratives, these stories we tell help us decide who is right and who is wrong. The power of a good narrative is among the most potent tools in the political arsenal. In fiction, narratives help us determine which characters are the good guys and which ones are the bad guys. They help us take a side in a conflict, assign motives to the actors, and determine whether justice was done.

Narratives can be true, false, or a matter of opinion. They help us make sense of our world, but as Hillary Clinton demonstrated, they can also be used to manipulate us. In the age of Donald Trump, the spinning of increasingly implausible narratives has gone into overdrive.

Without congressional majorities, Democrats in the first two years of the Trump administration were limited in their ability to initiate the types of investigations that help build election-year narratives. But even in the minority, they demonstrated just how far they are willing to go to take down this president. Traditional norms no longer apply. The confirmation hearings of Justice Brett Kavanaugh were a window into the scorched-earth approach Democrats will take to tell the stories that protect their power.

Democratic senator Dianne Feinstein of California, ranking member of the Senate Judiciary Committee, would be the Democratic lead in the confirmation hearings. To this point, Feinstein had been very outspoken about her principles when it comes to congressional oversight, posting to her website in 2009: "So amid all the quarreling and confusion, I say this: Let's not prejudge or jump to conclusions. And let's resist the temptation to stage a Washington spectacle, high in entertainment value, but low in fact-finding potential."

Unfortunately for Feinstein, the Kavanaugh hearings would pit her stated principles against her partisan interests. To disrupt the Kavanaugh nomination, Feinstein and her Democrat colleagues would have to cast off long-standing traditions and violate some of their own deeply held beliefs. They would do it. This confirmation hearing would be like nothing that had come before it. No one would contest that congressional hearings are inherently political. But this time Democrats would have to cross lines they had never crossed before.

Having lost the presidency, Democrats in July 2017 were now facing a second existential threat as President Donald Trump would have the opportunity to replace retiring swing justice Anthony Kennedy. A qualified and energetic young conservative could occupy that seat for three decades. Having gambled and lost on the president's first Supreme Court nominee, Neil Gorsuch, Democrats were now without the filibuster that would have given them the votes to block Kennedy's replacement. They needed to do something drastic. They needed a narrative that would be disqualifying. Without a valid reason to reject the president's nominee, they would have to create one.

The Kavanaugh Spectacle

The coordinated attempt to commit reputational murder for political gain is becoming a favorite trope of the left. The trope is effective, but only if people believe it. We should familiarize ourselves with the basic components of this screenplay, because we'll be seeing a lot more of it now that House committee gavels are held by Democrats. If we are to push back against the false narratives, we have to be able to spot them quickly and expose them fully.

That segment of the Democrat Party that is unmoored from truth is particularly adept at the smoke-and-mirrors game. Not being limited by the constraints of truth, these people project false narratives in hopes of producing short-term gains for their party, sometimes at the expense of third parties whose lives are never the same afterward.

You can often distinguish the fictional narratives from legitimate ones by the extent to which they conform to a pattern. If a story is shaping up like it's straight out of Hollywood, you know it's probably fake.

Conflict is accentuated, with clear markers indicating who is on the right side. Plotlines are sensational enough to capture attention. A boring character is imbued with fictional characteristics that cast him as a hero or a villain. Plot developments are timed just right to wow the audience.

Stories like the Trump-Russia collusion narrative and the Brett Kavanaugh sexual assault narrative conveniently match the story arc that is most compelling to audiences, but do so at the expense of the truth. It's easier than ever to dismiss truth and the rule of law when you're in the grip of anti-Trump hysteria.

The Kavanaugh hearings showcase that hysteria at its apex. Just as it had at my town hall meeting, the opposition followed a prepared playbook. It goes like this.

1. THE MEDIA MACHINE: Democrat allies deliver a highly choreographed and coordinated rollout.
2. UPPING THE STAKES: Senate Democrats open with attempts to tie the nomination to their ongoing collusion investigation.
3. STALLING AND DISTRACTION: Democrats seek to obscure their specious narrative with pointless procedural posturing, followed by a race to amp up the drama.
4. MOVING THE GOALPOSTS: Once the narrative is finally exposed, there's the age-old tactic of moving the goalposts at the finish line. It's a high-stakes game of Calvinball.

We saw many of these same elements as the Mueller investigation into Russian collusion drew to a conclusion. As long as the pattern provides short-term political gains, it doesn't have to be true to be useful. The public provides those short-term gains when we uncritically accept the narratives being fed to us.

The Media Machine

The Kavanaugh narrative started with a plotline scripted long before the nominee was ever chosen.

Under the direction of seasoned veteran senator Dianne Feinstein, Democrats planned to create a narrative that the nominee (whoever it was) would be unfit, unqualified, and unacceptable for the Supreme Court. If the public didn't buy it, they would come up with some sort of dramatic disqualifying event from the person's past that would cause most Americans to unite against the nominee. The clock would run out on the 2018 midterms, the Democrats would take the House and Senate in a landslide, and the Supreme Court seat would be held open until 2020, when a presumably Democratic president would nominate a liberal judge to the Court, saving mankind and restoring balance to the universe. For Democrats, that would have been the best-case scenario.

In retrospect, the hearings did not turn out according to plan. Kavanaugh's confirmation was not blocked, the narrative Democrats spun did not turn out to be credible, and at least one incumbent Senate Democrat believed the hearings cost the party her seat in the 2018 midterms. There were two problems: First, the nominee was miscast. Democrats were hoping for a radical extremist, a misogynist, or an inexperienced partisan. Kavanaugh was demonstrably none of those. Second, Democrats would inevitably do what people always do when not constrained by truth: overreach.

On cue, the July 9, 2018, announcement of Kavanaugh's

nomination triggered the first scene of any Supreme Court battle. This is the part where the nominee is cast as an extremist. Despite characterizations of being the moderate pick among those on the short list, Kavanaugh was immediately demonized as a radical. Never mind that just two days before the July 9 nomination, the *Hill* newspaper reported that Kavanaugh was facing pushback from social conservatives for being too moderate. According to the reporting, he would likely need Democrat votes to get confirmed. An opinion piece appearing in the *New York Times* the day of the nomination even made a liberal's case for Brett Kavanaugh.

Undaunted by those facts, Senate Democrats and their allies pressed on with a script that sounded as though it had been designed with another nominee in mind. Senate Democrat Chuck Schumer of New York rolled out the strategy with a July 10 floor speech setting out all the talking points—that Kavanaugh was "way out of the mainstream," believed "the president doesn't need to follow the law," and had a long paper trail that would require lots of time for review.

The staging for this phase of the performance is well documented. A September 4 *Politico* story reported on a Democratic strategy session pitting the Senate Judiciary Committee's "aggressive, often younger senators" against "veterans who prefer to adhere to the chamber's norms." Those norms would be not only challenged but in fact sacrificed in the days to come.

Vermont senator Bernie Sanders tweeted (without evidence, as Democrats like to say), "President Trump's Supreme Court nominee Brett Kavanaugh will be a rubber-stamp for an extreme, right-wing agenda pushed by corporations and billionaires. We must mobilize the American people to defeat Trump's right-wing, reactionary nominee." Connecticut's Senator Chris Murphy chimed in to call Kavanaugh a "Second Amendment radical" who was "way out of the judicial mainstream" and "far to the right of even late Justice [Antonin] Scalia." The hyperbole didn't end there.

Betting that most Americans were unaware of Kavanaugh's mainstream record, the Senate's outside allies were even more strident. Former Virginia governor and Hillary Clinton confidant Terry McAuliffe went so far as to make the outlandish claim that Kavanaugh's nomination would "threaten the lives of millions of Americans"—a claim that would be uncritically repeated by many others, including student groups at Kavanaugh's alma mater, Yale University.

Not to be outdone, the Women's March organization tweeted that Kavanaugh's nomination was a "death sentence" for women. Incidentally, the Women's March receives funding from none other than Planned Parenthood, in addition to dozens of other left-wing nonprofit groups.

In a revealing slip, the Women's March statement came with an introduction that read, "In response to Donald Trump's nomination of XX [*sic*] to the Supreme Court of the United States, The Women's March released the following statement . . ." Had they prepared the statement before they even knew the identity of the nominee? It sure looked that way. Just how coordinated was this rollout?

In a case of foreshadowing, NARAL Pro Choice America (short for the National Abortion and Reproductive Rights Action League) appeared to get ahead of the script with a statement reading, "We'll be DAMNED if we're going to let five MEN— including some frat boy named Bret—strip us of our hard won bodily autonomy and reproductive rights." Many people on the right focused on the hypocrisy of the fact that NARAL had no objection to *Roe v. Wade* originally being decided by an all-male Supreme Court. But the other interesting thing about this tweet is the reference to Kavanaugh as a "frat boy" with a frat boy name. That scene was slated for later in the show. How did NARAL already have the script?

Upping the Stakes

Having cast Kavanaugh as an extreme choice, Democrats next moved to connect him to their favorite narrative—the special counsel's investigation into the Trump campaign's alleged collusion with Russia. This messaging would deflect attention away from the challenging battleground of Kavanaugh's unquestionably stellar judicial record and move back to the familiar territory of Russian collusion—a story line that had not yet lost its potency. At this point, they still believed with near-religious devotion that Mueller would ultimately indict the president. They were interested, not in determining whether Kavanaugh was qualified, but only in tying him to what they thought would become a slam-dunk case against the president. Democrats conflated accusations related to the president and his political team with reasons to question Kavanaugh's fitness to serve on the Supreme Court.

Judiciary Committee Democrat and presidential hopeful Cory Booker, of New Jersey, sent a series of tweets before the hearings began in which he attempted to float the constitutionally suspect idea that a president who has been merely accused of something nefarious should not be permitted to make Supreme Court appointments. He tweeted:

> The President of the United States was implicated in open court of a federal crime by his longtime personal lawyer. It's increasingly urgent we stop Trump's handpicked Supreme Court nominee Kavanaugh from getting a lifetime appointment to the highest court in our land.

Booker repeated the argument less than two hours later, trying again to sell the idea that allegations against a president were sufficient reason to keep him from doing his constitutional duty. Booker tweeted:

> *A president who is named by his longtime personal lawyer as an un-indicted co-conspirator should not be nominating Supreme Court judges for lifetime appointments.*

On the opening day of Kavanaugh's testimony, Judiciary Committee Democrat and presidential hopeful Amy Klobuchar continued trying to tie Kavanaugh to the Mueller investigation in her opening statement, saying that Democrats' duty in these hearings was to figure out whether Kavanaugh viewed the president as above the law and to delve into his view of "laws protecting the special counsel." Once again, it was all about the Russia story.

A comparison of former senator Sessions's statement at the Sonia Sotomayor confirmation hearing in 2009 with Feinstein's statement at the Kavanaugh hearing shows just how politicized this latter hearing had become. Sessions criticized Sotomayor but based his criticism on the nominee's record and views pertinent to her role as a Supreme Court justice. By contrast, Senator Feinstein's statement at Justice Kavanaugh's confirmation hearing lists a series of criticisms of President Trump.

Stalling and Distraction

Having established the narrative, the Democrats now merely have to distract the public from looking too closely. Believe it or not, the boring function of requesting documents can be weaponized to create quite a distraction. Document requests can be written in such a way that they build narratives that manipulate public opinion and contribute to the pointless circus surrounding false narratives. This tactic wasn't unique to the Kavanaugh hearings, but the hearings are a textbook example of how the play is run. Pay close attention to how this particular tactic is deployed. As long as we have a Republican president in the White House, they'll run this play again and again.

The trick with this gambit is making the public believe Senate Democrats actually cared about reviewing hundreds of thousands of pages of documents on a nominee many had already pledged to oppose. The narrative depended on projecting a sincere desire to vet the man's record, when the reality was a covert desire to delay the confirmation hearings.

The first step is the submission of a document request sufficiently broad that it will prove impossible to fill in any reasonable amount of time. The intent is not to review the resulting documents, but to rail about documents that are missing. If the document request is not broad enough, they run the risk of actually getting all the documents. Then they would have nothing to complain about.

In the case of Kavanaugh, Democrats wanted every document Kavanaugh had touched during his time as a White House staffer for the George W. Bush administration. In an unprecedented move, Chairman Charles Grassley, Republican of Iowa, told the committee that Senator Feinstein demanded "the search of every email and every other document from every one of the hundreds of White House aides who came and went during the entire eight years of the Bush Administration."

These documents would be difficult to get and of little value. Feinstein would have known many of these documents would be protected by executive privilege. All the better.

According to comments from Republican senator John Cornyn of Texas during the hearings, every single Democrat on the Senate Judiciary Committee had announced opposition to Kavanaugh before the very first hearing. Their minds were made up. No volume of documents was going to change them. It was all a sham.

By demanding an impossibly broad series of documents they knew would be both difficult to get and of little value, they had a pretext to do what they likely would have done anyway—refuse to meet with the nominee, a move that might conveniently also delay the hearings. Many of them did refuse, waiting until the cameras were on to ask Kavanaugh simple questions that a genuine seeker of facts could have ascertained long before the hearings.

Senate minority leader Chuck Schumer continued framing the Democrat narrative, gaslighting the public into thinking Kavanaugh was hiding his record.

In August, Schumer tweeted:

Republicans' mad rush to hold this hearing after unilaterally deciding to block nearly all of Judge Kavanaugh's records from public release is further evidence that they are hiding important information from the American people, and continues to raise the question, #WhatAreTheyHiding?

In a subsequent tweet, he wrote:

Republican efforts to make this the least transparent, most secretive Supreme Court nomination in history continue. They seem to be more frightened of this nominee's record and history than any we've ever considered.

In reality, more documents were produced on Judge Kavanaugh's record than on any of the previous nominees'. Over a two-month period, Democrats had access to the following documents:

- An 18,000-page response to the committee's Senate Judiciary Questionnaire (SJQ)
- All of Kavanaugh's published writings
- 307 judicial opinions Kavanaugh wrote
- Hundreds of opinions Kavanaugh joined
- All available footage and transcripts of Kavanaugh's public appearances

- All books that used him as a resource
- More than 500,000 pages of documents related to his past legal service in the executive branch
- One-on-one meetings with Kavanaugh (65 senators took advantage of the opportunity).

Subsequently, senators heard thirty-two hours of testimony from Kavanaugh, then received responses to 1,300 post-hearing written questions. A memo from Senate Judiciary Committee Republicans notes this was "more questions than have been asked of all prior Supreme Court nominees combined."

Even the White House, whose right to withhold documents under executive privilege was held sacrosanct by these same Democrats during the Obama administration, reported having turned over more documents on Kavanaugh than on the five previous nominees combined. The opposition had to know that executive privilege would apply to some of the documents that they were requesting. Nevertheless, the Democrats insisted that Kavanaugh was hiding something.

Feinstein doubled down on the Schumer tweet, releasing a statement the same day with the same gaslighting technique Schumer had used to make the public question the facts:

Scheduling a hearing in early September, while more than 99 percent of Kavanaugh's records are still unavailable, is not only unprecedented but a new low in Republican efforts to stack the courts.

Aside from the obvious hyperbole of suggesting that Republicans filling Supreme Court vacancies constitutes "stacking the courts," Feinstein's numbers are problematic. The *Washington Post* called out the obvious exaggeration in her messaging, noting that she had to massage the numbers by excluding large volumes of documents produced to the Senate, but not made public. The

Post also noted her false assumption that the White House record being held back was millions of pages more than it actually was. Furthermore, the *Post* correctly pointed out that many of the records not produced were duplicates of emails sent and received among multiple people.

Democrats would have you believe they were waiting to assiduously review every last page of every last document so they could be certain how they would vote. But if that were actually true, they probably would have shown up to see the documents that had already been produced. Especially the ones designated "committee confidential" that were considered too sensitive for public release. Did they? You won't read about it in any mainstream source, but none other than Chairman Grassley himself provided the answer just before the hearings got under way:

"The most sensitive presidential records remain committee confidential under federal law just as they were during the nominations of Kagan or Gorsuch," he said. "But we have expanded access to these documents. Also, instead of just providing access to committee members, we've provided access to all 100 senators. Instead of just providing access to a very few committee aides, we've provided access to all committee aides. And instead of just providing access to physical binders of paper, we've provided 24/7 digital and searchable access. This is unprecedented access to committee confidential material. I would also like to add that my staff set up work stations and have been available 24/7 to help senators who are not on the committee access confidential materials . . . but not one senator showed up."

Any journalist with a laptop and a shred of integrity could have blown up the Senate Democrats' false narrative with one story. (Of course, few did.) The document demands were nothing more than a ruse to delay the hearings and prop up the false narrative that Kavanaugh must be hiding something. But that would not stop Judiciary Committee Democrats and 2020 presidential hopefuls from doubling down on the overreach in the opening day of the Kavanaugh confirmation hearings.

If this play sounds familiar, it's because Schumer ran it again immediately after Attorney General William Barr released his summary of the Mueller report in late March 2019. Knowing that an investigation involving a foreign power would necessarily have to be redacted and that grand jury material is never made public, Democrats made a show of demanding the entire Mueller report with underlying documentation. They know it can't all be produced. They don't even necessarily disagree with the reasons. But if they want to run with a narrative that the Trump administration is "hiding something," they have to create the appearance that they didn't get everything they needed.

To this point in the confirmation process, the behavior of Democrats trying to stop the Kavanaugh nomination was aggressive, opportunistic, and misleading. But not necessarily unprecedented. All of that would change once the hearings got under way. That's when a new narrative would need to be built—a narrative powerful enough to take down a highly qualified Supreme Court nominee.

The first day of the confirmation hearings was carefully scripted by Schumer, according to CNN. Citing an anonymous source, CNN reported that Schumer himself had worked through the preceding weekend with Judiciary Committee Democrats to lay out a plan. "Democrats agreed to protest the document issues at the beginning of the hearing with the goal of slowing down the process," CNN reported.

That's when the real show began. Who can forget the drama of those hearings and their immediate aftermath, with all the suspense of carefully timed plot twists, last-minute bombshells, emotional outbursts, and Oscar-worthy performances by Democrats on the Senate Judiciary Committee? Perhaps the influence of the Democrats' Hollywood acolytes had rubbed off on them.

The drama was just getting started. Cue the choreography between Senate Democrats and nonprofit political groups. On the opening day of the hearing, *Politico* reported, "They created a spectacle by hijacking the hearing as soon as it started and calling for the committee to adjourn against a backdrop of liberal activists being arrested in protest."

The DNC's surrogate Planned Parenthood was in the thick of the battle, announcing on the hearing's opening day a six-figure ad buy against Kavanaugh in Washington, D.C., and Alaska, where moderate Republican Lisa Murkowski was expected to be a swing vote. In a tweet on the hearing's opening day, the nonprofit posted:

The disruptions we're seeing during Brett Kavanaugh's hearing pale in comparison to the disruptions and lengths women already take to access safe, legal abortion. This is what the resistance looks like, and we're going to fight like hell to #StopKavanaugh.

Yes, they would. At one point in the hearings, Republican senator Thom Tillis of North Carolina referenced a tweet from NBC suggesting that the protests, which were supposedly in response to a late document released the night before, had been coordinated by Leader Schumer in a conference call prior to that document's release. He asked point-blank whether committee Democrats were involved in that call. Democratic senator Dick Durbin of Illinois admitted, "Mr. Chairman, there was a phone conference yesterday and I can tell you at the time of the phone conference many issues were raised." The protests were just part of the script.

Presidential hopefuls on the committee capitalized on progressive anger to jump-start fund-raising for their nascent presidential campaigns, with CNN reporting, "As the hearing was under way, both Booker and Senator Kamala Harris of California—often cited as potential 2020 presidential contenders—sent emails to supporters asking them to sign up with their names and contact information to stand against Kavanaugh, often seen as a way for senators to build contact lists."

Senator Booker had one of the most memorable moments of the hearing when he pointlessly broke committee rules to score political points. In promising to release a classified email he had inappropriately referenced publicly, Booker declared, "This is about the closest I'll probably have in my life to an 'I am Spartacus' moment," thus becoming a meme and a mockery. Later the public learned the disappointingly benign document had been cleared for release the previous night. But Booker's intended unauthorized release of classified information was one more Senate norm sacrificed in the effort to score points against Donald Trump.

Despite all the drama, the wall-to-wall news coverage, the screaming from activists, and the scheming from Senate leadership, the hearings weren't going well. The radical extremist narrative predictably didn't stick. The Russia collusion narrative was implausible given the paucity of evidence at the time. The #whataretheyhiding narrative didn't stand up to the fact-checkers. But Senator Feinstein still had one card left to play.

In a departure from long-standing Senate norms, Feinstein held that card back until the very last minute. She was sitting on a new allegation—a new plot twist—for which there had been no foreshadowing. Sensational allegations that Kavanaugh had sexually assaulted a woman in high school were being made by an unknown source. Although Senator Feinstein had known of these allegations for weeks, she never so much as hinted at them until just prior to the confirmation vote.

This craven attempt to amp up the drama and suspense was not the act of a person making a sincere attempt to get to the truth. It denied Kavanaugh that most fundamental right of due process. This was someone fearful the show would not go on if she took time to actually vet the allegations.

Kavanaugh had come to the confirmation process with a long

record of mentoring and empowering female law clerks, volunteering in the community, and coaching girls' sports teams. The narrative Feinstein needed to build would have to turn him into a beer-guzzling college frat boy who forces himself on unsuspecting innocents.

A letter to Chairman Grassley from Senate Democrats dated August 24, 2018, cited "unprecedented lack of transparency" as justification to delay the hearings slated for the following week. Yet even as Feinstein and colleagues were demanding transparency, they themselves were holding back information Feinstein would later describe as critical to the nomination. "From the outset," she would later say, "I have believed these allegations were extremely serious and bear heavily on Judge Kavanaugh's character." If that is true, her failure to produce that evidence at the appropriate time was a significant departure from standard investigative procedure and an indication that fact-finding was not her priority.

When news of the allegations finally dropped, it didn't come from Feinstein, who had briefed committee Democrats days after the Kavanaugh hearings concluded but chose to keep Republicans in the dark. Once again, this was a departure from the way such investigations typically operate, particularly when a committee believes there is a sexual assault victim to protect.

Details about the allegations leaked out slowly (some might say strategically) starting with a September 12 *Intercept* story the same day Feinstein briefed committee Democrats. The first story only described the existence of a document, but reported that the content was unclear. More details dribbled out in a *New York Times* story the next day suggesting the incident involved sexual misconduct and then a *New Yorker* article a day later that suggested an assault by Kavanaugh. Two days later, Chairman Grassley learned of the identity of Kavanaugh accuser Christine Blasey-Ford from the *Washington Post*. The coordinated rollout was now a full-scale public relations offensive.

I have worked with investigations that involved victims of sexual assault. They require great sensitivity and discretion. Never have I seen a witness treated the way Ford was treated by committee Democrats and by her own lawyers. To them, she seemed to be more of a political commodity than a human being.

The response from Blasey-Ford's lawyers to Senate Judiciary Committee efforts to investigate seemed calculated to maximize the drama rather than to expose the truth or protect the witness.

According to the Senate Judiciary Committee memo released after the whole process concluded, Dr. Ford's attorneys refused all committee requests for an interview with their client, either in California or in Washington, missed deadlines to respond, and delayed the investigation. When they finally did respond, they insisted on controlling the "number of witnesses, the order of witnesses, the number of cameras, the specific reporters and media outlets granted access, Justice Kavanaugh's location during Dr. Ford's testimony, and the Committee's manner of questioning Dr. Ford." Breaking with another Senate norm, the committee accommodated many of those requests. Despite those great efforts, Ford's attorneys refused to turn over evidence they claimed was in their possession—specifically polygraphs, videos of the polygraph examination, and therapy notes Dr. Ford claimed would substantiate her story.

For a witness to make such an incredible claim and then refuse to produce evidence she uses to support that claim was unusual. In my experience, witnesses are anxious to document their claims. Not Dr. Ford—if you believe her lawyers.

We later learned that Dr. Ford's attorney was a Democrat activist and self-proclaimed member of the resistance movement who had been recommended by none other than Senator Feinstein. Was Senator Feinstein coordinating with the witness and her legal team prior to the testimony? If so, that behavior would be far outside the norm for congressional investigations.

Rather than conduct an investigation using Democratic investigative staff, Senator Feinstein chose to believe Dr. Ford sans evidence proving her claims. She leaned on the earlier FBI investigation—perhaps because she could be critical of an FBI investigation rather than an investigation by her staff.

Meanwhile, Feinstein criticized GOP senators in an October 5 statement, saying, "They refused to gather evidence or do an impartial investigation into [Dr. Ford's] allegations." In contrast to Feinstein's complete failure to investigate, Senate Republicans included in their memorandum on the investigation an exhaustive list of the forty-five witnesses they spoke with and the twenty-five written statements they collected in their effort to validate the claims of Dr. Ford. They concluded, "Committee investigators found no verifiable evidence that supported Dr. Ford's allegations against Justice Kavanaugh. The witnesses that Dr. Ford identified as individuals who could corroborate her allegations failed to do so, and in fact, contradicted her."

Feinstein instead tried to argue that the FBI, not the Republican committee staff, should investigate the allegations. But as news organizations widely reported, sexual assault allegations are the jurisdiction of local police, not federal law enforcement. The FBI had no jurisdiction beyond the six FBI background checks performed over a twenty-five-year period that included interviews with 150 individuals who knew Justice Kavanaugh personally. Feinstein was surely aware of this fact. It was all part of the #whataretheyhiding strategy. As with document requests, they intentionally ask for something they know they can't get. Then, when they don't get it, they use that fact to shore up the narrative that someone is afraid of the truth.

Just ten days after the Ford allegations surfaced, a second allegation emerged, this one from Debra Ramirez, who claimed to remember an incident at Yale in which Kavanaugh supposedly exposed himself. The allegation was published uncritically by the *New Yorker*, after which the *New York Times* acknowledged passing up the story when witnesses would not corroborate it. Without vetting the allegations, Democratic senators responded by releasing statements demanding the White House rescind the Kavanaugh nomination. The committee would later reveal that Ramirez had contacted witnesses asking them to verify her story. None did.

Three days later, with the Ramirez allegations not yet discredited, another accuser came forward, this one represented by attorney Michael Avenatti. The accuser, Julie Swetnick, had a wild story involving a gang rape in high school. Like Ford's attorney, Swetnick's attorney played cat and mouse with committee investigators, promising evidence, but never producing it. Avenatti refused to allow Swetnick to be interviewed by the committee but did allow her to be interviewed by the media, where she would ultimately discredit herself.

The next morning, Ford testified for the first time—in public. While her story was heartbreaking, there was not one element of it that could be positively verified; this left the public and the committee to make their judgments based solely on emotions. Honestly, if I had such a witness testifying to something so personal and so painful, but who I knew could not corroborate her story, I would not put her in front of cameras for all to judge. If Democrats truly believed the allegations, why would they politicize, package, and market her pain for public consumption? Particularly given her inability to remember anything verifiable. They had to know her testimony would be deeply scrutinized. Why expose her in that way? It was a reprehensible and opportunistic display.

She told the Senate Judiciary Committee she was "100 percent certain" Kavanaugh was the one to abuse her. Later that day, Kavanaugh appeared before the Senate Judiciary Committee to defend himself. In no uncertain terms, he denied the allegations. During the follow-up questioning, Senate Democrats sought to shore up their narrative of Kavanaugh as a hard-partying frat boy. He was asked about a fourth accuser, Judi Munro-Leighton, who had emailed the committee claiming Kavanaugh raped her.

The media breathlessly reported, analyzed, and researched

every word. For days the allegations against Kavanaugh filled every newsfeed, newscast, and newsmagazine. In the stampede to get the story first, news outlets relaxed their standards for vetting, airing allegations that would later prove demonstrably false. Kavanaugh would forever be associated with the narrative Democrats had created around him.

Moving the Goalposts

Now, of course, the speciousness of the Democrat narrative could no longer be hidden. With the realization that none of the accusers could produce verifiable evidence of their claims, the narratives Democrats had so carefully spun began to fall apart. Democrats have an answer for that, too. It's called moving the goalposts.

Changing the criteria by which one party can declare victory is a political norm, but disingenuous nonetheless. They were frustrated over how many documents they hadn't received. Then it was frustration over the volume of documents they received the night before the hearing. Then it was frustration over the volume of documents marked as committee confidential, as explained by Senator Durbin during the hearing. They argued that the public needed to see these documents. Then, as every document that they requested be reviewed and made public was approved, they started releasing committee-confidential documents and claiming they were breaking the rules. They later demanded an FBI investigation. Then, when it was completed, it wasn't good enough.

A similar evolution would repeat the following year as the special counsel investigation similarly failed to produce evidence to confirm the narrative that the Trump campaign colluded with Russia to steal the presidential election. Once the results of Mueller's investigation became public, the collusion narrative would be old and busted. An obstruction narrative would become the new hotness.

Kavanaugh's nomination to the Supreme Court was ultimately confirmed. When all was said and done, some of the truth came out. One accuser, Judi Munro-Leighton, would later recant, admitting she had made up the allegation. The progressive activist from Kentucky said, "I was angry, and I sent it out." Likewise, Julie Swetnick walked back her allegation, claiming Avenatti "twisted" her words. Had the media vetted her claims more carefully, they would have discovered a long history of false allegations as well as a prior connection to Ford's lawyer, Debra Katz.

Planned Parenthood stood behind the discredited accuser, tweeting in late October, "We still believe Julie Swetnick. #BelieveSurvivors." Nevertheless, the committee found Swetnick and Avenatti had criminally conspired to make materially false statements to the committee to obstruct the investigation. Munro-Leighton, Swetnick, and Avenatti were all referred for criminal prosecution.

Democrats had a choice. They could have adhered to the process and procedures that have guided congressional investigations for decades. They could have thoroughly investigated the Ford allegations behind closed doors in a bipartisan manner. But they chose not to do that. They could have used transcribed interviews to keep her identity secret and protect her from a lifetime of harassment and notoriety. They could have sought for the truth as best they could find it. But they opted for the sensational. They opted for the theatrics. By choosing not to act in a bipartisan way, refusing to conduct private interviews, failing to keep the accuser's name private, and not involving the FBI until the allegations went public, Democrats backed themselves into a corner.

The Cost of the Kavanaugh Approach

While Democrats realized short-term gains from their scorched-earth strategy for derailing the Kavanaugh nomination, there are long-term costs. Those costs come in credibility, damage to the Senate's norms and institutions, and the opportunity costs of spending their political capital on partisan warfare rather than public policy achievements.

They also imposed a cost on Ford, Kavanaugh, and their families. Despite the lack of evidence, many Americans are left believing the false caricature of Kavanaugh as a drunken frat boy who routinely assaults women. As I was looking to refresh my memory of the outcome of the investigation, I tried a basic internet search using the names of the accusers. When I looked up Swetnick, Ramirez, and others, the only stories I could find were the ones reporting the allegations. Stories reporting the results of the investigation were few and far between. I finally had to turn to the memorandum released by Senate Republicans, which contained the full record of emails, text messages, interviews, and results from their investigation. The correction to the narrative was not amplified and was reported a small fraction as much as the original allegations. That is the danger of this false narrative strategy. It spreads misinformation and leaves broken hearts and broken lives in its wake.

In her urgent need to score political points, Senator Feinstein revved up the media machine to trample fundamental principles of due process and presumption of innocence. Unconstrained by truth, Democrats upped the stakes and lost sight of the boundaries of believability. As the plot became more and more sensational, the stalling and distraction came across as contrived, even forced. As the show wore on, our ability to suspend disbelief on so many inconsistent plot points evaporated. They unwittingly cast themselves as the antagonists. As they continued to move the goalposts, they came across as Keystone Cops who badly bungled this investigation. Dr. Ford herself came out of this all right, but the circus that surrounded her was so over-the-top it would have made P. T. Barnum blush.

Missouri senator Claire McCaskill, who lost a close race to

Republican Josh Hawley in 2018, told news outlets the "spectacle" created by the Kavanaugh hearings hurt her with voters. "I don't think my vote [against Kavanaugh] hurt me as much as the spectacle that occurred," McCaskill told NPR after her defeat. "There were mistakes made by my party in terms of how that was handled."

With Democrats now in control of the House, there are lessons to be learned from the Kavanaugh hearings—for all parties concerned. While I won't be holding my breath for Democrats to learn them, I do think there is value for voters in seeing the show for what it is. The sooner voters are able to see through the smoke and mirrors, the sooner we can unite to reject these damaging and divisive truth-free theatrics for the power grab they are. We can start by recognizing elements that are sure to be repeated as the House majority looks to set new narratives ahead of the 2020 presidential election.

CHAPTER 5

DOUBLE STANDARDS

The 2018 midterms saw Democrats convert forty-one seats in the House of Representatives to take over the majority and re-install Nancy Pelosi as Speaker of the House. With a Republican president and a Republican Senate, Pelosi now finds herself in the role she criticized during the Obama presidency—that of the obstructionist.

She's no doubt hoping that it will be a short-term role, necessary to play while Democrats wait out the remainder of the Trump presidency. Meanwhile, Pelosi is positioning her House majority to pursue an agenda that should scare the living daylights out of any true American patriot.

Resistance Is the New Obstruction

The mirror image of today was 2010, when Republicans took the House and Democrats still maintained the presidency and the

Senate majority. What the media now refers to as resistance was what they then called obstruction.

Back in those days, obstruction was bad. Connecticut Democrat Chris Dodd's take was typical of the narratives we heard from Democrats at the time. He told *Politico* in late 2009, "History will judge harshly those who have chosen the simple path of obstruction over the hard work of making change. It always does." In a 2014 weekly address, President Obama blamed obstruction for his failure to grow the economy.

> *The problem is, Republicans in Congress keep blocking or voting down almost every serious idea to strengthen the middle class. We could do so much more as a country—as a strong, tight-knit family—if Republicans in Congress were less interested in stacking the deck for those at the top, and more interested in growing the economy for everybody.*

Ironically, when the tables turned and Democrats had the opportunity to vote for a tax reform plan that would help the middle class, every last Democrat in the House resisted. They characterized the tax policy as a giveaway to the wealthy. But today the middle class is reaping the dividends as the economy continues to add new jobs, payrolls increase, new workers enter the workforce, and unemployment rates among women, Hispanics, and blacks hit record lows.

Of course, obstruction against the Trump agenda is given a very different treatment in popular media and culture than was obstruction against the Obama agenda. What was once obstruction is now resistance. What was once bad is now good. This time, by some strange coincidence, we are not being spoon-fed a steady diet of obstruction narratives by the media.

Back then, you could search the words "House obstruction" and "party of no" and come up with hundreds of current results— as though every media outlet were coordinating on their narrative of the day. In reality, the "party of no" and obstruction messaging originally came from the Democratic Congressional Campaign Committee (DCCC), the congressional campaign arm of the Democratic National Committee. But to read the reporting at the time, one would have believed there was some kind of national consensus against obstruction.

A search of those terms today will still show some of the old stories about Republicans, who deeply resented the label at the time and worked hard to dispel it. Far from resenting the label, Democrats, including former president Obama, now embrace it. The media cheerleads it. Suddenly resistance is all the rage.

But just because obstruction won't be marketed as such doesn't mean it won't be noticed by voters tired of political brinksmanship and hypocrisy.

I watch the obstructionists' resistance and I see them opposing policies they supported in the past, betraying their own principles in the pursuit of power. Voters would be right to wonder—are both parties willing to go that far? Did I?

Speaking for myself and other members of the freshman class elected at the same time as President Obama, we genuinely wanted to find ways to work together. I particularly remember how strongly we felt about health-care reform. It was going to impact all of our districts. We knew there was a problem. We wanted to see Congress get it right. And we really believed it was possible to come up with a bill that could garner bipartisan support. All of our efforts to engage on that legislation were rebuffed.

I look back at a January 2010 meeting of the House Republican Conference in which President Obama made an appearance. Our interaction with the president that day highlights the huge chasm between where we were at that time and where Democrats are with President Trump today.

At the beginning of each new Congress, Democrats and Republicans go off campus and spend two or three days in planning and strategy sessions. House Republicans, rather than going to the posh comforts of West Virginia's Greenbrier Resort, as they had in years past, elected that year to go to a Marriott hotel on the Baltimore waterfront so that President Obama could come to address us. At the time Mike Pence was our GOP conference chair, which meant that he would be conducting the meeting and calling on members to ask questions. The night before the meeting, I approached Pence and said, "I have a question for the president. If you have a list of people to ask questions, put me on that list." I didn't tell him my question and he didn't ask.

As a freshman legislator, I was surprised when Pence called on me to ask my question. I said to the president,

I'm one of twenty-two House freshmen. We didn't create this mess but we are here to help clean it up. . . . There are some things that have happened that I would like your perspective on. Because I could look you in the eye and tell you, we have not been obstructionists.

The Democrats have the House, the Senate, and the presidency. When you stood up before the American people multiple times and said you would broadcast the health-care debates on C-SPAN, you didn't. I was disappointed, and I think a lot of Americans were disappointed. You said you weren't going to allow lobbyists in the seniormost positions within your administration. And yet you did. I applauded you when you said it, and [was] disappointed when you didn't. You said you'd go line-by-line through the health-care bill. There were six of us, including Dr. Phil Roe, who sent you a letter and said we would like to take you up on that offer. We'd like to come. We never got a letter. We never got a call. We were never involved in those discussions. And when you said in the House of Representatives that you were going to tackle earmarks, in fact you didn't want to have any earmarks in any of your bills, I jumped out of my seat and applauded you, but it didn't happen. More importantly, I'd like to talk about moving forward, but if we could address—

He cut off my question. There went his narrative about Republican obstruction. He knew our exchange was being broadcast and it completely undercut the false narrative he had been trying to sell. Democrats wanted the public to believe that Obama was trying to work with Republicans in a bipartisan way while we were being the "party of no." It wasn't true. We had been trying to engage. In no uncertain terms, our efforts had been rejected. Remember, just the previous year President Obama had rebuffed Republican leadership at the White House when they tried to negotiate with him on a stimulus package. In a remark that reportedly poisoned the well with Republicans, Obama said, "Elections have consequences. And at the end of the day, I won. So I think on that one I trump you." (It would take a few more years before Democrats would get Trumped.) I felt he needed to own that noncollaborative attitude and America needed to know it.

President Obama really wanted the optics to show that he was coming to us, reaching out his hand, and we were reflexively rejecting anything he attempted to do. That's not what I saw. We had stood ready to work with him—not to cave to him—but to work to find common ground on a health-care bill we believed (and time later proved) would drive up the cost of health care. That bill had too many mandates and used too much force to implement its policy prescriptions.

The next week, President Obama's chief of staff came to see me in my office. In retrospect, I can only guess that they needed the optics and the story that they had followed up with me because they certainly weren't interested in making changes to their health-care bill. After that one meeting, I never heard from them again until Republicans won back the House.

Today, we don't really expect to hear anyone from the freshman class of Democrats listing a series of issues on which they think the president should be applauded. This freshman class wears the term "obstruction" like a badge of honor. Their resistance-obsessed base eats it up. But what about the average American, who is working hard and playing by the rules?

With the script flipped, the hypocrisy is laid bare. Much of what they told us two years ago is suddenly heresy. Obstruction is good now. Solving real problems, such as the border crisis, is considered bad strategy. Nobody is offering to work with the president on immigration the way my freshman class begged to work with President Obama on health care.

Meanwhile, Pelosi has implemented changes in the body intended to stifle the minority, impose a double standard, obscure transparency, and entrench her party's hold on power. All of that works to set the stage for the kinds of reforms that will dramatically raise taxes and spending, reduce individual liberties, and appropriate vast local government and free-market powers. The strong central government her party envisions will be more socialist, less free, and completely under the unfettered control of the Democratic Party.

Stifling the Minority

Not sixty days into her new speakership, Nancy Pelosi was being urged by members of her caucus to remove a long-standing tool of the minority that was exposing divisions between moderates and liberal progressives in the caucus. The little-known motion to recommit (MTR) allows the minority party to force an immediate vote on an amendment to a bill.

In the House, the majority rules. Anything can pass with just 50 percent plus one vote. Without a few tools to give the minority input, they might as well go home. The MTR is one of the times that the minority can put something forward and force a vote on it.

Republicans masterfully used the procedure in a February 2019 vote on the barely bipartisan piece of legislation called the Bi-partisan Background Checks Bill.

While the bill itself had the support of only eight Republicans, it had broad support from the Democratic caucus. An MTR offered by Republican representative Doug Collins of Georgia forced an immediate vote on an amendment previously voted down in committee. That amendment, which would report illegal alien gun purchasers to U.S. Immigration and Customs Enforcement (ICE), received twenty-six votes from moderate and swing district Democrats—enough to pass.

With the amendment added to the background checks bill, Democrats from safe liberal districts now had a dilemma. A vote for background checks would also be a vote for reporting illegal aliens to ICE. In an interview with the *Daily Caller*, Republican congressman Richard Hudson of North Carolina recalled, "I thought it was pretty amazing to watch the Democrats try to decide 'Do we want to protect illegal immigrants or do we want to confiscate guns more?' It was kind of funny."

House Minority Leader Kevin McCarthy responded to the threat to do away with minority rights that date back to 1909. During a press conference, McCarthy said:

> *Democrats are now thinking about changing the rule. Rather than reconcile the differences within their party that are driving this division, Democrats want to rig the rules and suppress the minority party's speech on the House floor.*
>
> *I want to be very clear and make no mistake:* changes to the MTR would be a nuclear option. *And it would leave a stain on this majority.*
>
> *You all know the history. In the last twenty-four years in America, Republicans have been the majority party for twenty of them. Never once did we discuss, bring up the option, or even entertain the idea that we would silence the minority. Never once. Not during a sit-in, not during anything that we did.*

Why didn't the MTR threaten the Republican majority the way it now threatens Democrats? This is where we get into how the sausage is made in Washington, D.C. MTRs never posed a threat to the Republican majority because House Republicans united to treat the motion as a procedural vote, not a policy vote. If the full GOP conference was united in voting no on every motion to recommit, there was no need to justify those votes on policy grounds. The minority could access valuable floor time to express opposition, but a united majority could still ensure bills did not get derailed by a minority picking off votes from moderate members. MTRs simply weren't treated like policy votes.

But with Democrats winning their majority primarily from swing districts, many of their newest members felt they could not afford to vote no on an amendment reporting illegal gun buyers to ICE, for example. They treated the MTR as a policy vote. That decision made the MTR far more powerful in the hands of the minority. Democrats now face the threat of actually having to take votes on difficult issues. This is something members of Congress try to avoid at all costs. But with the caucus fractured and inconsistent, every Democrat is now expected to explain, from a policy perspective, why they voted no on a provision Republicans selected. This has made the tool far more potent with a very real chance of altering legislation.

As of this writing, Pelosi has not opted to eliminate the MTR. Instead she has instructed her caucus to adopt the Republican strategy of voting no across the board. Unfortunately for her, that genie can't be put back in the bottle. Her members have established that votes on minority amendments are indeed policy votes for which they must answer. When the House subsequently passed H.R. 1, Republicans offered an amendment condemning illegal alien voting. This time only six Democrats supported the amendment. But that many, combined with the previous precedent, means every Democrat will have to go home to the district and answer questions about why they voted no on condemning illegal immigrant voting. Furthermore, MTR votes now engender headlines like this one from FoxNews.com: "House Dems overwhelmingly reject motion to condemn illegal immigrant voting."

Imposing a Double Standard

For anyone who was paying attention to the work of oversight during the Obama administration, prepare to get whiplash. The script has flipped. With Democrats in the majority and a Republican in the White House, leadership has succumbed to the temptation to revert to a whole different standard of rules. We've seen a 180-degree shift in the Democrats' attitude toward witness preparation and what they used to refer to as taxpayer-funded fishing expeditions. Behavior they routinely engaged in during the Obama years is now considered reprehensible. Behavior they routinely and inaccurately accused Republicans of engaging in is now virtuous.

I've been around long enough to remember way back two years ago when it was inappropriate for witnesses to meet with committee members or partisan staff outside the presence of the other party. I was routinely questioned by my Maryland Democratic colleague Elijah Cummings as to whether I or my staff had interacted with a witness prior to a hearing. I never dreamt of having those types of meetings without inviting the Democratic staff. It just didn't happen.

Likewise, if we wanted to go on an overseas trip to perform oversight, with few exceptions we had to get a member of the other party to join us. The only time I got an exception to that rule was immediately following the 9/11/12 attack in Benghazi when I traveled to Tripoli. Time was of the essence and no one on the Democratic side had accepted my invitation to go. Because of the emergency nature of the incident, I was permitted to go without a Democratic counterpart, but only after offering them the opportunity and having them turn it down.

That rule is not being observed in Speaker Pelosi's House. When former Trump attorney Michael Cohen testified before the House Oversight Committee, Cohen sheepishly admitted to Republican ranking member Jim Jordan of Ohio that he had spoken with Democratic Intelligence Committee chairman Adam Schiff of California "about topics that were going to be raised at the upcoming hearing." After the hearing, Republican Oversight Committee member Mike Turner of Ohio sent a letter to Cohen's team asking for more information about those contacts. All of us who have served on the House Oversight Committee know that such a meeting is far outside the norm. Turner wrote, "These questions are important for the public to understand whether or not they were watching witness testimony, a public hearing, or well-rehearsed theater."

Cohen later acknowledged to House investigators that Schiff had traveled to New York four times (presumably at taxpayer expense) and that he or his staff spent ten hours meeting with Cohen. Democrats played it off as standard procedure. Schiff told CBS News' Margaret Brennan, "that's what you do in any credible investigation." Committee spokesman Patrick Boland, in response to Turner's letter, said:

We are running a professional investigation in search of the facts, and we welcome the opportunity to meet with potential witnesses in advance of any testimony to determine relevant topics to cover in order to make productive use of their time before the Committee. Despite this professed outrage by Republicans, it's completely appropriate to conduct proffer sessions and allow witnesses to review their prior testimony before the Committee interviews them—such sessions are a routine part of every serious investigation around the country, including congressional investigations.

No. They are not routine. There is nothing standard about this procedure. Keep in mind, this is not a court proceeding where the rules of discovery are in play. But there is a long-standing norm and a deep understanding that the minority has rights. The minority should be invited to such meetings. They are not held with staff or members from one party except under very unusual circumstances. Certainly not in dealing with a scheduled witness. And certainly not when that witness has an attorney through whom the staff should be communicating.

For Schiff and his partisan staff to meet a scheduled witness in person, without the minority present, is not remotely appropriate or routine. These responses are incredibly dishonest in that they conflate routine bipartisan investigation and witness preparation with partisan witness tampering and testimony rehearsal. These two things are very different. Chairman Cummings would have been livid had I pulled such a stunt. I never did. I'm sure if a reporter pressed him, he would have to acknowledge that Schiff's behavior was inappropriate. But no reporter will.

Other rules and norms have also shifted with the flipping of the script. Remember when taxpayer-funded fishing expeditions were a bad thing? Those days are over as far as Democrats are concerned. Remember when executive privilege was a valid defense for withholding information from Congress? No more. And remember when failing to respond to congressional subpoenas was okay with the Democrats? Suddenly they don't feel that way anymore.

With Democrats now on offense, their strategy has changed. During the Obama administration, Democrat members of Congress saw themselves as a defensive team for the president. They went to great lengths to keep embarrassing information from being discovered or revealed. With President Trump in office, Democrats have miraculously discovered a newfound commitment to accountability.

One of our Republican Oversight Committee staffers tells the story of a meeting she once attended in which the chief counsel for the Democrats introduced herself and said, "I'm in charge of defensive investigations." She was paid by the legislative branch, but her job was literally to defend the administration. That really set a tone. The staff all knew that was essentially her job, but for her to openly admit it was audacious. If congressional Republicans got caught using a term like "defensive investigations" I wouldn't be surprised to see a dozen mainstream stories within twenty-four hours.

The Democrats were very aggressive at playing defense for President Obama. Not for one minute should we let them get away with pretending to be offended by behaviors they routinely engaged in. Republicans should not be the least bit embarrassed to call out witness tampering, defend executive privilege, protect classified and grand jury information, or point out what they see as taxpayer-funded fishing expeditions.

The Democrats' newfound commitment to executive branch transparency and simultaneous commitment to legislative branch secrecy are predictable. Their sudden conversion to the need for subpoena compliance is welcome, but it must be channeled into permanent solutions that hold both parties to the same standard. They don't seem to want that.

They are using their oversight power to let the Deep State off the hook—losing interest in any investigations that might negatively impact their constituents in the civil service. They are instead using the subpoena power to engage in the very fishing expeditions they decried under President Obama. In the case of the Mueller Report, many called it contempt of Congress when Attorney General Barr wouldn't give them access to grand jury material he is legally prohibited from providing. I remember well how vociferously my Democratic colleagues defended the need to withhold grand jury materials when those materials involved Hillary Clinton's emails. Now they express shock and horror if the executive branch does not immediately turn over evidence they seek—as though they had not themselves promoted and defended the very practices now relied upon by the Trump administration to withhold documents or testimony.

Some of their complaints are certainly valid, but unless they are willing to close the loopholes in the law that they themselves exploited under President Obama's leadership, their complaints will continue to ring hypocritical and opportunistic. I wouldn't object to reconsidering congressional access to grand jury materials under certain circumstances, for example. But Democrats don't necessarily want to have that debate. They want Attorney General Barr to go to the courts and seek approval to release the information in this case and this case only. They have no interest in opening up a potential future Democratic president to congressional oversight of grand jury materials.

Obscuring Transparency with Strategic Rule Changes

Fulfilling the quixotic promises Democrats made to win the House majority will require some heavy, unpopular, and economically debilitating tax and spending increases. To mitigate the damage and protect her members from the inevitable real-world consequences of those policies, Pelosi needs to obscure the harsh realities of the policies. Furthermore, she needs to shield the government from scrutiny that might undermine faith in the bureaucracy. She needs them to manage the decisions Americans have traditionally been free to make for themselves.

Speaker Pelosi crafted a rules package that better serves her agenda to grow government, shield incompetence, and stay in power. These rule changes will also help facilitate her escalation of the war on the administration in the short term.

Rules packages are introduced at the beginning of each two-year cycle in the House. With the ending of the 115th Congress and the seating of all newly elected members on January 3, 2019, all previous bills and rules expired and the 116th Congress began. With it came a new rules package developed by a new Speaker. By and large, the House of Representatives still follows the original parliamentary rules crafted by Thomas Jefferson and adopted in 1837. But each new Congress can adapt those rules to suit the body's purposes. Upon her taking the gavel, the crafting of the new rules package was Pelosi's first opportunity to set the stage for future power grabs. Predictably, she did just that.

The rules package adopted in January 2019 acted as a preview of coming attractions. Some of the power grabs we've seen since Pelosi took the gavel—and what we will continue to see through the 2020 election cycle—were foreshadowed from the very first day of the 116th Congress.

Comparing the new rules package to the one it replaced paints a vivid picture—if you know what to look for. Specifically, the new package does five things that signal where Pelosi is going. It eliminates government from the reform mandate, shields members who vote for tax and spending increases, hides debt ceiling increases, removes barriers to new taxes and spending, and finally, it changes the way Congress forecasts the impact of tax increases. Any question what Pelosi needs to do to get her agenda enacted?

1. Eliminating Government Reform

Right out of the gate, we saw what looked like a minor change to the standing rules—the Committee on Oversight and Government Reform became just the Committee on Oversight and Reform. The removal of one word my not seem like a big deal. But it foreshadows a completely different approach to oversight. For Democrats, government is never the problem. Government is always the solution. I predict we are unlikely to see any serious oversight of actual federal employees from Chairman Elijah Cummings's House Committee on Oversight and Reform unless they are Trump appointees. Democrats have effectively taken the "government" out of government reform.

We can expect Cummings's focus to be twofold: providing political advantage for the 2020 election cycle, and expanding the committee's oversight reach deep into the private sector. Such reach would take investigations beyond the proper role of government or the historical authority of the committee. Look for him to use his congressional authority to target and intimidate individual businesses and people who are perceived as harmful to the progressive agenda. We'll dive deeper into that problem in the next chapter. Suffice it to say that the federal workforce can rest easy with Democrats at the helm. There will be little transparency to check their power as long as the Oversight Committee is focused on the private sector.

2. Changing Rules for Accounting for Taxes

Other changes to the rules package portended big changes in the way new taxes and spending would be adopted and accounted for. Unfortunately, we're used to seeing Congress spend a lot of money no matter who is in the majority. The rules package indicated Democrats would be looking to take taxes and spending to a whole new level, but without having to answer for those votes. Indeed, their subsequent proposals have borne that prediction out.

Pelosi's agenda is aggressive enough that even the scant spending restraints still in place were too much for her. Furthermore, she believes her members need to be protected from the blowback that will come when votes touted as "high taxes on the rich" inevitably morph into high taxes for everyone who works for a living. The Green New Deal is being pitched as something to be funded by raising tax rates on top earners. We are now seeing what Pelosi must have always known—top earners can't generate enough pay for the Green New Deal. Massive tax increases won't be limited to the wealthy.

Perhaps the most convincing illusion in the package was a provision called PAYGO—which projected fiscal responsibility but in this case was actually designed to do the opposite. Pelosi ignited a show of controversy within her own caucus by inserting a PAYGO provision (pay-as-you-go) that ostensibly required lawmakers to offset spending increases with cuts elsewhere in the budget. That idea likely pacified the moderate members and their more conservative districts. But the small print of the provision was designed to please the most extreme members of the Democratic caucus. Pelosi's version of PAYGO was designed to be easily waived either by a majority vote or for emergency spending. Is there any spending (other than for the Wall) that Democrats do not consider to be emergency spending?

Inserting PAYGO was a great piece of theater, with members like Alexandria Ocasio-Cortez actually voting against the rules package, basically citing objections to paying for things we can't afford. In reality, the pliable nature of the PAYGO rule was an open secret on Capitol Hill, with Progressive Caucus cochairs Democrats Mark Pocan of Wisconsin and Pramila Jayapal of Washington even issuing, prior to the adoption of the rules, a statement that read: "Chairman [Jim] McGovern and House Leadership have committed to us that PAYGO will not be an impediment to advancing key progressive priorities in the 116th Congress."

In other words, as long as the spending is considered a "key progressive priority" it won't be subject to PAYGO. What will be subject to PAYGO? Spending Democrats don't like—such as defense and border security. Meanwhile, members in swing districts will be able to go home and tout their commitment to fiscal discipline.

3. Hiding Debt Ceiling Increases

PAYGO is just the beginning of the sleight of hand in the House rules package. Pelosi also removed one of the few tools the minority could use to rein in spending, by reinstating the 1980 Gephardt Rule. Except this time the rule was "turbocharged"—as *Roll Call* described it—to remove what little leverage remained to constrain debt. Designed by Democratic former representative Richard Gephardt of Missouri, the rule shields House members from unpopular debt ceiling votes by conjuring up (what they refer to as "deeming") a debt ceiling resolution automatically whenever a budget resolution is adopted.

In other words, members don't ever have to go on the record voting to raise the debt ceiling. That happens every year if we want to keep the government open. Does that fulfill Pelosi's commitment to be more transparent? Not at all. It obscures from the public the realities of the skyrocketing debt ceiling.

The Senate has never used such a rule, so Pelosi neatly shifted the tough on-the-record vote to the Republican Senate and left her members unscathed. Only this time, the rule goes one step further by triggering an independent piece of legislation that does not require Senate agreement. In the past, the Senate could trigger a subsequent on-the-record vote in the House. Now her caucus can drive up the debt as high as they wish without having to go home and justify votes for debt ceiling increases.

The idea of ending the perpetual fights about the debt ceiling may sound appealing to voters fatigued by past conflicts over spending—especially since Republicans did little to rein in spending on their watch. But eliminating the debt ceiling vote is a very dangerous precedent. It truly was the only speed bump left on the soaring trajectory of the national debt.

Upon taking the gavel in January 2019, Pelosi stood up and said that "transparency will be the order of the day" on her watch. But one of her first actions as Speaker was to change the rules and shield her members from a difficult vote to increase the debt ceiling. That's certainly not transparent. She hopes to deemphasize the fact that the growth rate of our debt is screaming toward all-time records, yet a member can be there for two years and never have to take a vote on the debt.

4. Removing Barriers to New Taxes and Spending

To add insult to injury, the new rules remove the supermajority requirement for increasing taxes—further paving the way for the

Democrats' ambitious government growth agenda. In the House, a supermajority is 290 votes, which means Democrats have to be able to garner some minority support to raise taxes. With Pelosi's rule change, they don't need any minority votes whatsoever. They need just 218 votes from their 235-vote majority to ratchet up taxes as high as they want. If you consider the cost of their legislative agenda this is a frightening development.

Senator Sanders's College for All Act will cost $750 billion in the course of a decade. Representative Jayapal's Medicare for All bill will run $28 trillion to $32 trillion over a decade, according to the Committee for a Responsible Budget, which cites five other estimates in the same range. Jayapal's estimate is half that number. Democrats are pushing to spend $1 trillion on infrastructure investment. A national paid family leave entitlement program, like the one implemented recently in Washington, D.C., would cost between $306 billion and $1.9 trillion. The American Action Forum estimates a 4 percent payroll tax at all levels would be needed just to fund the lowest-cost projection.

American Action Forum also published a study estimating the cost of the Green New Deal at $94 trillion. This organization, run by economist and former director of the nonpartisan Congressional Budget Office Douglas Holtz-Eakin, concludes, "The Green New Deal is clearly very expensive. Its further expansion of the federal government's role in some of the most basic decisions of daily life, however, would likely have a more lasting and damaging impact than its enormous price tag."

Those are just the beginning. Pelosi's rules package contains another provision to drive spending higher by allowing amendments on spending bills, even if those amendments increase net spending. Previously, on appropriations bills, all members could introduce an amendment but they had to offset the spending by cutting something else. The way the process is meant to happen, the House considers twelve separate spending bills individually and members can amend each bill as it is considered.

When the system works properly, any member at any point can offer an amendment, but it's only ruled in order if the overall spending is offset or reduced. When I added an amendment to a spending bill to fund roads on the Navajo reservation in my district, I had to offset that $2 million in spending with cuts elsewhere in the Interior Appropriations bill. With school buses unable to navigate dirt roads on the reservation, kids were missing school every time it rained. I felt this was a high enough priority to justify cuts elsewhere in the bill.

Democrats, however, hate this rule—as they hate any and all restraints on government spending and growth. So they nixed it. The new rule will allow Democrats to lard up spending bills with pet projects at the last minute and to pass the bill with a simple majority. Their members will be able to attempt to shirk responsibility for these votes by claiming the last-minute spending wasn't in the bill when they read it. How much restraint do you think they'll exercise when there is no limit to how much they can spend?

5. Changing the Way We Forecast the Real Impact of Legislation
Meanwhile, Speaker Pelosi is paving the way to hit voters where it hurts at tax time. In a transparent bid to control the narrative on tax increases, Democrats are also changing the way tax legislation is scored. Ultimately, this move helps stack the deck by producing incomplete data that obscures the negative economic impact of tax increases while overplaying the cost of tax cuts. Here's how it works.

Scoring is the process of forecasting the ten-year economic impact of legislation. The conventional scoring system is fundamentally flawed because it measures only the direct impact of tax policy changes. Republicans modernized the scoring process when they ran the House to estimate indirect impacts and give members of Congress a more complete fiscal picture. Dynamic scoring uses forecasts that take into consideration the inevitable behavioral changes that result when taxes go up or down. This reveals the part of the picture Democrats prefer to keep hidden from the public.

Conventional scoring methods that Democrats favor assume tax policy does not impact behavior. That's why the Congressional Budget Office (CBO) scoring for Obamacare was so inaccurate. The number of people who buy private policies did not remain steady when the cost of insurance on the exchanges multiplied. But CBO missed that dynamic because they only looked at direct impacts—how many people would qualify to buy private plans on the exchange. CBO projected 21 million people would pay for these plans. But only 12 million did, because of an indirect impact—the rising cost of plans on the exchange—which CBO did not account for.

Even more significant was the CBO's estimate of the number of people who would enroll in Medicaid. Their estimates assumed all fifty states would expand Medicaid, as the law required prior to a Supreme Court decision allowing states to opt out. But with only thirty-one states expanding, the number of people enrolling was still 50 percent higher than CBO estimated, according to research reported by the Mercatus Center. Once again, CBO was only measuring the direct impact—how many people were eligible at that moment and how much were states spending for Medicaid enrollees at the time? In reality, the incentive to enroll in the best insurance that money can't buy (truly—you cannot buy insurance as rich as Medicaid at any price in the private market) caused many more people to enroll or to adjust their income downward slightly in order to become eligible to enroll.

Furthermore, the cost per newly eligible enrollee was much higher than the scoring estimated, largely because states and medical providers were responding to perverse incentives in the bill that encouraged them to set higher payment rates than they had previously used. Mercatus's Brian Blase reports:

Medicaid expansion is proving much more expensive than CBO expected, largely because the agency failed to anticipate how states would respond to the elevated reimbursement rate for ACA Medicaid expansion enrollees. Many states have set very high payment rates to insurers for the expansion population with the cost dispersed to federal taxpayers.

The scoring method used to project the cost of the Democrats' health-care policy misled many states to enter into expansions that are proving unsustainable. This flawed projection model is the one Nancy Pelosi's rules package dictates we use going forward.

Democrats don't like seeing the economic trade-offs of tax increases—and they certainly don't want you to see them. The new rules package removes dynamic scoring to create the illusion that tax increases are harmless to the economy and to hide the economic growth generated by tax cuts.

Are Earmarks Next?

Much to my surprise, Speaker Pelosi's rules package did not contain language reinstating the corrupt federal earmarking practice. Watch closely. That debate is yet to come. We can expect to see supporters of earmarks marketing them as a solution to gridlock and government shutdowns. Young voters may not even remember what they are, as Speaker Boehner did away with the practice in 2011. Earmarks were lawmaker-requested spending provisions that bypassed the merit-based funding process. They were a treasured institution in their day.

Earmarks enabled lawmakers to bring home federal dollars, take credit for generating jobs in their districts, pick winners and losers, and elicit campaign contributions. They included projects like $250,000 for a farmers' market in Kentucky or $750,000 for the World Food Prize in Des Moines, Iowa. The Department of Defense was particularly plagued by companies lobbying their home-state senators and representatives for appropriations to buy products the military did not even want. In one notable example published by the *Seattle Times*, the Pentagon made a decision in 2003 to move away from using decontaminant powder and to instead use more effective lotion to protect soldiers from exposure to nerve agents.

Although the Pentagon told Congress in 2005 of its plans to switch to the lotion, lawmakers who represent the powder producer used earmarks to force the Department of Defense to keep buying the less effective product. That year, after a powder company spent $830,000 on lobbyists, the Department of Defense stockpiled enough powder to last seven years.

Daniel Kohn, president of a New York company involved in the powder production, told the *Seattle Times*, "In self defense, we've gone to our representative in Congress and we've said, 'You know, let's lay our cards on the table. We're in business to provide a living and jobs in your district.'" Despite the large stockpiles already purchased, New York senators Charles Schumer and Hillary Clinton added a $2 million earmark for more powder in the 2007 defense bill. In 2008, another $5.6 million was added. The military in 2010 had 2.2 million unwanted powder kits in stock. Meanwhile, manufacturers of the lotion did some defensive lobbying of their own, hiring lobbyists who got a $3.2 million earmark for the lotion in the 2009 defense bill.

In the 2010 Department of Defense appropriations bill, 532 of the 1,083 House earmarks were requested on behalf of private companies within the requesting member's home district. Although the total amount spent on earmarks was only slightly more than what we spend on foreign aid—about 1 percent of the federal budget—they became grease for the wheels of corruption. In one of many pitches to end the practice, I wrote in the 2010 issue of the *Hinckley Journal of Politics* that lawmakers who wished to reform the practice had traditionally been left with two untenable choices: shortchange America by participating in a corrupt system, or shortchange constituents by refusing to request earmarked dollars that everyone else is receiving. Fortunately, the wave election that was the 2010 midterms drove the political will for congressional Republicans to end earmarks. Reversing that progress would be tragic. Voters should keep an eye out for candidates and representatives calling to restore earmark spending, as there are many in Congress who still deeply regret the loss of this spending tool.

Pelosi Protects Her Power

The selection of Nancy Pelosi as Speaker of the House gave Democrats in Congress a general to lead them in battle. Whereas Speaker Paul Ryan was a policy wonk, Speaker Pelosi is a political strategist. Ryan is the leader you choose when your priority is policy. Pelosi is the one you want when you're going to war.

Make no mistake. The Democrats have gone to war. For them, Donald Trump is an existential threat. The last thing they want to do is find common ground on public policy to drive solutions for which Trump can take credit. Only when their voters are angry and motivated do they donate large amounts of money to get Democrats back in power. You don't accelerate the Trump Bump by passing budgets and growing the economy. To grab power in 2020, they need to create division, build damaging narratives, discredit the Trump administration, and convince Americans their lives are worse despite a booming economy. It's a tall order. Pelosi is poised to use her new majority to deliver.

One rule change that may surprise those who weren't watching C-SPAN at the time is an insurance policy for Pelosi in case she once again proves to be a political liability to her caucus. While I oppose the change on the grounds that it is bad for the institution, it may offer some political advantages for Republicans, who would surely be happy to see Democrats stuck with a wildly unpopular Speaker who drives voters to Republican candidates on election day.

In a move to cement her hold on power during a time when support for her speakership was weak, Pelosi changed the rules to make calling for a mid-session vote for Speaker more difficult. Republicans had used this particular vote process on Speaker Boehner in 2011, with Congressman Mark Meadows introducing a mid-session motion to vacate, which would declare the office of Speaker vacant and force a new vote. Although the bill was never passed, it was in the wake of that effort that Speaker Boehner stepped down. Pelosi will face no such threat.

The new rule requires a majority of members of Congress to call for the motion to vacate, therefore making a threat nearly impossible to carry out successfully. This was a tool of the minority—even the minority within the party in power. It was rarely used, but an important step when leadership needed to change or a re-vote was needed to send a message. This change is bad news for Pelosi's far-left flank. They want impeachment and they want it yesterday. But with no ability to introduce a motion to vacate, they pose little threat to her speakership.

This may have a silver lining for Republicans, who rode anti-Pelosi sentiment to a crushing victory in 2010. It leaves little flexibility for Democrats if they once again see Pelosi driving their party over an electoral cliff.

If there's one bet you can never lose, it's predicting that Nancy Pelosi will overreach. She cannot help herself. There are few lines she will not cross to get a political win. That trait sometimes serves her well, but also threatens to be her downfall. When she was serving as Speaker during my first term in the House, Pelosi overreached to such a degree that she helped spawn the Tea Party movement.

Her policy prescriptions were so bad and her marketing of

them was so deceptive that the resulting electoral backlash cost Democrats the House and Pelosi the speakership. Remember how her deceptively named Affordable Care Act actually did the opposite of what she marketed it to do? How she told *Meet the Press* in 2012 that "everybody will have lower rates"? How she told MSNBC in 2009 that "if you like what you have and you want to keep it, you have the choice to do that"?

In a rare moment of candor, Pelosi did tell us we had to pass the bill before we could know what was in it. I applaud her for her honesty on that point; it was probably the most truthful statement I'd heard from any Democrat on Obamacare. Hundreds of times the bill said, "the secretary shall" or "the secretary may"—which gave so much power to the administration that no one could possibly know what implementation would look like. While Pelosi is a disaster on public policy, Democrats know she'll be a rhetorical warrior in their battle against Donald Trump and she won't let truth stand in her way. That's what they think they need going into 2020.

Did she learn any lessons from her downfall in 2010? If the first year of her return to the gavel is any indication, she did not. Apparently, neither did most of her caucus, who overwhelmingly voted to restore her to the gavel despite the disastrous results of her last performance. If anything, she is doubling down on the strategies that failed Americans less than a decade ago.

In truth, one could fill a book with the many examples of Pelosi overreaching and power grabbing on her agenda, strategy, and tactics. But I predict the 2020 election cycle and her own severe case of Trump Derangement Syndrome (TDS) will drive her to new lows. Despite her party's narrowly winning many tight races, she will attempt to lead as though Democrats had been given a mandate to destroy the Trump administration at all costs. Lawmaking will be a forgotten responsibility as Pelosi looks to convert every legislative shield into a political sword.

The risk for Pelosi has always been that people might see

through the act. This time, with social media even more ubiquitous than it was in 2010, she will need all the help she can get from her Silicon Valley allies to keep the deplorables from exposing the hypocrisy that will undergird the congressional investigations her new committee chairmen will undertake.

Notwithstanding the steady weakening of legislative branch powers in recent decades, many powerful tools remain in the hands of the majority—the ability to set the agenda, make law, control the purse strings, subpoena documents and testimony, and block a president's agenda. Those tools can and should be used to solve problems for the American people. That's not how Democrats will use them. In their hands, every tool that can conceivably be weaponized in the battle for 2020 will be used in the pursuit of power—to destroy enemies, weaken the minority, raise money, and influence elections.

We can expect Pelosi and House Democrats to overreach by completely neglecting to govern as they repurpose every available legislative tool toward the goal of destroying President Trump. How will they do it? In the coming chapters, we'll explore how Democrats in the House are changing rules to facilitate their embrace of radical and unpopular taxes and spending, compromising transparency to shield themselves from accountability to their voters, violating long-standing bipartisan norms to enable wider fishing expeditions, suppressing documents that don't fit their narrative, and abusing their oversight authority to politically target individuals and businesses over which they have no jurisdiction.

In doing so, not only are they missing the opportunity to accomplish anything positive on behalf of the American people, but they are obstructing any efforts by the administration and the Republican Senate to do so. So keen on their agenda to hedge up Donald Trump's way, Democrats are ultimately blocking policies they have long promised voters to support.

The media is not calling them on it, of course. Recognizing the overreach for what it is requires us to pay attention.

With Democrats now in control of the House of Representatives, they are doubling down on the false narratives they use to sell their agenda—and this time they have all the tools available to a majority party in Congress at their disposal.

In the coming pages, we'll look at the tools and tactics used by the Democrats to indelibly paint President Trump and his supporters as enemies of the state as they make their own pursuit of power in 2020 their highest priority. How are the Democrats leveraging these tools? I know. I've been there.

The tip of the spear for the Democratic resistance in the House of Representatives will be the House Oversight and Reform Committee—a committee I once chaired. The other will be the House Judiciary Committee, on which I once served. Most of the aggressive action from the House will occur via these two committees, but other committees will also engage in a coordinated charge against the president and his administration. Though Republicans still hold the majority in the Senate, the Kavanaugh confirmation hearings demonstrated just how far Democrats will be willing to go in the quest for political power.

The newly won control of House committees, gavels, and formidable committee resources has opened new lines of attack. But those very benefits are creating new vulnerabilities for a party that just can't help but go too far.

Despite the legislative, financial, and cultural tools the left can wield, the right retains certain advantages—not the least of which is an American public that increasingly rejects identity politics, cultural manipulation, biased media, and the politics of personal destruction. Democrats can't see outside the Beltway into the hearts of the American people. We want our nation to be strong. That's why America elected a disruptive and unconventional president. Having tasted the fruits of a president who focuses on solutions, Americans prefer the thriving economy, favorable trade environment, dominant foreign policy, and America First agenda promised and delivered by Donald J. Trump.

At what point does the political obstruction go so far that it undermines the very institutions that undergird our republic? Though Congress has always been a political battleground, there is a price to be paid for pursuing political agendas rather than doing the job voters elect representatives to do.

There are constitutional limits to legislative power that must not be breached. There are opportunity costs to squandering all available political capital on the war against President Trump. Whether that gamble pays off or whether it doesn't, the opportunity cost will be high. And it will be working Americans who pay it as we experience more gridlock, more debt, more polarization, more economic disruption, and more incursions on our freedoms.

The strategy to refuse to engage the president on public policy (in other words, do their jobs) does not build confidence in Democrats' ability to actually govern.

Representative Debbie Wasserman-Schultz in 2014 published an op-ed in *Politico* decrying the fact that Republicans were spending some of their political capital on a lawsuit to fight executive overreach—a lawsuit Democrats are now using to push back against President Trump. Back then, Democrats didn't approve of limits to executive authority. In the wake of that lawsuit, Wasserman-Schultz described what she saw at the time as a majority party "deeply unserious about the challenges facing the country."

The phrase applies to Democrats today, not because they're going after the president, but because they are more openly obstructionist than Republicans ever dreamed of being with President Obama. They're not just obstructing the Trump agenda—they're willing to obstruct their own agenda. Look at how they threw away the chance to resolve the conflict over so-called Dreamers. After years of demanding solutions for people brought to the United States as young children, they blew the chance to extend protections to that group because they determined a government shutdown was more politically beneficial to them than a solution for Dreamers that might be seen as a win for the president.

Such will be the story of the 116th Congress. Lawmaking will take a backseat to "oversight"—but this new oversight will not look much like the oversight we're used to. Speaker Pelosi is changing the rules of the game to help her party win what she sees as the most important battle yet—the quest for power. Exhibit A in that quest can be found in the Democrats' priority legislation for the 116th Congress, a bill referred to as H.R. 1.

CHAPTER 6

DEMOCRATS' FIRST PRIORITY: PROTECT THE SWAMP

The first bill introduced in a new Congress is often a symbolic piece of legislation that indicates what is most important to the incoming majority.

For the 115th Congress under Speaker Paul Ryan, H.R. 1 was tax reform. This was the policy Republicans had run on and it was ultimately the signature accomplishment of President Trump's first term. The passage of that bill gave middle-class families a huge tax cut, resulting in more jobs, higher wages, low inflation, low unemployment, and robust consumer spending.

What was the symbolic introductory legislation of House Democrats? The For the People Act, which had overwhelming support from Pelosi's 235-member caucus, with 227 signed on as cosponsors. When the bill came to a vote on March 8, 2019, it passed along strict party lines and with the full support of the House Democrat caucus, 235–193. Even the very moderate and endangered swing district Democrat now holding Representative Mia Love's seat in Utah, Ben McAdams, voted for it.

To read the promotional materials posted to social media by leftist political groups, the bill was about draining the swamp and ending corporate dominance in elections. At first glance, the issue may not be a priority for most Americans, but everyone wants to drain the swamp, right?

But digging a little deeper reveals the bill was far more sinister. It was written by the swamp, for the swamp, and the provisions it aims to impose are specifically designed to protect the swamp.

This bill was no far-left fringe pipe dream. It represented the agenda and priorities that unite the House Democrat caucus. Above all else, this is what Democrats believe America needs most.

What might be the top priority of American voters? We don't need to guess—the Pew Research Center routinely surveys the public on this question. Their January 24, 2019, polling identifies the public's political priorities for the 116th Congress and cross-tabulates those answers by partisan affiliation.

According to Pew, 70 percent of Americans identify improving the economy as a top priority. The next-highest level of support is for health care, with 69 percent calling it one of the top priorities. Rounding out the top four are improving education at 68 percent and defending the country from future terrorist attacks at 67 percent. If you just look at Democrat voters, preserving Social Security comes out on top, with 65 percent of Democrats identifying it as one of the top priorities, followed by the economy, Medicare, health care, and education.

H.R. 1 addresses none of these issues. In fact, it doesn't address any of the issues listed in the top eighteen for which Pew released numbers.

What is the great priority that Democrats believe must happen before anything else?

Securing power.

That's what becomes clear when you look past the marketing

rhetoric and read the actual bill. But let's explore the provisions of the bill. Readers can decide for themselves what to call it.

Democrats marketed it as an ethics reform bill. The nearly six-hundred-page bill addressed election reforms, campaign finance rules, redistricting, and judicial ethics reforms, among other things. The *New York Times* described the bill's purpose this way:

Democratic leaders view the voting and ethics measure—named the For the People Act—as the opening salvo in a two-year campaign to either make law or drive a wedge between Mr. Trump and the voters who supported him.

That's right. This bill is basically a campaign piece designed to position the party for a new round of smoke and mirrors. It was really not about the priorities "For the People." Clearly it was about setting the table for the priorities For the Democrats in the 2020 election cycle.

H.R. 1 imposed more than thirty consequential new federal mandates on state governments, along with dozens of other changes in policies and standards, essentially reversing our election process from a bottom-up approach to a top-down approach guided by the interests of politicians.

A deeper analysis shows this bill was designed to ensure a permanent hold on power for Democrats. If one were to create a road map for perpetuating mass voter fraud, it would look a lot like this bill. Had H.R. 1 become law, it would have eliminated tools for detecting voter fraud. Blatantly unconstitutional provisions imposed sweeping limits to free speech. In a violation of the Fourteenth Amendment, it superseded state laws and state constitutions to award voting rights to felons. It empowered the Justice Department to more easily prosecute political targets and politicized the Federal Election Commission. It created a new avenue for political campaigns and political consultants to fleece taxpayers.

Like the deceptively named Affordable Care Act, the For the People Act was named to create the illusion that it would do exactly the opposite of what it actually does. This was not an anti-corruption bill. It legalized corruption. This is a bill designed For the Democrats, For the Incumbents, For the Consultants, and For the Deep State.

Fortunately, this bill is dead on arrival in the Republican U.S. Senate. Even if by some miracle it were to pass the Senate, it would certainly be vetoed by President Trump. The bill itself has no path to become law in this Congress, but that didn't stop Speaker Pelosi from wasting valuable floor time to pass it. Nor is it a reason to write the bill off. The provisions of this legislation are a chilling indication of where Democrats want to take this country. Even though the For the People Act will not become law as long as Donald Trump is president, we need to understand what Democrats will do if they regain power.

That preserving their power was their highest priority should be a wake-up call to every American. The For the People Act is a manifesto of everything the Democrats need to do to manipulate the electoral process in their favor and insulate themselves from the will of the people.

Facilitating Voter Fraud

Whether by design or by accident, the Democrats' signature legislation removed important safeguards used to prevent voter fraud (which Democrats claim to be a myth). Whatever their justifications, a professional fraudster could hardly have designed a system more susceptible to abuse than the one dictated by this bill. No one tell the Russians.

Theoretically, if you were serious about stealing national elections, you would need to figure out how to exploit vulnerabilities in more than three thousand different counties, all of which operate their elections differently. Having one unified electoral system to exploit would almost certainly be easier. President Obama said as much in an October 2016 speech at the White House. "There is no serious person out there who would suggest somehow that you could even rig America's elections, in part because they're so decentralized, and the numbers of votes involved," he said.

On this point, President Obama was right. Decentralized elections are a deterrent to fraud and corruption. Not if the Democratic Party gets its wish. The For the People Act reverses that protection—abandoning our federalist tradition of locally controlled elections and empowering Congress and the Federal Election Commission (FEC) to take charge. Federal bureaucrats and politicians would take over decisions about how to secure election integrity, manage voter lists, and ensure ballot access. What could possibly go wrong?

Now, instead of being run by someone chosen within the community, elections would be run by 535 members of Congress, only three of whom represent any given voter. They would be regulated by appointed federal bureaucrats at the FEC (newly empowered with openly partisan agendas under this bill). Say good-bye to trying to influence election policy in your county. To effect change, you would need to persuade a majority of the 100 senators and 435 House members to listen to you. But they only meet with people who live in their districts. Good luck with that. How this can be described as "For the People" is a mystery.

When Congress sets the rules for elections, that body will not be able to resist the urge to set those rules with an eye to the political implications. This should frighten both Democrats and Republicans, as we know both parties would be loath to give up such an advantage once secured.

Fortunately, H.R. 1 gives us the perfect preview of what elections will look like if we put Congress in charge. The bill is replete with provisions that would secure electoral advantages for Democrats.

By some strange coincidence, the vast majority of the election provisions in the bill make elections less secure rather than more secure. By another strange coincidence, the very provisions that help Democrats win elections also help fraudsters manipulate them.

Weakening Election Security

The list of unfunded federal mandates imposed upon states by this bill is too long to exhaustively catalog here, but we can hit a few of the highlights of those that make our elections less secure.

NO-FAULT ABSENTEE BALLOTS: The Heritage Foundation calls these ballots the "tool of choice for vote thieves" because they are so easy to manipulate. But Democrats have long dismissed these claims, pointing to what they call a dearth of voter fraud convictions.

Nonetheless, they could hardly ignore what happened in North Carolina's 9th Congressional District in 2018. This time election fraud was used by a Republican campaign to narrowly win a tight race against a popular Democrat. Had the parties been reversed, who knows how much coverage the race would have gotten. But with a Democrat losing and the race being rerun, there was no way to avoid shining a spotlight on a key vulnerability.

North Carolina's absentee ballot provision actually has more security than the one H.R. 1 will impose nationwide. It requires ballots to be signed by the voter and witnessed by another person attesting that the voter is who they say they are. Campaign operatives in the North Carolina race violated state law by collecting absentee ballots on behalf of voters and turning them in.

This process, called ballot harvesting, is illegal in North Carolina for very good reason. Campaign operatives or nonprofit political groups could harass voters to turn in ballots, "assist" them in filling them out, and potentially "lose" ballots that don't support the candidate the ballot harvester is paid to help. In North Carolina, officials estimate as many as a thousand ballots supporting the Democrat candidate may have been destroyed. One witness testified she was paid $150 for every fifty ballots she collected, acknowledging that in many cases she signed as a witness for ballots she had not actually watched the voter fill out.

The same ballot harvesting process used illegally in North Carolina was recently legalized in California, where it helped Democrats flip seven previously Republican seats in 2018. The process Democrats hate in North Carolina they defend in California, where third-party organizations like Grassroots Campaigns Inc. or labor unions are permitted (one might even say encouraged) to collect ballots directly from voters and turn them in on their behalf without a secure chain of custody. Prior to that change, only close relatives or those living at the same address could turn in another person's completed ballot.

The indication that ballot harvesting made the difference can be found in the vote proportions. Studies of absentee voters have consistently shown they tend to reflect the population or lean slightly to the right. But when ballot harvesting was deployed in California, we saw late ballots break heavily for Democrats.

Take, for example, the race between incumbent Republican David Valadao and Democrat T. J. Cox in California's rural 21st District. When polls closed, Valadao led Cox by 6,000 votes—or 8 percent. That margin was wide enough for media outlets to call the race for Valadao. But late ballots delivered by the hundreds from third-party groups broke for Cox so strongly that Cox ultimately eked out an 843-vote victory.

The *San Francisco Chronicle* reported that elsewhere in the state, Orange County voters were calling the registrar's office asking if it was legitimate for someone to come to their door and ask if they could take their ballot.

Who was coming to the door? According to a January 2019 *Los Angeles Times* story, illegal Dreamers were deeply engaged in the process—not just delivering ballots, but helping voters fill them out. The *Times* reports on the experience of one Dreamer, Gabriela Cruz, who "found" a voter smoking a cigarette on a tattered old couch behind a group home hours before election day.

> *He politely tried to wave her off until she reminded him he had a right that she as an immigrant without citizenship didn't have. "It could really make a change for us," said Cruz, 29.*
>
> *Half an hour later, she was helping Silva look up candidates as he filled out his ballot by the light of her phone.*

What are the implications of activists with an agenda "helping" voters look up candidates and fill out ballots? How many of those activists are willing to turn in a ballot that doesn't help their cause? Should we be exposing people's ballots to that kind of temptation?

In this case, Democrats got a head start in California, which gave them an advantage. But that won't always be the case. What happens when the only way to win elections is to have the biggest army of ballot harvesters?

In an ironic exchange, Democratic representative Joe Kennedy of Massachusetts tweeted during the debate over H.R. 1, writing:

> *As GOP stands unified against a bill to strengthen our democracy & increase transparency in our elections, it's important to remember that the #NC09 seat is vacant because a GOP candidate tried to steal an election.*

In reply, Republican representative Dan Crenshaw of Texas responded:

> *You do realize your bill #HR1 would actually make that kind of fraud in #NC09 LEGAL. Right?*

TRUTH: it would legalize vote harvesting across the entire country, use your tax $ to do it, and limit free speech drastically. All in the name of "democracy."

Even the ACLU opposes it.

And there's an interesting tidbit. The Donald Trump–hating, Democrat-aligned, Grassroots Campaigns Inc.–consulted ACLU was opposing H.R. 1. Given that they were likely funding some of the vote harvesting, that was hard to believe. But according to their letter to members of Congress opposing the bill, there were many provisions ACLU strongly supported and long championed— likely no-fault absentee voting is among them. Their reasons for objecting to the bill have more to do with transparency provisions for donors that we'll talk about later in this chapter.

Meanwhile, one can't miss the irony of Representative Kennedy using the vote fraud in North Carolina to whip up support for a bill that, at a minimum, does nothing to prohibit the very practices used to commit that fraud. Of course, Democrats denied that their bill actually imposes ballot harvesting since there is no explicit language doing so—only a failure to prohibit the practice. Senate Majority Leader Mitch McConnell described the bill's position on ballot harvesting as "suspiciously silent on the murky ballot harvesting practices that recently threw North Carolina's 9th Congressional District into chaos."

Of course, Republicans gave Democrats an opportunity to make the bill more explicit on the issue of ballot harvesting by offering an amendment prohibiting the practice. Democrats promptly rejected the amendment.

RESTRICTIONS ON VOTER LIST MAINTENANCE: Voter list maintenance is one of the most egregious targets of the bill. Democrats have branded such activities as a form of voter suppression. The bill uses the sinister term "voter caging" to describe basic list maintenance activities required by the National Voter Registration Act (NVRA). The process by which election officials periodically mail "non-forwardable" correspondence or even ballots is used to confirm whether a voter remains eligible. If the mail is returned because the voter no longer lives there, election officials can flag that voter registration. If the voter doesn't cast a vote in the next two elections, that registration becomes inactive. It's important to understand that the NVRA does not allow voters to be removed from voting rolls until either a voter confirms in writing that he/she has moved *or* the voter fails to respond to the notice sent to the address on the voter registration *and then* fails to vote in the next two consecutive elections. This is a process Democrats want destroyed.

If you move, Democrats want you to stay on the list. If you die, they still want your name there. If you haven't voted for decades, they still want you to receive a ballot. If the bill had become law, verifying current addresses of registered voters against the U.S. Postal Service's national change-of-address system would become virtually impossible. This is a database that stores submissions of change-of-address requests that people submit when they move. State and local governments should not be prohibited from utilizing this tool in their efforts to maintain accurate voter lists.

According to an analysis by the Lawyers Democracy Fund, "the overly broad language of the bill would essentially prohibit the transmission of voter registration lists from one election official to another locality to update its voter records, thus dramatically restricting the current ability of localities to interact with each other to maintain the integrity of the voter rolls."

To further nullify this provision of the NVRA, Democrats inserted a provision to their bill requiring notification of inactive voters be sent via email rather than mailed to the address on file. Obviously, an email will not detect whether the person has moved and would invalidate the use of such notifications as a means to clean up voter lists.

Democrats have consistently challenged the provision allowing removal of inactive voters in court—and lost. The bill seeks to nullify a 2018 Supreme Court ruling in *Husted v. A. Philip Randolph Institute*. The Court held that list maintenance was valid, given that as many as 40 percent of Americans fail to inform the USPS when they move. The volume of outdated addresses on state voter lists compromises the lists and makes them more vulnerable to fraud.

In testimony before the House Judiciary Committee in January 2019, former Federal Election Commission member and election expert Hans von Spakovsky told the committee, "The proposed change would directly interfere with the ability of states to maintain accurate, up-to-date voter registration lists." Maybe that was the point.

The Court in *Husted* noted that "24 million voter registrations in the United States—about one in eight—are either invalid or significantly registration inaccurate. And about 2.75 million people are said to be registered in more than one state."

The millions of voters registered in multiple states are another vulnerability Democrats seem to want to protect. States would be unable to voluntarily participate in cross-check programs like the Interstate Voter Registration Crosscheck (IVRC) and the Electronic Voter Registration Center (ERIC). These voluntary state-run programs compare voter registration lists to identify voters with multiple active registrations. Since their inception, these programs have been targets of Democrats' wrath. Not every state participates in these systems, but if H.R. 1 became law, election officials would lose yet another tool to help maintain accurate voter lists.

Beyond opposing the cross-checking of voter registrations, the bill goes a step further, eliminating methods of detecting people who vote in multiple jurisdictions. It compels states to stop using provisional ballots for those who show up on election day asserting that they have moved into the precinct. Those people would now be given a regular ballot, which cannot be later retrieved if the person's address proves invalid. This creates an opportunity that a corrupt campaign operative or a foreign government could exploit. If someone were to lie about where they live, there would be no way to recall that ineligible vote. Nothing would stop a would-be fraudster—or an organized group of them—from going to one polling place after another claiming to live in that district.

Even if the crime were later discovered, the damage would be irreversible. Election officials are unlikely to audit the election and find such cases. But such illegal voting is sometimes discovered and challenged. Unfortunately, H.R. 1 removes that option as well.

PREVENTION OF ELIGIBILITY CHALLENGES: Challenging fraudulent votes would become much more difficult under H.R. 1, which would override existing state laws governing such challenges. The new federal mandate would require such challenges to be sworn under oath and penalty of perjury. State laws authorizing poll workers, poll watchers, or any other person to legally challenge a vote would be nullified and replaced by a more bureaucratic process that could place a person in legal jeopardy if they report potential fraud.

It's true. Not only does this bill discourage routine maintenance of voter lists, but it is also written to expose voters to criminal penalties for eligibility challenges that can't be confirmed. Under current law, if you suspect someone does not actually live in the precinct where they voted, you can challenge that vote. If the validity of that voter is not confirmed, it can be thrown out. Under this bill, many of those votes will be irretrievable once cast and a person who challenges a suspicious vote is at greater risk of criminal penalties than the person who cast the vote.

Why would anyone risk exposing our elections in this way? As we discussed in an earlier chapter, the bill's proponents are responding to a narrative that any attempt to secure the election process is really just an excuse to suppress votes. They argue that election fraud simply doesn't happen, therefore security is unnecessary. Meanwhile, in a report shortly after the 2016 election, the Office of the Director of National Intelligence acknowledged Moscow's "longstanding desire to undermine the US-led liberal democratic order," noting that Russia's activities in that election "demonstrated a significant escalation in directness, level of activity, and scope of effort compared to previous operations." Although past efforts have been primarily hacking and influence campaigns, making voter fraud too easy risks inviting further escalation by the Russians or any other foreign government with a stake in our election outcomes.

NULLIFICATION OF VOTER ID LAWS: One provision of H.R. 1 enables voters in states with ID requirements to bypass that requirement by signing a statement agreeing that they are the person whose registration they are using.

Meanwhile, allegations of fraud in one 2018 race raise more red flags. An audit released in February 2019 found indications of fraud in a New Mexico House race called for the Republican on election night, but won by the Democrat. The tight 3,500-vote margin in that race reversed in favor of Democrat Xochitl Torres Small after absentee ballots broke for the Democrat in a county where voter ID laws are not enforced. The audit, paid for by Republican Yvette Herrell's campaign, found that a significant number of absentee ballots were time stamped after the 7 p.m. deadline on election night. The consulting company conducting the audit reviewed some 12,000 absentee ballot requests. According to a report in the *Daily Signal*, the audit found nongovernmental groups "are almost certainly engaging in at best aggressive—and at worst fraudulent—procurement of absentee ballot applications."

This conclusion is consistent with reports from other swing districts in which last-minute absentee ballots reversed the election night outcome.

ONLINE VOTER REGISTRATION: The very first provision in H.R. 1 was a new mandate to dictate that states must use an online voter registration process that does not require signatures to be verified. Already thirty-seven states use online voter registration, but some of those would have to reconfigure their systems to remove security features that match a voter to a state division of motor vehicles (DMV) record for signature comparison.

AUTOMATIC VOTER REGISTRATION: This sounds like a great idea. We want everyone to vote. But beneath the surface, there is a lot of work to do before we can safely implement such a provision without jeopardizing the security of elections.

The bill requires states to compel people to register to vote. This unfunded mandate forces states to reconfigure their voter databases to accept record transfers from what the bill calls "contributing agencies" such as the DMV, Social Security Administration, Department of Veterans Affairs, Medicare, and Medicaid, among others. Because the populations served by these agencies include many who are ineligible to vote, these agencies would be required to determine which records are eligible before they are transferred. Therein lies the problem.

Evidence suggests we should be skeptical of this process. The U.S. Court of Appeals for the D.C. Circuit ruled in 2016 that three states could not ask for proof of citizenship on federal voter registration forms, after left-wing nonprofit groups sued claiming documentation requirements disenfranchise voters.

If states cannot ask about citizenship, how are they to determine the eligibility of voters? We don't really know. California officials assure voters that no illegal votes are cast there, but refuse to divulge how they distinguish illegal voters from legal ones in the absence of valid data. The California Division of Motor Vehicles reported in April 2018 that more than 1 million illegal immigrants had obtained licenses to drive in the state over just a three-year period. The *Sacramento Bee* reports that election officials won't answer questions about how many of those may have been automatically registered to vote. Nor could they answer questions about how an ongoing investigation will determine which voters were eligible, since voters weren't asked to make a clear declaration at the time of registration. If California is certain there are no illegal votes, why won't they answer questions about the methodology for identifying more than one million automatically registered illegal immigrants?

The *Pittsburgh Post-Gazette* reported in 2018 that Pennsylvania's motor-voter system registered more than 8,000 ineligible voters, including many who were not U.S. citizens. And in an ongoing mess in Texas, election officials never could determine how many illegal immigrants were automatically registered to vote through federal motor-voter laws. Initial estimates of 95,000 noncitizen registered voters proved inaccurate, demonstrating the difficulty of accurately confirming eligibility after a person has been automatically registered. The Democrats' answer to this conundrum is not to clarify citizenship status, but instead to make verifying that status more difficult. Mistakes in Texas's initial attempt to count illegal voters triggered a lawsuit by the League of United Latin American Citizens. As a condition of settling that lawsuit, LULAC demanded Texas cease some voter list maintenance activities that Democrats consider to be a "purging" of voter rolls.

While there is bipartisan support for procedures to make voting more convenient, voters should still have a choice to register to vote. Noncitizens should not be compelled to register and risk subsequent pressure by activist groups to submit illegal ballots.

MANDATORY SAME-DAY VOTER REGISTRATION: The practice of registering voters on election day and during each day of the early voting period has several unintended consequences, not the least of which is the inability to confirm registration information. Polling places can be chaotic on election day, but more so when counties cannot anticipate the number of voters to expect, ballots to have on hand, and precinct workers to manage the volume of voters. Of greater concern, however, is the potential for crooked campaign operatives to exploit the weakness in this system as part of a larger ballot harvesting initiative. These are problems state and local election offices should be free to address in a customized way.

These are just a few of the thirty different federal mandates Democrats wish to impose on state governments, all of which nullify existing state and local laws.

An "Independent" Redistricting Commission

Democrats paid a heavy price for the Republican wave election of 2010, not only losing the House in those midterms, but losing 19 Democrat-controlled state legislatures and 650 legislative seats nationwide. Those losses came just as state lawmakers were poised to redraw the maps for House districts that would dictate boundaries for a decade.

With redistricting again on the horizon in 2018, Democrats tried to use H.R. 1 to stack the deck in their favor. H.R. 1 transfers state legislatures' authority to draw voting districts to a so-called independent redistricting commission. The bill's provision compelling states to create redistricting commissions is blatantly unconstitutional. Although some states have created such commissions, frequently the legislature still holds the ultimate authority. Instead of being drawn by those who are accountable to voters, districts would now be drawn by people who have no fear of being voted out. If voters don't like the results, they have no recourse.

The Supreme Court has upheld the rights of states to choose to use independent commissions, but that 5–4 decision included a dissent by Chief Justice John Roberts and depended on a swing vote from Justice Kennedy. There is a strong likelihood the current Court would strike down the redistricting provision.

The bill bars these federally imposed redistricting commissions from considering "the political party affiliation or voting history of the population of a district." This is intended to prevent gerrymandering, but it also prevents any pursuit of partisan fairness, which is supposedly the whole goal of an independent commission.

But the most egregious provision in the bill is the one governing conflicts between state legislatures and independent commissions. If they can't agree, state maps will be drawn by judges in Washington, D.C. This is an unmitigated violation of the separation of powers. Elections expert Hans von Spakovsky, in his testimony before the House Judiciary Committee, explained, "The bill transfers to the judiciary a power that the Elections Clause of the Constitution exclusively gives to the legislative branch. That violates basic separation of powers principles as well as the delegation doctrine. It is antidemocratic and unconstitutional."

Protecting the Green Wave

One of the bill's strongest selling points was the promise to end corruption. While chomping at the bit to impose campaign finance reforms, Democrats are careful not to endanger what many dubbed the Green Wave of small-dollar contributions that helped flip the House for Democrats. Speaker Pelosi referred to campaign finance reform as "the people's interests not the special interests." That's cute. But if you understand how Democrats have gamed the campaign finance system in the last election cycle—and they're hoping you don't—you'll see that this legislation not only protects the Democrats' Green Wave of ostensibly grassroots contributions, but drastically expands it at your expense.

Remember the settlement slush funds we discussed in chapter 2? Democrats have new plans for that money they were collecting from civil and criminal financial penalties. Instead of diverting it to their nonprofit allies, which is now illegal, they want to create a fund, ironically called the "Freedom from Influence Fund," that will now be used to fund political campaigns—providing a 6-to-1 match for all donations under $200. To qualify, candidates have to forgo contributions larger than $1,000.

Why the focus on small donors? Democrats would have you believe they are motivated by a commitment to reducing the influence of money in politics. But a closer look at where Democrat candidates are getting their campaign funds tells a different story.

In the 2018 midterms, Democrats in vulnerable House districts outraised Republican candidates more than 2 to 1. The difference? Small donors. The *New York Times* reported that in the 69 most competitive House races, Democrats raised a total of $46 million from small donors compared to just $15 million for Republicans. "[T]he influx of Democratic donations touched every corner of the House map," reported the *New York Times* story, "from high-profile races in the suburbs of New York and California, to more rural, conservative-leaning stretches of Indiana, Kansas and Alaska."

While Republicans were using the two old-school methods of disclosing donors, disavowing corporate donations and sticking to campaign finance limits—or funding with traditional Super PACs—Democrats pioneered a clever new method of small-donor fund-raising that diminishes their reliance on Super PAC money. It's a good idea and one that Republicans should have replicated long ago. But it may not be everything it appears to be. The mechanism for this new Green Wave of Democrat fund-raising is called ActBlue. The *New York Times* calls ActBlue the "piggybank of the Democratic resistance," having raised a mind-blowing $1.6 billion for Democratic candidates in the 2018 cycle.

ActBlue is a technology company founded in 2004 that uses inventive online fund-raising software to distribute donations to Democrat candidates and causes at the federal, state, and local levels. What was once an inconvenient and unwieldy process to donate to multiple campaigns can now be done with the click of a button. According to the ActBlue website, their mission is to "democratize power and help small-dollar donors make their voices heard in a real way."

According to ActBlue's own numbers, the website facilitated 42,093,173 individual contributions during the 2018 election cycle, with an average contribution size of $39.50. There are 14,997 individual groups raising money on ActBlue—that number includes local, state, and federal campaigns as well as 501(c)(4) organizations doing political work on behalf of Democrats. These donations represented huge infusions of cash that likely made the difference on election night. Indeed, ActBlue brags on its website:

> *Small-dollar donors proved over the past two years that people power is a winning strategy. Grassroots donors fueled the Democratic takeover in the House, as well as hundreds of victories at the state level. In total, these donors gave more than $1.6 billion through ActBlue during the 2018 election cycle—double the 2016 cycle total—and powered the campaigns and organizations changing the direction of our country.*

It's a great narrative. The little guy is taking back power from the corporate Super PACs imposed on America when the Supreme Court ruled in *Citizens United* that campaign donations were protected speech.

One problem: Some of it is smoke and mirrors. It's not just little guys using ActBlue. Studies show most of the money comes from coastal states. An analysis of campaign finance data by FiveThirtyEight and the Center for Public Integrity reviewed 38 million FEC records of ActBlue contributions between January 2017 and October 2018. Their analysis revealed:

- Since the beginning of 2017, donors in states Clinton won have given $157 million to support House and Senate candidates running in states Trump won. That's more than five times the amount of cash flowing from Trump states to Clinton states.

- Donors in California and New York combined to contribute roughly one-third of the dollars that have flowed through ActBlue to House and Senate candidates since the beginning of 2017.
- Fifty-seven percent of dollars directed to congressional candidates via ActBlue went to out-of-state races.

The study went on to identify hundreds of donors who had contributed more than 500 times during one election cycle, with some contributing thousands of times. Instead of making large donations to local candidates, coastal elites in the Democratic archipelago that runs from urban New England through America's large coastal cities and over to the Pacific Coast are dividing their donations into smaller amounts to create the illusion of broad support from the little guy. Under H.R. 1, each of those donations would be matched 6-to-1 from the Freedom from Influence Fund, giving Democrats a huge advantage.

For their part, Republicans are far behind the curve on technology to facilitate small-donor contributions. It's no secret that technology entrepreneurs overwhelmingly lean left. Academic research backs that up, with one study finding more than 75 percent voted for Hillary Clinton in 2016. Democrats have long had the advantage in deploying cutting-edge technology.

The Republican alternative to ActBlue, reportedly called Patriot Pass, is expected to be up and running in 2019. President Trump himself has shattered records for small-dollar donors, but 2020 is expected to be the first cycle in which the Republican Party will embrace a one-click donation platform.

For all the talk about reducing the influence of big donors in elections, the real motivation for public campaign financing provisions in H.R. 1 is to stack the deck in favor of Democrats and ensure their permanent hold on power.

The DISCLOSE Act

Now we get to the part where Democrats manage to go so far that they even lose the ACLU. Perhaps confident in their ability to rely on small-dollar donors and the corresponding 6-to-1 match from financial institutions through the payment of federal fines, they decided to include language in this bill exposing the dark money donors of nonprofits like the ACLU. They incorporate the provisions of a previous bill known as the DISCLOSE Act (Democracy Is Strengthened by Casting Light on Spending in Elections Act), which imposes mandatory disclosure of private associations.

They even went a step further, according to the ACLU's letter to lawmakers opposing the bill. They expanded the definition of campaign-related disbursements covered by the disclosure requirement to include communications that "support or promote or attack or oppose" the election of a candidate, without regard to whether the communication expressly advocates the election or defeat of a candidate. Remember, the ACLU's home page is all about fighting (not defeating, but fighting) Donald Trump. By this standard, that home page would subject the ACLU to disclosure requirements they currently don't have to worry about.

Now, I'm actually with the ACLU on this one. In fact, they end up making the very argument Republicans have used to defend the *Citizens United* decision and the use of undisclosed donors (what Democrats derisively refer to as dark money). In their letter, the ACLU passionately defends the very free speech Democrats are seeking to jeopardize, writing:

Should the DISCLOSE Act, as currently constituted, become law, it will have one of two effects. First, donors could choose not to give to organizations, even if they support their messages, or could be forced to give less than they otherwise might. Second, organizations, especially small organizations that either cannot afford the compliance costs or simply refuse to breach the trust that donors expecting anonymity have placed in them, could choose to refrain from speaking at all. Either way, the public discourse and the First Amendment lose.

The FEC as a Partisan Weapon

There are many more troubling provisions in this one bill, much less the next nine bills that round out the Democrats' legislative priority list. But we'll conclude our analysis with one final unnecessary and baffling provision. That is the partisan weaponization of the currently nonpartisan Federal Election Commission (FEC). Weaponizing federal agencies like the Internal Revenue Service and the Department of Justice is certainly not new. But never have we seen Democrats do it so boldly and so openly.

Since 1974, the six-member FEC has operated as a bipartisan commission, with Democrats and Republicans each more or less controlling three seats. Four votes are needed to initiate an investigation or prosecute an FEC violation, thus always depending on bipartisan support before the body can proceed with an action.

This legislation changes the FEC to a five-member commission that can proceed with a simple majority vote, making it possible for the party holding the majority to steamroll the minority. Democrats tried to hide this reality by dictating that no more than two members may belong to any one political party. The Institute for Free Speech points out that this requirement would not be a barrier to partisan control, explaining that "under this criteria, Senator Bernie Sanders, who nearly gained the 2016 Democratic presidential nomination, would not count as a Democrat on the Commission (technically, Sanders remains an 'independent'), allowing him to join two other Democrats in a Commission majority. The same would be true for Angus King, the Maine senator elected as an independent, but who caucuses with Democrats."

H.R. 1 goes even further, allowing the president to appoint a powerful chairman of the FEC to serve as a sort of Speech Czar, with vast powers to appoint staff, control budgets, issue subpoenas, and compel testimony. This person is required to consult with the commission, but has no limitations on his own authority to act.

Finally, the bill is timed to ensure Democrats will be the ones to control the commission. The Institute for Free Speech analysis found that while most provisions of H.R. 1 (the ones that favor Democrats in the election) are effective in 2020, this provision does not take effect until 2021—when Democrats hope Donald Trump will have been replaced with a president from their party. That person will appoint all five commissioners and choose the first chair. Those appointments will last through 2027, regardless of whether the next president serves a second term, and that chair will be able to appoint the staff director and general counsel for the FEC. Ultimately, the Institute for Free Speech wrote:

> *That means that all the new regulations required under other provisions of H.R. 1 will be written by the initial appointing president's team of the Chair, supportive commissioners, and their appointed General Counsel, and can be written (and if necessary re-written) with a specific eye to the 2022 midterms and the 2024 and 2028 presidential races. That same group would also respond to Advisory Opinion Requests and approve or disapprove of all enforcement actions.*
>
> *Working with these potential advantages, if that president is re-elected in 2024, he or she could appoint a Commission majority through 2033.*

It's a big gamble that rests upon the assumption that President Trump loses in 2020. Should that happen, Democrats will get the short-term results they seek. But at what cost? They will have completely undermined any credibility the FEC once had. When the FEC becomes a partisan attack dog, who will police the side in power? No one. The institution that had traditionally played that role will have been sacrificed on the altar of Democratic power grabbing.

Beyond the many provisions of this bill that provide advantages to Democrats, the real casualty of this power grab is the institutions that have to be sacrificed to give Democrats what they want. The bill is riddled with constitutional violations that undermine natural rights. One could fill a book with the list of ways H.R. 1 violates the Constitution, but for our purposes, we'll conclude our analysis of this bill by looking at just a few of them.

Violating the Constitution

You don't have to spend too many minutes on your browser's search engine to find a reference to Donald Trump as an authoritarian who is a threat to our institutions. Nicholas Kristoff in a January 2019 *New York Time* piece reiterated the old criticisms of President Trump as someone who is "unraveling democratic norms" and who seeks to "undermine institutions and referees of our political system."

Don't look now, but the Democrats made unraveling our democratic norms and undermining our institutions their top priority in the 116th Congress. The first institution on the chopping block: the Constitution. More specifically, the Bill of Rights. H.R. 1 runs afoul of many constitutional provisions, including federalism (the Tenth Amendment), voting rights (the Fourteenth Amendment), free speech (the First Amendment), and the separation of powers set forth in Article III. In addition to usurping local control of elections, the bill restores voting rights to convicted felons, a move that illegally abridges the authority of states explicitly granted in the Fourteenth Amendment. It forces taxpayers to fund campaigns, imposes restrictions on political speech, and empowers Washington, D.C., judges to decide state redistricting conflicts.

H.R. 1 would be more aptly named the "From the People Act" because that's what it is. It takes power away from the people— from the representatives in their communities whom they know and interact with—and invests that power in decision makers who are completely inaccessible to the average American.

Federalism, the constitutional innovation that created a division of power among federal, state, and local governments, enables diverse communities to self-govern. As a result, communities holding very different values can still be part of a larger whole without compromising their priorities. The process of transferring power away from state and local governments and into the hands of the federal government is a process of taking power from the people.

The advantages of an approach that allows California voters to tax themselves into oblivion without harming nearby Utah voters who overwhelmingly support smaller government are many. Federalism is a far better tool for promoting diversity than identity politics could ever hope to be because it does not impose the values and policies of one group over another. It disperses power, which protects against tyranny. It allows government to be more responsive to local issues and problems in a more efficient way than a slow and unwieldy federal bureaucracy. And federalism creates an environment in which more people can interact with the policy makers who represent them, even as more policy makers can be drawn from local communities.

Federalism has been under attack since Alexander Hamilton first proposed the formation of a national bank in 1791. Politicians have been at work trying to grow the federal government ever since. Let's look at how the "For the People Act" actually takes power *from* the people.

Wresting control of local elections seems to top the Democratic wish list in this bill. The bill seeks to penalize routine voter list maintenance, micromanage online registration and voting processes, dictate the use of no-fault absentee ballots, and neutralize the impact of voter ID laws.

Democrats justify this power grab with wild claims that states are deliberately attempting to suppress votes. But research from the left-wing Brennan Center for Justice at New York University contradicts that narrative. They report, "More broadly, 31 states have filed or pre-filed at least 230 bills that would expand voting access. That far surpasses the 14 states, at least, where lawmakers have filed or pre-filed at least 24 bills thus far that would restrict voting access." The Brennan Center considers any bill that requires photo ID to be a bill that restricts voting access.

In reality, states are working hard to find solutions that expand ballot access without damaging election integrity. This is exactly the process by which such issues should be addressed. States have long been the laboratory of ideas in which new solutions can be tried and shared.

Democrats love to invoke the Fourteenth Amendment and the Voting Rights Act when trying to make the case that election security measures are equivalent to voter suppression. They seem to believe secure elections are a threat to them politically. But what about provisions of the Fourteenth Amendment that don't cut their way at the ballot box? Section 2 of the Fourteenth Amendment explicitly grants to states the ability to abridge voting rights "for participation in rebellion, or other crime" as long as they do not discriminate. Yet this H.R. 1 legislation tries to do by statute what can only be done by constitutional amendment. It imposes a federal mandate restoring voting rights to all felons upon their release. This is not only unconstitutional, but it is a direct assault on states' rights and in some cases, directly violates state constitutions. Why are Democrats so interested in forcing this policy from the top down?

Coincidentally, studies show that the vast majority of convicted felons identify as Democrats. A 2013 study published by professors from the University of Pennsylvania and Stanford University offered more recent confirmation of what earlier studies have often shown. Democrats benefit when felons vote. This massive pool of voters—about 2.5 percent of the national voting age population—overwhelmingly register as Democrats. In New York, the study found 61.5 percent register Democrat to 9 percent Republican. In swing state North Carolina, 54.6 percent register Democrat and 10.2 percent Republican.

Our policies on felon voting rights should not be dictated based on political fortunes. States retain the power to enact policies that reflect the will of their voters. Those voters have a great deal more influence at the state level than at the federal level. Thorny questions involving whether criminals should have voting rights restored, which criminals, and at what point are not federal decisions.

The priority bill for Democrats in the 116th Congress has absolutely no chance of becoming law so long as Donald Trump remains president of the United States. But it does provide a useful road map of the power grab Democrats have in mind when they do return to power. More important, it shows us the institutions that will be sacrificed. The FEC will never function objectively once Democrats are finished reorganizing it.

Infringements on free speech and federalism in this bill are just the beginning. H.R. 1 is just the first of ten priority bills Democrats will introduce—many of which follow the same formula of sacrificing long-term institutions, rights, and credibility for short-term political gains. Let's look at what else is on the Democrats' priority list. H.R. 3 addresses high prescription drugs prices by imposing market-distorting price controls on drugs, a move that will lower prices in the short term but cripple innovation in the long term, and put government bureaucrats in charge of health care. H.R. 4 addresses voting rights. It is expected to impose even more (politicized) federal control over local elections. H.R. 5, the Equality Act, imposes criminal penalties on religious dissent and overrides the rights of states to dictate who can be in the public restroom with our sons and daughters. H.R. 6, the DREAM Act, undermines the rule of law by doubling down on our system of rewarding citizenship to lawbreakers while continuing to penalize with long delays and high fees any who attempt to come here legally. The bill is anticipated to offer citizenship not only to a greatly expanded category of children of illegal immigrants, but to immigrants with Temporary Protected Status from El Salvador, Haiti, Nicaragua, Sudan, and Liberia at a minimum. H.R. 8, a background checks bill that further restricts Second Amendment rights, was passed by the House in February. H.R. 9 is expected to be a climate bill that will almost certainly restrict rights as well as markets.

The legislative agenda of House Democrats will undoubtedly go nowhere this time. But that won't stop Democrats from attempting to insert various provisions into must-pass budget legislation. In the Senate, Minority Leader Schumer demanded that "election security" measures be added to the defense spending bill. This implies that Schumer wants to protect elections from Russian interference. But when he talks about election security measures, he isn't talking about voter ID, voter list maintenance, or other measures that might potentially ferret out voter fraud. He's talking about the provisions of H.R. 1, which do just the opposite.

Given the heavy reliance of Democrats on small-donor contributions from deep Blue states, we can likely expect legislative efforts to function as a marketing campaign to draw donations from the left's wealthy coastal enclaves. Those donors don't get excited by bipartisanship or problem solving. They open their checkbooks when they see their policy prescriptions imposed on everyone. But legislation is not the only way to draw the attention of potential donors. Newly won control of House committee chairmanships gives Democrats a new platform for stoking anger and raising funds for 2020 campaigns.

Democrats have shown that they have little regard for constitutional norms when short-term partisan wins are at stake. While Republican policy tracks closely to the things people actually want, Democrats are more concerned with preserving the conditions that have kept them in power. How do you recognize the swamp? The swamp always protects itself first.

CHAPTER 7

OVERSIGHT WITHOUT GOVERNMENT REFORM

The transformation of congressional oversight from its function as a government watchdog to an anti-Trump opposition research function happened fast. Suddenly the imperative to root out waste, fraud, and abuse became an imperative to root out a sitting president. Democrats are not even trying to make a pretense of pursuing government reform. Instead of addressing government corruption, they are fully focused on politically motivated investigations into the president's personal and professional life.

During each of the eight years Barack Obama was president, I was a member of the House Oversight Committee. Never once did we attempt to target the president personally. We certainly never went after his family. We never delved into his personal financial records or his or his family's business dealings, never targeted his legal counsel or spiritual leaders, nor asked them to testify. Not because there were no scandals. But because we were there to identify and solve systemic executive branch problems.

Government abuses were the scandals we targeted. Using the investigative tools of Congress to perform political opposition research on a single individual—even the president—is simply not appropriate. It is an abuse of power that undermines the authority and credibility of the entire legislative oversight process.

Republicans could have easily opened politically motivated investigations. There were calls to look into President Obama's association with anti-Semitic radicals Louis Farrakhan and Reverend Jeremiah Wright, former terrorist Bill Ayers, and other virulently anti-American characters. Some wanted an investigation into a sweetheart mortgage Obama was given by convicted felon and Obama campaign bundler Tony Rezko. Some wanted us to look into the mysterious disappearance of Obama's college transcripts or even the legitimacy of his birth certificate!

None of these questions have anything to do with the purpose of oversight: crafting legislation and overseeing government expenditures. Such investigations would have been criticized as political stunts, and rightly so. My colleagues and I weren't willing to misuse the committee resources for that purpose. Nor would our leadership have supported such a ploy. Yet that is exactly how the new batch of Democratic committee chairs have been approaching the awesome responsibility of government oversight.

At a time when the president's opponents are hyperventilating over whether a nondisclosure payment qualifies as a campaign contribution, far too much of the investigatory apparatus of Congress has been converted to the unofficial opposition research arm of the Democratic National Committee. The Federal Election Commission might want to consider the value of *that* campaign contribution.

The prerogative to investigate the executive branch does not rest solely with Chairman Elijah Cummings and the House Oversight Committee. Each House and Senate committee has jurisdiction over specific parts of the government and can thus launch limited investigations that involve specific agencies within that committee's jurisdiction. For Democrats, it's all hands on deck to target the president of the United States.

Certainly the most high-profile theater of battle between House Democrats and the Trump administration leading up to the 2020 presidential election will be in the committee I once chaired. The committee, now named the House Oversight and Reform Committee, is ground zero for investigations of the Trump administration, although other committees are ramping up aggressive presidential investigations as well.

The House Oversight Committee has the broadest mandate of any House committee. It can look at any government agency or expenditure. But the real focus of Speaker Pelosi's leadership team is on President Trump. Already, Chairman Cummings has launched probes targeting the president, looking into the activities of the president's personal attorney Michael Cohen, investigating White House security clearances, and questioning White House dealings with Saudi Arabia. It remains to be seen what, if any, legislative goals they hope these investigations would achieve.

In the House Judiciary Committee, Democratic chairman Jerry Nadler of New York can go after anything involving federal law enforcement, including the DOJ, the courts, immigration, and even internet and intellectual property issues. He started with investigations of obstruction of justice by the president in a counter-intelligence operation, violations of the Constitution's emoluments clause by the president, and what the committee is calling abuses of power—a reference to Trump's insults against the media. But that was just the beginning.

Over in the House Intelligence Committee, Chairman Adam Schiff can investigate the most highly classified subjects involving counterterrorism, defense intelligence, and advanced research. He is using his authority to pursue a do-over of the Mueller investigation, going after President Trump for discredited connections with Russia, determining whether foreign actors have sought leverage over the president, and investigating obstruction of justice.

Schiff, who thought the investigation of the murder of four Americans in Benghazi was duplicative, "a colossal waste of time," and "a tremendous red herring and a waste of taxpayer resources," has had a change of heart about duplicative investigations now that President Trump is the target. He has hired his own experts to prosecute a case against President Trump. Former NBC News legal analyst Daniel Goldman serves as a senior advisor to the House Select Committee on Intelligence. His experience as an assistant United States attorney for the highly politicized Southern District of New York makes him a seasoned prosecutor. Instead of addressing foreign threats to the United States, Schiff seeks to second-guess the outcome of Special Counsel Robert Mueller's investigation, which involved more than 2,800 subpoenas, 500 search warrants, 500 interviews, and more than $25 million in costs.

House Financial Services Committee chairman Maxine Waters, Democrat of California, is using her committee oversight of financial institutions to investigate President Trump's charitable foundation. She is also attempting to compel financial institutions with which Trump does business to divulge information to the committee that regulates them.

In the House Ways and Means Committee, Democratic chairman Richard Neal of Massachusetts is probing the president's tax returns, working with Waters to compel Capital One and other financial institutions to turn over documents. The House Energy and Commerce Committee chairman, Frank Pallone, Democrat of New Jersey, vowed "robust oversight of the Trump administration's ongoing actions to sabotage our healthcare system, exacerbate climate change and weaken consumer protections."

Not to be outdone, House Foreign Affairs Committee chairman and New York Democrat Elliot Engel chose to eliminate the Terrorism, Nonproliferation, and Trade Subcommittee and replace it with a new Oversight and Investigations Subcommittee that is investigating all things Trump. Who cares about terrorism or nuclear proliferation when you can be the seventh House committee to try to duplicate the Mueller investigation?

This highly coordinated and targeted effort to take down the sitting president sucks all the oxygen from the room, leaving no one to do the real work of congressional oversight. I fear that when oversight is seen as nothing more than a political operation, it loses its legitimacy and weakens our republic. All of this occurs even as Democrats promote ambitious plans to overhaul our society, damage what's left of our free markets, and transform our government. Without congressional oversight, what's to stop them?

How Oversight Should Work

Our sprawling federal bureaucracy and multitrillion-dollar budget need more oversight, not less. My belief in the importance of congressional oversight does not diminish when the tables turn and my party holds the presidency while the opposing party holds the House majority. The more government grows, the more oversight it requires.

The Office of Inspector General (OIG) is an independent executive branch agency that does a great job policing the various federal departments, but that role is different from the one Congress can play. OIG investigations, audits, and reviews are often limited in scope, authority, and impact. Congress has broader authority, it has subpoena power, and it has the media megaphone to call attention to things administrations or partisan media may prefer to bury.

I know the public gets frustrated that Congress cannot do more to expose and punish wrongdoing. That frustrated me as well. They don't give members of Congress handcuffs, nor should they. As I outlined in my previous book, *The Deep State*, there are specific fixes we should implement to address the shortcomings of the oversight process. While Congress should never be given the power to prosecute lawbreaking, it does need the ability to enforce its access to documents and testimony. Nevertheless, the weaponization of the Department of Justice in the first two years of the Trump administration proves why oversight from outside the executive branch is such an important function of Congress.

To the extent congressional investigations can expose what happens in darkness, they serve as one of the few disincentives to abuse power in the executive branch. As I've often said, absent market forces to constrain behavior, the federal bureaucracy needs the threat of public exposure to keep it in line. The fact that the exposure may be motivated by political considerations makes the tool no less potent.

Legitimate oversight is nothing to be feared. If someone inside the Trump administration has legitimately broken the law, compromised national security, or abused their power, they should be held accountable like anybody else. I think President Trump would agree. It was my experience that President Obama did not. Nevertheless, rooting out waste, fraud, and abuse should be a priority in any administration. Oversight is not overreach simply because the target of an investigation shares our political views.

I had the opportunity to work with Chairman Elijah Cummings while he served as the House Oversight Committee's ranking member. Despite some of our public disputes during hearings, we made a serious effort to work collaboratively on many investigations. We developed a mutual respect and a friendship that would probably surprise people. Together we pursued dozens of bipartisan investigations that often drew little media coverage, but ultimately helped hold people accountable.

I'm proud of the work we did on prescription drugs, Freedom of Information Act reforms, legislation to empower inspector generals, uncovering misconduct and improving security with the Secret Service, exposure of wrongdoing at the Drug Enforcement Administration, and efforts to uncover the truth of the Flint, Michigan, water crisis. We were able to work together to root out some of the incompetence that can inevitably be found in large bureaucracies and to be a catalyst for effective reforms. This is oversight as it is meant to be conducted. Now that Cummings holds the chairmanship, I would like nothing better than to see him continue that bipartisan tradition of working together to root out the problems within the federal bureaucracy.

Policy Replaced with Politics

Unfortunately, I think Speaker Pelosi believes the tools Chairman Cummings now controls are far too valuable politically to waste on government accountability or problem solving. These are not her priorities. They don't excite the base to donate to political campaigns and nonprofits. They do not generate invitations to Sunday news shows or get members featured in viral media clips. Instead, she wants the oversight tools for her war on Donald Trump.

Make no mistake. The transformation taking place right now is not merely a change of partisan control. What is coming is a fundamental transformation of the oversight role. The Oversight, Judiciary, and Intelligence committees' investigative powers are becoming primarily a political weapon. Pelosi sees them as a tool to build narratives. She has little care whether those narratives are true or false, only that they move the needle in the next election.

Don't expect to see much energy being devoted to bipartisan efforts to clean up government in the run-up to a high-stakes presidential race. Those types of efforts may well become another casualty in this political war for dominance. While Cummings is very capable of providing substantive and effective oversight, he is also a loyal soldier for Speaker Pelosi and unfortunately seems to concur with her inclination to convert oversight resources to weapons on the political battlefield.

The renaming of the committee to remove the word *government* was the first signal that the 116th Congress will have little interest in traditional investigations of waste, fraud, and abuse in executive branch agencies. The decision also signals a metamorphosis of congressional committees to extend their oversight jurisdiction beyond mere government entities and into the furthest reaches of the American economy. Targeting individuals and private sector entities is an abuse of the committee's power. But it's already happening.

In fact, when Chairman Cummings was interviewed by *60 Minutes* just after taking the chairmanship, he indicated a belief that his committee could investigate anything, without limit and without regard to whether the subject of the investigation is government related at all.

Coincidentally, this threat to dramatically expand the committee's scope brings some financial perks to the campaigns of committee members.

The House Oversight Committee is considered a "C" committee, meaning seats on the committee are not as difficult to get as the more choice "A" and "B" committees. "A" committees are designated as such primarily because of the ability of committee members to fund-raise off those with business before the committee. Freshman members seldom get "A" committee assignments— those are generally reserved for more senior members. When members are competing for spots and ranking their choices, Oversight has not traditionally been very competitive. Everyone wants a coveted seat on the Appropriations Committee, which regulates spending, the Financial Services Committee, which regulates banks and Wall Street, or the powerful Ways and Means Committee, which regulates the tax code. These "A" committees have the power to tax, spend, and regulate some of the deepest pockets in America, so their members are an important target for donors and lobbyists.

Traditionally, the House Oversight Committee has not been a

threat to many private entities. It only engages with government entities, and its legislative jurisdiction primarily covers federal operations. With Cummings repositioning the committee to exercise jurisdiction over the entire American economy, K Street lobbyists will show a lot more interest. Members on the committee will find campaign contributions much easier to solicit. Perhaps more senior members will seek seats on the committee. We can expect to see government oversight and legislative reform take a backseat to campaign-driven priorities.

The only government waste, fraud, or abuse we can expect Democrats to pursue will be that which can be pinned to the Trump administration and its appointees. They will use every tool they once derided, taking each a step further, confident in the belief that the public will have forgotten their previously held positions and trusting that their media allies will remain silent.

Subcommittees Get Woke

Every committee chairman gets to exercise the prerogative to restructure the committee when taking over the gavel. When I took the Oversight chairmanship, I created two entirely new subcommittees—the Information Technology Subcommittee and the Subcommittee on the Interior. Likewise, Chairman Cummings gets to create a committee structure that reflects his priorities. Although the act of reorganizing subcommittees is nothing to fear, the changes Cummings made signal the committee's coming metamorphosis.

Both of the new subcommittees I created in 2015 were eliminated by Democrats. They do not make very good weapons for 2020. Instead, Chairman Cummings replaced them with his own new subcommittees that are better suited for political warfare. The Committee on the Environment will help him promote the Democratic priority to use climate change as a pretext to grow government—a very useful tool on the political battlefield, but hardly one that lends itself to the committee's core mission of rooting out government waste, fraud, or abuse.

The Civil Rights and Civil Liberties Committee will be useful in producing fodder for Democratic identity politics in the 2020 political campaigns. Perhaps it is just a coincidence that Pelosi has assigned many of her best icons of identity politics to Cummings's committee, including Representatives Alexandria Ocasio-Cortez, Rashida Tlaib, Ayanna Pressley, and Debbie Wasserman-Schultz. This committee will also be primed to promote the voter suppression narratives upon which Democrats depend to fend off election security measures. I know from experience that Democrats on the committee firmly believe that election security is used as a pretext by racists to keep black and Hispanic people from voting. Don't expect to see Democrats looking to secure elections, even in the face of Robert Mueller's documented conclusion of Russian interference. For Democrats, identity politics and voter suppression narratives will trump election security every day of the week.

Most disturbingly, an Economic and Consumer Policy Committee will presumably allow Cummings to fulfill the Democrats' wish to expand their limited oversight jurisdiction over the federal government into broad oversight of the entire U.S. economy. This committee in particular will be helpful in targeting (and conceivably destroying) private companies and organizations that do not align with the Democrat agenda. Alternatively, it can be used to back up Financial Services Committee chairman Maxine Waters's efforts to target deep-pocketed financial institutions whose fines Democrats hope to use for public funding of political campaigns.

Sacred Cows: Protecting Federal Employees

Each new committee chairman brings certain priorities—often those that impact the constituents back home. That's generally a good thing. In my case, I represented a large geographic area that was rural. The vast majority of land in this country is rural and I felt rural communities were not getting enough attention in the United States Congress. I created the Interior Subcommittee to address issues ranging from rural economies to tribal issues and from grazing to energy. There were many issues I felt were getting glossed over or didn't neatly fit in other committees.

Likewise, Chairman Cummings will be able to prioritize the things that matter in his district. I have no objection to that. He and I visited one another's districts in 2013. He learned a lot about public lands. I learned about inner-city challenges like intergenerational poverty.

Unfortunately, I'm afraid the home constituency that will matter most to committee Democrats will be the one that writes the biggest checks.

Chairman Cummings's home state of Maryland in 2018 had 144,542 federal employees according to figures published by *Governing* magazine. Cummings's district includes anywhere between 25,000 and 50,000 of those, depending on whether retirees are counted. Taking care of federal employees is and always has been a high priority for Democrats in general and for Chairman Cummings in particular. Yet his job as Oversight Committee chairman is theoretically to expose waste, fraud, and abuse within that very constituency.

He isn't the only one.

Pelosi has inexplicably stacked the Oversight Committee with members from districts with heavy concentrations of federal employees. Doesn't it seem strange that the Democrats would choose people to oversee federal mismanagement who are beholden to the very people they must hold accountable? If you really want effective oversight, wouldn't you choose someone less vulnerable to such conflicts? You would if you actually intended to conduct effective oversight of the federal employee population.

For example, the Government Operations Subcommittee, which

traditionally investigates much of the wrongdoing by federal employees, is now chaired by Virginia representative Gerry Connolly, whose 11th District has more federal employees than any other district in America, save Washington, D.C. (whose delegate in Congress, Eleanor Holmes-Norton, incidentally also serves on the Oversight Committee). Connolly literally cannot win reelection without the support of federal employees. His donor list reflects this reality, with public sector unions consistently numbering among his top contributors.

Why is he the man Democrats chose to investigate the operations of the federal government? Because when it comes to the federal employees who predominantly vote Democrat and whose unions donate richly and almost exclusively to her caucus, Speaker Pelosi doesn't want Connolly there to play offense. He's there to play defense. We'll still see him play offense—against President Trump and his appointees. He'll be aggressive and persuasive on those issues. But we won't see him go anywhere near the systemic problems in the civil service.

In my experience, Connolly was sympathetic to individual cases of wrongdoing brought up by Republicans. He was not happy about Environmental Protection Agency employees who spent hours of every day watching porn on their office computers or National Park Service managers who sexually harassed women they supervised. But he was never interested in systemic solutions like giving agencies more power to fire the bad apples in their ranks, nor was he one to draw attention to such cases. I don't see him using his authority to shine a light on situations that might reflect poorly on federal employees. Fearful of upsetting federal employee unions, he will handle the civil service with kid gloves.

I learned during my tenure that there is no such thing as an offense committed by a federal employee that is severe enough to rattle federal employee unions. They will simply never concede that behavior of one of their members rises to a level justifying rule or policy changes. Connolly will never cross those unions.

Lying in a Bed of Their Own Making

We may actually see some chickens come home to roost for congressional Democrats after they stood against their own institution during the Obama administration. They stood by supportively while the Obama administration ran roughshod over our congressional subpoena authority and while it invoked an unprecedented expansion of executive privilege.

Though the Trump administration has not as yet gone to the same audacious lengths the Obama administration went to withhold information, Democrats will have a hard time enforcing subpoena compliance or piercing executive privilege without intervention from the courts, a process that could take many years to come to fruition.

During the Obama administration, the government routinely ignored our subpoenas. They claimed executive privilege, even for documents that had never previously enjoyed such protection. When they did produce requested documents, those were often either heavily redacted or they were copies of publicly available documents we could have downloaded from a government website. They were seldom responsive to our document requests and often rejected our demands to hear from government witnesses. To remember how Democrats responded to these practices, the case of the Fast and Furious gunrunning investigation is instructive.

Republicans in early 2011 sought records pertaining to the failed Bureau of Alcohol, Tobacco, Firearms and Explosives (ATF) program that allegedly facilitated the flow of thousands of weapons to drug cartels across the U.S.-Mexico border. The Obama administration withheld 15,000 documents, inappropriately claiming executive privilege, while simultaneously arguing the president had never been briefed on the operation. This was a completely new and expanded use of executive privilege to shield documents the president had never even seen. I believe in executive privilege, but how can it be invoked when the chief executive was not directly involved? Yet it was.

We attempted to push back on the expansion of executive privilege and the refusal to comply with congressional subpoenas by introducing a resolution to hold the attorney general in contempt of Congress. Warning our colleagues about the future implications of this vote, we reminded them the resolution wasn't just about Attorney General Eric Holder or Fast and Furious. It was about protecting the right of congressional committees to access documents in the future.

When the committee voted, not a single Democrat was willing to defend our congressional subpoena authority. When the resolution went to the House floor, some Democrats actually walked off the floor in protest.

In the floor debate on the contempt resolution, Democratic California representative Adam Schiff argued forcefully against the very position he now takes against the Trump administration. He argued:

> *What we are doing today is simply a partisan abuse of the contempt power. What we do will cause no injury to the department but will cause great injury to this house. The Justice Department, after providing 8,000 documents and extensive testimony is now being required to turn over privileged materials, and like all administrations before it, it has reluctantly used executive privilege to respectfully refuse to provide materials it cannot provide.*

By June 2017, Schiff's opinion on privilege had changed dramatically. No more was executive privilege something presidents did "reluctantly" to "respectfully refuse" to provide documents. In the heady days before the Russia collusion narrative fell apart, Schiff was anticipating a damning report from the special counsel investigation led by Robert Mueller. But there was one problem—

Trump could legitimately use executive privilege to shield the report from public view.

Suddenly executive privilege became a relic that needed to be sacrificed for the greater good of the Democratic quest for power. "Privilege cannot be used as a shield to protect or hide potential impropriety or illegality. So we may have to go to court to pierce that privilege," Schiff told PBS.

But wasn't that precisely the point of Holder's refusal to comply with the Fast and Furious subpoena? We know that it was. Details about the documents (though not the documents themselves) Holder sought to withhold were later released in response to a court order. According to a recipient of that information, Judicial Watch's Tom Fitton, the withheld documents showed conclusively that Holder himself had directed the cover-up of the Fast and Furious scandal—personally crafting talking points and responding to congressional inquiries.

Schiff is right—privilege should not be used as a shield to protect impropriety. But he himself is on record defending its use for just that purpose. This issue is too important to be viewed strictly through a partisan lens.

Because of their failure to defend our institution, we now have strong precedent for an administration routinely and consistently ignoring congressional subpoenas. We have precedent for a president to use executive privilege to shield documents upon which he was never even briefed. We now have precedent for an administration to wait out the subpoenas and let Congress fight for them in court, where those disputes can languish until the scandal is ancient history and the administration has left office.

The right of a president to withhold information from Congress through executive privilege, though not enumerated in the Constitution, dates back to the presidency of George Washington. The two branches have been fighting over it ever since, with the Supreme Court stepping in to resolve disputes. Though it's not unusual for partisans to take a different approach to executive privilege when the opposing party is in power, Democrats now find themselves on the other side of a battle they were winning under the Obama administration.

The Democrats' failure to push back against the Obama administration's blatant attempts to shield Attorney General Eric Holder from embarrassment has set a precedent they now have to live with.

At the time Holder refused to produce the documents, Cummings was reticent, denying that Holder had failed to comply. He instead took the position that the Justice Department was "still producing documents" long after the deadline had passed. Will he be happy to live with that precedent if the Trump administration engages in those same delay tactics?

Now Democrats need that congressional authority they so casually ceded to the presidency. As they subpoena government witnesses in their effort to second-guess the results of the Mueller investigation, they are faced with a president who already cooperated with an in-depth investigation and is disinclined to do so again.

An exasperated Judiciary Committee Democrat, Rhode Island's David Cicilline, in an April interview with MSNBC, parroted Republican talking points his party had vociferously rejected during the prior administration. "First of all, Congress cannot allow the president to prevent us from oversight," he told *Hardball*'s Chris Matthews in a discussion. But that's exactly what his party did during the Obama-era Fast and Furious gunrunning operation.

Cicilline went on to outline the options Congress has to enforce those subpoenas, telling Matthews:

> We have three things Congress can do if witnesses refuse to comply with a lawfully issued subpoena. One is, refer to the Department of Justice for prosecution because that's a crime. We don't have a lot of confidence Mr. [William] Barr will do

*that. The second is to start a civil proceeding and get a citation
from the court to bring that person into contempt and do it that
way. But there's a third method we can do right away. Since
1821, the Supreme Court has recognized the inherent right
of Congress to hold individuals in contempt and to imprison
them. That was reaffirmed in a case in 1935. Congress has the
responsibility, and I would say the obligation, to hold individuals in contempt who do not comply with a lawful subpoena,
who do not produce documents, and we ought to be prepared
to imprison them because we have the inherent right.*

Now he sounds like me. I also raised the question of whether
Congress would have to resort to imprisonment to enforce
subpoena power. I have a little bit of experience pursuing
those avenues outlined by Cicilline. He is not going to be very
happy when he finds out what's at the end of each of those
paths.

Waiting for the Justice Department to prosecute itself is a
fool's errand. Cicilline admits this, saying he has no confidence
Attorney General Barr would prosecute anyone for failing to
comply with a congressional subpoena. He's right. Barr probably won't. His predecessors didn't. And Barr has a better case for
failing to comply. His agency has already conducted a full-scale
investigation, with full cooperation from the president, including the waiving of executive privilege. They aren't necessarily
hiding anything from Congress. They're simply refusing to do
the same thing twice.

Given that fact pattern, do Democrats really want to proceed to
the next option on Cicilline's list? Is this really the case Democrats
want to take to court to defend congressional authority? As much
as I would like to see Congress's authority affirmed, this is not the
case I would want to bet the farm on. And if they take this case
before the courts and they lose, how do we recover from that?
Better to take a stronger case.

As for the imprisonment route, that is perceived as an extreme response for which there may be a political price to pay. Personally, I think they should go for it. But I have my doubts whether Pelosi's team will be any more supportive of it than my leadership was, particularly since Democrat leadership thus far has been squeamish about pursuing limits to executive power that might apply when their own party is in power.

They'd like to prevent President Trump from unilaterally changing immigration enforcement policies. But they are not willing to rein in the very power President Obama used to offer short-term amnesty to Dreamers through his Deferred Action for Childhood Arrivals (DACA) program. They'd love to stop the president from using his national emergency authority to build a wall, but they stop short of actually legislating away the president's power to declare national emergencies. Likewise, I think it's unlikely Democrats will pursue a congressional imprisonment option that could be used to give Republicans the upper hand against a Democratic president.

They could go the route of legislating limits on executive privilege. But that, too, would cut both ways. I am a big believer in executive privilege. We want the president to get the widest perspective on anything that happens or that could potentially happen. His advisers should be able to be candid without fear that their counsel will ultimately be publicly disclosed.

That said, I believe the Democrats were wrong to defend the abusive expansion of that privilege by the Obama administration and they would be wrong to deny President Trump the legitimate use of it today. We have to be willing to consider what is best in the long term, regardless of which party is in power. I still believe the administration cannot claim executive privilege unless the chief executive was briefed. But neither can we afford to risk destroying the protection that privilege provides.

Going Fishing for Evidence

Chairman Cummings, a longtime opponent of what he called congressional fishing expeditions, instituted another change to the committee that I never expected to see from him. In fact, he would have come unglued had I made the same change. Apparently Oversight Democrats are ready to put their waders on.

I have to bring you in on a little bit of insider baseball to show how Democrats hope to expand their capacity to fish through mountains of irrelevant testimony in an effort to find that one fish that can help build a damaging narrative against the president.

Here's how it works. The committee will no longer defer to the wishes of witnesses or minority members to have a member of Congress present for depositions. That may not seem like a big deal, but let me show you what happens when they make that one small change.

For every public hearing you see on television, there can be numerous private depositions that take place as part of the fact-gathering process. In the past, the minority was consulted and had the right to request that a member of Congress be present at such depositions even though staff attorneys conducted them. Witnesses could also make such a request.

That rule meant depositions could only be conducted when Congress was in session, which limited the number of depositions that could be done. Sometimes the minority or the witness would waive that right, but I can assure you that Cummings, as ranking member, would have been very upset had we proposed such a rule change. The reason is that we could have fired up the accelerant on investigations of the Obama administration. Without a need to have a member of Congress on hand, we could have had staff doing depositions day and night, even when Congress was in recess. That rule limited the committee's ability to go on broad fishing expeditions by interviewing an endless string of witnesses.

Members' time is tight, between floor votes, legislative work, meetings with constituents and lobbyists, and the necessary evil of fund-raising. When a member is required to be present for a transcribed interview, the staff has to make sure that interview is going to be worthwhile. Without that requirement, Cummings's staff will be able to go on extended fishing expeditions without any factual evidence that the witness has something relevant to share.

This practice also compromises the legitimacy of these interrogations. The committee's members, not its staff, hold the constitutional authority to engage in this work. With no member present for transcribed interviews, constitutional legitimacy is in doubt. These congressional depositions carry great weight. They can also be expensive for the witness, potentially incurring significant travel costs and attorneys' fees, not to mention damaging media attention.

For a public company, the news that the company has even been called in for a transcribed interview can have consequences as devastating as anything that might be revealed in the actual interview. With the considerable expansion of the committee's scope, Cummings has theoretically empowered his staff to impose the functional equivalent of financial fines and penalties against anyone they believe does not sufficiently align with the Democrat agenda.

Ranking member Cummings once called the Benghazi investigation "an abusive effort" to "derail Secretary Clinton's presidential campaign" and called for Republicans to "end this taxpayer-funded fishing expedition." (It wasn't one, but more on that later.)

Nonetheless, Democrats' aversion to taxpayer-funded fishing expeditions seems to have subsided. As Chairman Cummings told *60 Minutes* in January, "we can look at anything" to get Donald Trump. That's a far cry from 2016, when he complained in an Oversight Committee hearing on the IRS, "Unfortunately, Republicans have become obsessed with investigating any and every allegation relating to the IRS, no matter how small." Sound familiar?

With the shoe firmly on the other foot, Cummings came out of the gate with fifty-one different requests for documents from the Trump administration and a long list of subpoena threats. Unless there is evidence of wrongdoing, Cummings's investigations meet the very definition of the obsessive fishing expeditions he once condemned.

Not to be outdone, Judiciary Committee chairman Jerry Nadler, a New York Democrat, issued more than eighty subpoenas in March 2019, all seeking information targeting President Trump. Will either of them pull back because it's an election year? To the contrary. But back in 2012, Cummings called the Fast and Furious investigation "an election-year witch hunt," even as he acknowledged that the investigation into the botched government gunrunning operation "uncovered a pattern of problems."

Thus far, the Democrats can only wish the results of the election-year witch hunt into President Trump had produced as much evidence of wrongdoing as that Fast and Furious investigation did. Even the vaunted special counsel investigation turned up less substantive evidence of wrongdoing than we found in just that one Obama-era investigation of the gun-walking scandal. It's safe to say Democrat committee chairmen appear to have overcome their objections to witch hunts, fishing expeditions, and obsessive investigations.

Crying Wolf: False Investigations

Further undercutting the credibility of legislative branch oversight is the pursuit of false claims and meritless investigations. It doesn't take many to convince the public that oversight is not credible.

We all saw what happened when the Justice Department announced prior to the release of the Mueller Report that there would be no indictments of Trump campaign operatives for Russian collusion. This came as an obvious shock to anyone who had been listening to Intelligence Committee chairman Adam Schiff's assurances over the previous year. He had seen the evidence himself, so he said. Even after the vast resources of the special counsel had exhausted every possible lead and come up empty, Schiff continued to insist the Mueller investigation had gotten it wrong. Schiff has indicated this is a hill he's willing to die on, undermining the legitimacy of the congressional oversight he oversees. The price is one he (and we) may have to pay.

The staff of the House Oversight Committee is fewer than one hundred people. Other committees are even smaller. The resources are simply not sufficient to pursue every potential investigative lead. That means the chairman has to pick his battles. Schiff has proven he'll choose the battle with Donald Trump every time. There is no rumor too speculative, no allegation too unfounded to attract the attention of the many committees itching to investigate the Trump presidency.

Before Donald J. Trump was even sworn in as America's forty-fifth president, Democrats began demanding that the Oversight Committee do to Donald Trump what they perceived we had done to Hillary Clinton. In their view, our attempts to investigate her email server during a presidential campaign were a political stunt. They wanted similar "stunts" aimed at Donald Trump.

My colleagues on the other side of the aisle had tremendous faith that there would be evidence—if we would just search for it. But when I did open investigations, there was nothing there. In the months before I left Congress, we opened several investigations into allegations Democrats made against Donald Trump.

For example, just a month after President Trump's inauguration, various outlets reported on a photo posted to social media by a member at Trump's Mar-a-Lago resort in Florida showing the president, top aides, and Japanese prime minister Shinzo Abe looking at a computer screen. The *New York Times* alleged, "President Trump and his top aides coordinated their response to North Korea's missile test on Saturday night in full view of diners at Mr. Trump's Mar-a-Lago resort in Florida—a remarkable public display of presidential activity that is almost always conducted in highly secure settings."

The social media post had not mentioned the North Korean missile test, but the article drew the conclusion based on the fact that shortly before the photo was posted, North Korea had test-fired a ballistic missile from its coast. Other outlets claimed cell phone lights had been pointed at sensitive documents during the briefing in "full view of fellow diners."

The story was widely picked up by news outlets around the world.

Immediately, Democrat politicians jumped on board to condemn the president, with Nancy Pelosi telling the *Times*, "There's no excuse for letting an international crisis play out in front of a bunch of country club members like dinner theater." Senators Tom Udall and Sheldon Whitehouse said in a statement, "This is America's foreign policy, not this week's episode of 'Saturday Night Live.'"

Unlike so many of the wild allegations against the new president, this one at least had a photo. On that basis, I went ahead and launched an investigation. The media covered that, too. What they didn't seem to want to cover was the inconvenient result of that investigation.

The investigation revealed that no classified documents were reviewed at that time, nor was classified information discussed. Nothing the president does in that setting is off-the-record. Every email sent, every word said, and every website visited can be validated. I ultimately went to the White House to receive a classified briefing. Ranking member Cummings chose not to join me, but he did send staff to receive the briefing.

As I recall, it turned out that newly minted President Trump and the Japanese prime minister were looking not at classified information, or even foreign policy information, but at pictures of Prime Minister Abe's father playing golf decades earlier. Does anyone remember seeing that reported in the media? Probably not. But the allegations themselves and the fact of my opening an investigation were broadly reported, fanning the flames of anti-Trump sentiment for several weeks. When the story turned out to be false, no one was interested in writing about that.

Was it legitimate to ask the question? Sure. But the breathless response and immediate condemnation were all about setting a political narrative—one that turned out to be false. I continued to receive pressure to open investigations into similarly unsupported allegations.

None of those early allegations against the president produced a shred of real evidence. There was a lot of speculation. But I wasn't willing to open investigations based on nothing more than speculation. I had not done so against Democrats and would not do so against Republicans, either. All of that has changed now that Democrats run oversight.

We never did open an investigation into the Russia collusion allegations, because at that time there was no evidence on which to base such an action, only speculation and the wild conjecture that he *must* have done something illegal or he wouldn't have won.

Breaching the Constitutional Limits of Oversight

As political opposition research activities morph into full-scale congressional investigations across multiple committees, it's fair to wonder what the actual constitutional limits of oversight are. What will happen if the Democrats breach them?

In truth, congressional oversight authority is broad—as it

should be. However, despite the widespread belief in Congress that the oversight role is boundless, the Supreme Court has not agreed. The primary role of Congress is quite clearly to legislate. Over time, the courts have rightly interpreted that role to include an oversight component. But the purpose of congressional oversight is to provide oversight of government expenditures and to inform pending legislation. In that role, Congress is able to obtain documents and testimony from the executive branch specifically for the purpose of informing the lawmaking process.

Back in 1957, the Supreme Court addressed the limits of congressional oversight authority clearly. In response to a subpoena, John Watkins testified and answered questions before the House Committee on Un-American Activities. Watkins was asked whether certain other named individuals were members of the Communist Party.

In refusing to answer, Watkins told the committee, "I do not believe that such questions are relevant to the work of this committee, nor do I believe that this committee has the right to undertake the public exposure of persons because of their past activities." That answer resulted in Watkins being convicted of contempt of Congress. In the ensuing court case, *Watkins v. U.S.*, the Court addressed the limits of congressional oversight jurisdiction, holding:

The power of the Congress to conduct investigations is inherent in the legislative process. That power is broad. It encompasses inquiries concerning the administration of existing laws as well as proposed or possible needed statutes. . . .

But, broad as is this power of inquiry, it is not unlimited. There is no general authority to expose the private affairs of individuals without justification in terms of the functions of the Congress. . . .

No inquiry is an end in itself; it must be related to and in furtherance of a legitimate task of Congress.

A subsequent 1959 Supreme Court ruling dealing with that same House Committee on Un-American Activities set broad, but clear parameters for congressional oversight. The Court in *Barenblatt v. U.S.* ruled:

> *Broad as it is, the power is not, however, without limitations. Since Congress may only investigate into those areas in which it may potentially legislate or appropriate, it cannot inquire into matters which are within the exclusive province of one of the other branches of the Government. Lacking the judicial power given to the Judiciary, it cannot inquire into matters that are exclusively the concern of the Judiciary. Neither can it supplant the Executive in what exclusively belongs to the Executive.*

When you look at the areas in which the House Oversight Committee has primary jurisdiction to make law, it's easy to understand why Democrats beholden to the civil service would prefer to gravitate to private sector work. Consider how difficult it will be to legislate only in the areas of the committee's primary jurisdiction and still hold harmless the federal employees and federal unions that fund the Democrat Party. The House Oversight and Reform Committee is responsible to vet laws that apply to:

- Federal civil service, including intergovernmental personnel; and the status of officers and employees of the United States, including their compensation, classification, and retirement;
- Municipal affairs of the District of Columbia in general (other than appropriations);
- Federal paperwork reduction;
- Government management and accounting measures generally;
- Holidays and celebrations;
- Overall economy, efficiency, and management of government operations and activities, including federal procurement;
- National archives;

- Population and demography generally, including the census;
- Postal service generally, including transportation of the mails;
- Public information and records;
- Relationship of the federal government to the states and municipalities generally; and
- Reorganizations in the executive branch of the government.

How hard is it to make laws in these areas that do not require anything inconvenient of federal employee benefactors?

No doubt there will be some lawmaking in these areas—but only to the benefit of the Democratic Party and its political donors at public employee unions. Instead of civil service reforms that promote accountability or empower managers to root out bad actors, expect to see Democrats tighten restrictions on disciplining or terminating federal employees.

One area where we may see some legislation movement is the census. This is one area that impacts elections and campaigns. Oversight Committee member Carolyn Maloney, a New York Democrat, introduced legislation restricting the census from collecting relevant information about citizenship. After all, the census can ask you how many toilets you have in your home, but Democrats consider it an invasion of privacy to ask if someone is here legally. Maloney says, "Every person must be counted." But no one is suggesting illegal immigrants not be counted. In fact, I believe Republicans are even more interested than Democrats in learning just how many people live in this country illegally. Accurate information about immigration could even hurt Democrats' 2020 election narratives. What Maloney wants, and what her party wants, is to count them for purposes of representation, thus ensuring that sanctuary states and cities are overrepresented in Congress.

In attempting to repurpose the tools of oversight for investigations of political targets and private entities, Democrats lose opportunities to legislate solutions and address the waste, fraud, and abuse that are inevitable in any large bureaucracy.

What's the Solution?

The answer to the problems plaguing congressional oversight is not less oversight. There is a right way and a wrong way to react to an oversight investigation.

For Republicans, we must resist the temptation to assume every investigation is politically motivated. Instead, we must demand evidence and act on principle. If legitimate wrongdoing is found, we ought to quickly acknowledge it and demand accountability.

The correct response to oversight from an administration is to be open and transparent, to signal to the federal workforce that inappropriate conduct will not be tolerated, and to work with Congress on legislative remedies to any wrongdoing uncovered. By handling the legitimate investigations in such a way, the administration retains greater credibility to fight any illegitimate or politically motivated investigations.

Not every investigation is legitimate. When the outcome of an investigation is predetermined, when the facts amplified are driven by personal agenda and political narratives, and when the target of the investigation is conveniently a political opponent, congressional oversight is undermined.

Does that happen? Unfortunately, it does—as we're about to see.

CHAPTER 8

OUTCOME-DRIVEN INVESTIGATIONS

Unbeknownst to incoming House Judiciary Committee chairman Jerry Nadler of New York, the woman sitting near him on the Amtrak Acela train just days after the 2018 midterm elections knew exactly who he was. She knew the responsibilities that would soon be his. With Democrats having flipped the House two days earlier, Nadler would take the gavel of the committee with jurisdiction over the Justice Department, putting him in prime position to investigate President Donald Trump.

As Nadler rattled off plans in phone call after phone call during that November 7, 2018, train ride from New York to Washington, D.C., *Federalist* reporter Mollie Hemingway was taking notes.

In a phone call with a friend whom Hemingway did not name, Nadler discussed two strategies for investigating Supreme Court justice Brett Kavanaugh, whose nomination to the Court had been confirmed the previous month. There was no new information at the time, but this wasn't good enough for Nadler, who must have known Kavanaugh investigations would whip up the base and drive fund-raising.

The first option, Hemingway reported, was to go after the FBI for mishandling the Kavanaugh background check. Oversight of the FBI rests with the House Judiciary Committee, making them an easy target.

The second strategy was to go after Kavanaugh for allegedly committing perjury. Nadler went on to describe a widely reported and now debunked perjury allegation that had Kavanaugh giving an incorrect answer about when he learned of allegations against him by Debra Ramirez. Ramirez's claims were never verified and, in fact, were contradicted by her own witnesses.

What's notable—and chilling—about this exchange between Nadler and his unnamed friend is the focus on the outcome rather than the problem. That is not how the oversight process is designed to work.

Yet here was Nadler, strategizing how to build an investigation around a desired outcome. Not a legislative outcome, but a political one.

When I first read Hemingway's story, I wanted to give Nadler the benefit of the doubt: to believe that perhaps he was genuinely concerned about Kavanaugh's fitness for office. Perhaps he was. But there is no escaping the rank political gamesmanship revealed by this conversation.

There was more.

Nadler went on to acknowledge that the plan to target Kavanaugh with investigations might fail. Hemingway overheard Nadler say, "The worst-case scenario—or best case depending on your point of view—you prove he committed perjury, about a terrible subject and the Judicial Conference recommends you impeach him. So the president appoints someone just as bad." The implication here is that they would have impeached Kavanaugh for nothing. The ends might not justify the means.

Apparently, the recipient of Nadler's suggestion told him impeachment might still be worthwhile because a new president in 2020 could nominate someone else. There's that political outcome again. But Nadler knew better. He responded that this investigation couldn't be dragged out long enough to get the desired outcome. "There are a finite amount of witnesses. I don't see why it should take long at all," he reportedly said.

Can there be any doubt what Nadler was trying to accomplish? This conversation was not about finding truth, or legislating solutions, but about removing a political obstacle. If this conversation is accurate, Nadler's goal appeared to be based in rank partisanship. He wanted to reverse the appointment of a Trump nominee to the Supreme Court.

Kavanaugh wasn't Nadler's only target that day. As Hemingway quietly tuned in, Nadler went on to discuss his party's plans to impeach the president of the United States. The Mueller investigation of the Trump campaign was the centerpiece, but Nadler said those investigations would be framed in the context of holding Trump accountable since that argument is more palatable to the public than impeachment. According to Hemingway's reporting, Nadler said Democrats would go "all-in" on the Russia conspiracy, with incoming Intelligence Committee chairman Adam Schiff, a California Democrat, taking the lead.

For his part, Nadler vehemently denied Hemingway's account, with a spokesman calling it "an absolutely false and deliberately inaccurate report." The truth of that statement would have to be measured by Nadler's actions once he assumed the gavel.

These conversations rightly provoked outrage. Nadler didn't even seem to make a pretense of objectively seeking truth. Outcome-driven investigations are an egregious abuse of power. He is focused on what he needs to prove to get the outcome he seeks. The establishment of guilt or innocence seems secondary.

Nadler comes off as a man whose mind is made up, like someone who doesn't need evidence, nor particularly care where it leads. He will search for something to satisfy the skeptics. But he comes across in this conversation as a man who has already decided what the facts will conclude and who is interested only in evidence to support those conclusions. Asked by ABC News' George Stephanopoulos if he believed the president had obstructed justice, Nadler in March 2019 replied, "Yes, I do. . . . It's very clear that the president obstructed justice." At this point, he had only been chairman for a few weeks. The summary of the Mueller Report had not yet been released. He had not had time to launch and complete an investigation. Yet he already knew what the outcome was going to be. And he was wrong.

In the hopes of building an impeachment case against the president, Nadler and Pelosi took the unprecedented step of hiring two outside lawyers to consult with the committee staff. Though NBC reported that committee officials stressed the move was not a precursor to impeachment, the selection of anti-Trump activists Norm Eisen and Barry Berke strongly indicated a prejudged investigation was on the way. Judiciary Committee ranking member Doug Collins, a Georgia Republican, noted in a letter to Nadler that the two attorneys had already published their conclusions widely, including in a Brookings Institution report they authored before they were even hired by Nadler. The two attorneys tasked with conducting an impartial investigation wrote that publicly available evidence "strongly supports that the president obstructed justice under ordinary application of relevant criminal law." They were not hired to investigate. Clearly, they were hired to prosecute.

That became even more clear in early May 2019 when Judiciary Committee Democrats insisted Attorney General William Barr come before the committee and agree to be questioned by staff attorneys rather than by lawmakers themselves. Barr refused. The full redacted report had been publicly released. The unredacted report was available for members of Congress to view. He had testified before the Senate Judiciary Committee. The point of having staff attorneys interrogate and cross-examine Barr was simply to relitigate the results of the criminal probe for political purposes. Testifying before the Senate Judiciary Committee on May 1, Barr told the senators, "We have to stop using the criminal justice process as a political weapon."

Nadler may well believe all the allegations against President Trump are true. But given his certainty about what he will find, can we be sure he will actually recognize, accept, or even share any evidence that contradicts his narrative?

When Truth Becomes a Casualty

When congressional committees give in to the temptation of pursuing outcome-driven investigations, truth can become a casualty of the process. However, valid oversight is important. It needs to be done, even in an election year. Even when it benefits one party and hurts another. The fact that an investigation may be politically convenient does not necessarily negate the value of that investigation. Truth can also become a casualty when we dismiss investigations against our own party that we would pursue against the opposition party. Congress has no credibility if the only standard for pursuing investigations is political expedience.

To get oversight right, we need to apply the same standards regardless of who is in the White House. Congress has broad authority to investigate—and it should. But all of us can benefit from recognizing the hallmarks and red flags that distinguish credible investigations from political witch hunts. Looking at these markers, we can compare the ongoing investigations into the Trump administration with those Republicans pursued against the Obama administration. It's helpful to ask three questions to determine if an investigation is justified.

1. Is Evidence the Impetus or the Outcome?
First, valid investigations will be a response to evidence of wrongdoing. Outcome-driven investigations will use the investigative

process to find evidence of wrongdoing. Broad document requests are the most obvious symptom of a fishing expedition looking for a specific outcome.

2. Is the End Goal to Find a Legislative Fix?

Second, a credible investigation will be solution-driven, not outcome-driven. The focus will be on crafting legislative remedies to the problems brought to light by the investigation. When the purpose of a hearing or an investigation is to politically embarrass someone, there will be no sign of lawmaking.

3. Is the Target the Government?

Third, legitimate oversight is focused on government waste, fraud, and abuse. If there is not government wrongdoing involved, Congress is overstepping constitutional boundaries. Congress is the wrong body to prosecute the wrongdoing of private individuals or companies. That is the job of the executive branch.

Let's apply these standards to major investigations under each administration.

Question I: Is Evidence the Impetus or the Outcome?

The role of evidence should come at the beginning of an investigation. If the purpose of document requests is the pursuit of evidence, they're doing it backward.

The obsession of House Democrats to get their hands on President Trump's tax returns is a compelling case study in foundation-free investigating. Congress has passed no law requiring presidential candidates to release tax returns. Candidates often do so voluntarily. But President Trump, citing an ongoing audit, has chosen not to release his.

This choice by the president is the only real evidentiary foundation of the investigation into President Trump's returns. Since he has, as of this writing, opted not to make his returns public, a decision I have criticized, the conclusion of Democrats is that he must be hiding something. We hear that from them a lot. This is a flimsy pretext for an investigation.

House Ways and Means Committee chairman Richard Neal, a Massachusetts Democrat, has asked for six years of returns. His justification? "Congress, as a co-equal branch of government, has a duty to conduct oversight of departments and officials," he said. So far so good. Congress does have that duty. If Neal believes the IRS has failed to address problems in the president's tax returns, Neal has the authority to investigate the IRS.

He goes on, "The Ways and Means Committee in particular has a responsibility to conduct oversight of our voluntary Federal tax system and determine how Americans—including those elected to our highest office—are complying with those laws."

Wait a minute. The justification is that Neal is curious about whether a single individual, a political opponent, not in government at the time, fully complied with tax laws? And he is claiming as his authority the committee's need to determine how Americans comply with tax law? What will Donald Trump's personal tax returns tell the Ways and Means Committee about how "Americans" are complying with tax laws? That one set of tax documents will only tell him how President Trump complied with tax laws—a question for the IRS and its auditors, not Congress. That rationale would entitle the committee to access the tax returns of any individual (or political opponent) in America for any reason or no reason.

Even if Neal had evidence of wrongdoing on the part of the president, adjudicating that tax conflict is the job of the IRS, not Congress. When constituents approach their congressional office for help with an IRS matter, we work with the taxpayer advocate at the IRS. We don't take that complaint to the House Ways and Means Committee, because they do not adjudicate individual tax filings. The committee's curiosity about what is in President Trump's tax returns is no foundation for an investigation.

Further intensifying the fishing expedition, three House committee chairs sent a letter to the president's financial institution in early March demanding to see anything and everything dealing with "potential foreign conflicts of interest, compliance with the foreign and domestic Emoluments Clauses of the U.S. Constitution, and any counterintelligence threats arising from links or coordination between U.S. persons and other foreign entities, including any financial or other compromise or leverage over the president and his business interests."

What's wrong with that request? It describes the crimes they are hoping the president committed and then asks his financial institution to fish for documents that might support those specific crimes.

They don't have evidence of crimes. They want to find some. That's not their job.

Do we want a Congress that can choose a political target, choose a crime, and then use the force of government to compel a private financial institution to be complicit in seeking evidence against its own customers?

Why would any financial institution compromise customer trust by complying with such a request? Possibly because the House Financial Services Committee, whose chairman—California Democrat Maxine Waters—is one of the three committee chairs who signed the document demand, has the legislative power to inflict great pain on those very financial institutions.

There is a reason Congress does not have law enforcement authority. Under our constitutional system of checks and balances, we separate lawmaking from law enforcement specifically to prevent just these types of abuses. The people enforcing the law should not be the same people writing the law. Yet that is precisely what Chairman Waters is attempting to do. I want to see Congress take back power from the executive branch that never should have been ceded, but this is an attempt to take power that

Congress is not entitled to have. Law enforcement is an executive branch power.

Congressional oversight is not law enforcement. It is oversight of government agencies. Congress generally conducts oversight when it receives evidence that something is not working within government. That evidence usually comes in the form of a report from the Office of Inspector General (OIG), an audit from the U.S. Government Accountability Office (GAO), a tip from a whistle-blower, or a very public government misfire. Even the most politicized investigations of the Obama era still had a solid foundation of evidence.

In the case of Benghazi, we had two solid evidentiary leads. One was the fact that four Americans, including our ambassador, were murdered at our own facility under the protection of our own State Department. The second was information we received from a whistle-blower in my own district in Utah. Lieutenant Colonel Andrew Wood had been among the security forces sent home prematurely just weeks ahead of the attack. With his testimony, we knew the State Department had violated its own safety protocols for the Benghazi facility. That is a matter worthy of congressional oversight. I spoke to more whistle-blowers in a subsequent visit to Tripoli, where I learned that the story of the attack being peddled by the administration about an anti-Muslim video was flatly false.

The Obama administration was either dangerously misinformed or intentionally misleading the American public. That was a matter worthy of congressional oversight. We had more than enough information to open an investigation of the State Department's security decisions. Still, the primary investigative role rested with the executive branch. There was an internal investigation. But the results of that investigation conflicted with the evidence before Congress from whistle-blowers.

To ignore the State Department's role in the incident given the red flags we received from whistle-blowers and the incongruent results of the internal investigation would have been malpractice. Following the facts led us to discover major lapses in security protocol, to expose Hillary Clinton's Accountability Review Board (ARB) investigation as a sham, and ultimately led to the discovery of a home-brew server—the contents of which can be accessed only by the owner of the server—in Hillary Clinton's private residence containing classified information in a nonclassified setting.

Had the ARB investigators done a thorough job instead of botching their Benghazi review, Congress wouldn't have needed to conduct separate oversight. But we learned that the ARB investigators never even interviewed Secretary Clinton for their report. They lied about having reviewed military after-action reports, which would have analyzed what happened, why it happened, and how to prevent it from happening again. Because they didn't ever get to the bottom of what actually happened, their report conflicted with the evidence, particularly the testimony of witnesses.

The ARB initially reported they had reviewed the after-action reports that would have been filed in real time. We knew that couldn't be true or their findings would have been different. When they were under oath in a public hearing, I pinned them down and got them to finally confess that they never even read the after-action reports.

Our committee wanted to review those reports to see what the ARB had missed in its investigation. The Pentagon first refused to produce them, and then later made the incredible claim that after-action reports were never written. Still, the ARB had previously reported having read them. Every time the military does something, there is an after-action report. No one who knows how the military works could possibly believe that in the lead-up to the attack, thirteen hours during the attack, and the aftermath, not one person wrote any kind of report summarizing what happened. No one ever wrote anything down? That was a ridiculous assertion and everyone knew it. To this day, it remains a complete mystery. That cover-up was successful because the president and the lawmakers in his party refused to cooperate with the oversight process. They were more interested in protecting the president than in following the evidence.

Incidentally, the House Oversight Committee wouldn't have touched the Benghazi tragedy had Democrats been running the committee. From what I could see, they had no desire to conduct any investigation of that incident whatsoever. Even as evidence emerged, they continued to insist there was nothing to see. Nonetheless, we had testimony from multiple witnesses in Benghazi that the story Secretary Clinton, Ambassador Susan Rice, Vice President Joe Biden, and President Obama had peddled to the media was a fabrication.

Given this fact pattern, we had every reason to pursue an investigation. We hadn't completed this investigation when even more damning information about Clinton emerged.

What became the Clinton email investigation actually began with an innocuous and unrelated Freedom of Information Act (FOIA) request. In response to that request, the State Department inadvertently released information that should not have been made public. All of this took place unbeknownst to Congress. Meanwhile, the IG for the intelligence community got involved to investigate how the State Department had released protected information. Their security protocols should have prevented that from happening.

When investigators dove into the record preservation process at the State Department, they discovered that Secretary Clinton and her team had their own way of doing things that was incompatible with cybersecurity. They told us they found evidence that more than three hundred people at the State Department were using Clinton's private email address to send unsecured messages to the secretary of state, creating an inexcusable security vulnerability. She had refused to participate in the secure systems put in place to protect the integrity and security of digital information at the State Department. She had her own equipment, her own server, and her own email account, and her own rules about what information would be preserved.

Congress only learned of Secretary Clinton's arrangement with herself when those findings were released by the IG. They didn't come to us as a result of a broad document request fishing for crimes to prosecute. With this report, Congress began to see why we were having such trouble getting relevant documents in the Benghazi investigation. We had a very real problem with serious implications for national security. This is exactly the kind of issue congressional oversight is designed to scrutinize.

The documents on Clinton's server had a level of classification (SAP) far beyond anything anybody in Congress was able to review. Remember, some of that information was so classified that, even as the chairman of the House Oversight Committee, with a high security clearance, I could not see it. Yet that information was floating out there on a home-brew server.

What I didn't know then that has only recently come to light, through the release of testimony from FBI investigator Peter Strzok, is that Clinton's operatives had already purged her server. Pursuant to a secret agreement with the DOJ, they were able to hold back tens of thousands of emails. I regret that the full scope of Clinton's duplicity was not known then—and is probably still not known now. But I am proud of the evidence-based investigation we ran.

I'm proud of the fact that I didn't start my tenure as the chairman of the Oversight Committee preannouncing eighty-one different investigations. We let facts dictate what drew our attention.

Contrast that with this batch of Democrat committee chairs whose goal is to, in their view, right the wrong of the 2016 election. Nadler, upon taking control of the Judiciary Committee, really did issue eighty-one document request letters to the Trump administration seeking an impossibly broad range of documents. This is a classic fishing expedition. No doubt if a single document is held back, Nadler will send a tweet asking, "What are they hiding?" He sees no need for an evidentiary foundation.

Neither do many other Trump opponents, who were calling for investigations of Donald Trump before the man was even sworn in. They believed if we looked hard enough, we would find something—anything.

That's not how this works.

That's not how it worked with Hillary Clinton, who served her full term as secretary of state before ever being formally investigated for anything. Until we had solid evidence of potential criminal wrongdoing, we left Clinton alone. Had my priority been politics, I would have called her to testify before our committee. That never happened, because it was not necessary. She only ever testified before the Select Committee on Benghazi, for good reason. She was a key witness. We were largely able to get information through private transcribed interviews to show what had happened.

The fact that these investigations had political overtones did not automatically disqualify them from legitimacy. Inevitably some congressional investigations will become political. For example, the timing of the September 11, 2012, terrorist attack in Benghazi, Libya, happened to coincide with an upcoming presidential election just eight weeks later. That meant any investigation of the incident would be viewed through the lens of President Obama's reelection race against Republican Mitt Romney. But that investigation was driven by an incident we did not control. We did not initiate it, plan it, script it, or collude with the media on it.

Our pursuit of that investigation was driven by evidence and guided by the next sign of a credible investigation—a search for legislative solutions.

Question 2: Is the End Goal to Find a Legislative Fix?

Congress is a lawmaking body. As discussed in the previous chapter, its oversight role is to evaluate and investigate the federal government for the purpose of proposing systemic changes. We have Supreme Court precedent setting forth this restriction on oversight. It is done for the purpose of informing legislation.

If Congress wants presidential candidates to disclose their tax returns, Congress can make a law that applies to all candidates. If Congress doesn't like a president declaring national emergencies to access funding, Congress has the power to change the law. If Congress is worried that Russians might meddle in our elections, Congress can appropriate money for cybersecurity efforts or enact security provisions such as voter ID.

None of those things are happening. Why? Because the House majority is only focused on this president. At best, they are not considering the long term. At worst, they want to limit this president without constraining a future Democratic president.

The first high-profile hearing of the new Democrat-run House Oversight Committee in February 2019 was a case study in oversight gone out of bounds. The witness, former Trump personal attorney Michael Cohen, had never worked for the executive branch. He was a private citizen. There was no pending legislation to which his testimony could have been relevant. The hearing was simply titled: "Michael Cohen, Former Attorney to Donald Trump." What else could they call it? It served no legislative or oversight purpose.

By contrast, Oversight Committee Republicans made sure even our most politically contentious investigations during my tenure were on solid jurisdictional grounds. That was very important to me as oversight chairman.

Both the Benghazi terror attack and the subsequent email scandal of Hillary Clinton involved wrongdoing within the executive branch and the potential failure of laws we had passed to protect our overseas employees and our classified information. You can go down the list—everything from IRS targeting to Fast and Furious gunrunning and from DEA prostitution scandals to Secret Service security failures—it's all executive branch malfeasance. Those investigations fell squarely within the committee's jurisdiction as they all involved the actions of executive branch officials within the context of their work for the government and for the purposes of considering legislation. By contrast, Michael Cohen was neither a government actor nor a person who could inform legislation. There was some attempt to argue that Cohen's testimony of a hush money payment to porn star Stormy Daniels might be considered a campaign contribution and thus have a tenuous link to something government related.

Of course, when Democrats were in the minority, they would have used a different argument to delegitimize a witness like Michael Cohen. If we ever called a witness who was also a witness in an ongoing third-party investigation, committee Democrats would always object, arguing that we could not possibly intervene with an ongoing investigation. They would say, Let them do their work! Let them finish their job!

They don't seem to feel that way anymore. Michael Cohen is reportedly under investigation for possible bank fraud, among other things. But suddenly Democrats have had a change of heart about interfering with ongoing investigations. They called on Cohen to testify in both open and closed hearings on Capitol Hill.

Too much of the oversight the House has embarked upon since Nancy Pelosi took the gavel falls outside Congress's legal jurisdiction. We've already discussed why real oversight of executive branch agencies—and the federal employees who operate them—is unappetizing to a party dependent on federal employee support and funding. More appealing to Democrats is the weaponization of oversight against people and entities outside of government.

This overreach won't stop at targeting private citizens who happen to be in President Trump's orbit. The new House majority's agenda is much broader and much more disturbing. The next step will be the usurpation of prosecutorial power from the executive branch to go after private sector companies and individuals. This is something Democrats have been chomping at the bit to do for as long as I was in Congress. They want to use the oversight authority to punish and embarrass private entities who come in conflict with the goals of the Democratic agenda. That could be anything from gun manufacturers to bakeries. Or, as freshman representative Alexandria Ocasio-Cortez suggested, financial institutions that loan money to projects of which she disapproves. In a March 2019 hearing, Ocasio-Cortez suggested Wells Fargo should be held responsible for cleanup costs on a pipeline spill simply because the bank financed the project.

This conflict came up numerous times during my chairmanship. For example, both parties have serious concerns about high-priced pharmaceuticals. Specifically, we were concerned about the inexplicable price gouging for common drugs such as EpiPen and insulin. Chairman Cummings has justifiably made this issue one of his first oversight investigations as chairman. But his approach to the problem is to focus on the private sector while ignoring the government's role in the crisis. This is a waste of his committee's resources because the government side of the equation is the one he can most directly and powerfully influence.

The Specific Legislative Decision Standard, articulated in several important Supreme Court cases, limits congressional oversight authority to areas upon which Congress can conceivably legislate. In *Barenblatt* the Court held:

> *With regard to oversight of the private sector, the court held in U.S. v. American Tel. & Tel. Co (1976) that "Congress is not invested with a 'general power to inquire into private affairs.' [The subject of any inquiry always must be one] 'on which legislation could be had.' "*

Sadly, congressional committees that perform oversight do not have a strong record of using information from investigations to craft legislative solutions. When I was chairman of the Oversight Committee, I wanted to change that. It can be done.

We successfully passed substantive bipartisan legislation as a result of our oversight work. For example, after a deep dive into the Freedom of Information Act, we were successful in pushing significant reforms all the way to President Obama's desk, where he signed them into law. As a result of our scrutiny of the Secret Service, the committee issued dozens of recommendations that ultimately resolved some of the problems plaguing the agency. We further legislated personnel reforms that addressed attrition problems that had contributed to the agency's failures. After several of our investigations revealed inspector generals were having difficulty gaining agency cooperation to access documents, we passed legislation beefing up their ability to get access to agency records and grand jury materials relevant to their oversight investigations.

If you want to measure the effectiveness of congressional oversight, a good place to start is by assessing the real legislative outcomes of high-profile hearings, not only in the House Oversight Committee, but in Judiciary, Intelligence, Financial Services, and any other committee engaged in an oversight role. Given what I've seen thus far, my guess is that with Democrats running the show, you won't find much. The best opportunities for reform are within the government agencies themselves. But this Congress will be more focused on private companies and individuals.

There is a way to address the pharmaceutical pricing problem without creating unprecedented new ways for government to usurp freedom. We simply have to address the incentives that the government puts in place and to which free markets respond.

My approach to this problem was to bring in Martin Shkreli (aka "Pharma Boy"), former CEO of Turing Pharmaceuticals, and get him on the record to testify about the ways in which he was exploiting the government's slow, costly, and prohibitive approach to generic drug approvals. The government's role in the process was something that was within the committee's jurisdiction.

When you watch the hearings Democrats are now doing with regard to pharmaceutical pricing, do you see them bringing in any government witnesses? Do they even have anyone on the panel from a government agency? The Oversight Committee's January 29, 2019, hearing had not a single government witness.

Whenever Congress holds a hearing, we should be asking ourselves: What legislation do they hope will arise from the information learned in this hearing?

Question 3: Is the Target the Government?

The tools of oversight were given to Congress in 1814 for a specific purpose—to check the spending and management of the federal bureaucracy. Rooting out waste, fraud, and abuse is a job Congress was designed to do. On my committee, we could have kept three committee staffs busy with just the investigative tips we received from whistle-blowers, audits, and OIG reports. There is that much.

The most valuable oversight happens when we undertake programmatic reviews of government operations. This type of work doesn't give us a YouTube moment or get our names in the headlines. But diligent work on government programs can lead to legislation that creates real results for the American people. That's what they elected us to do. That's what we give up when we allow the political opportunities to overshadow our legislative responsibilities.

Let me share an example of the kind of productive oversight that can happen when the committee is focused on doing its job. In 2016 the committee was approached by a whistle-blower for the highly secretive Federal Air Marshal Service. This person made an allegation about a scheme by a senior employee to manipulate sky marshal flight schedules to facilitate rendezvous with illicit lovers in high-demand vacation destinations. It turned out someone was scheduling optimal flights and then "accidentally" missing the return flights so they could have extended weekends in places like Miami, Honolulu, and other desirable locations.

For example, they might be scheduled on a flight from Los Angeles to Honolulu and the next day from Honolulu to Chicago. But they would somehow miss that flight back to Chicago, and the next available flight with an open sky marshal position on it would be three days later. That meant they would just have to spend four or five days in Honolulu. We discovered a staffer who had some say in the scheduling and who was allegedly somewhat of a sexual predator in that this person tended to have affairs with a variety of coworkers, many of whom were married. The individual was in a powerful position to dictate who went where and when. It had finally reached a point where one brave whistle-blower stepped up because the person wouldn't stop.

As a committee, we quickly engaged in a bipartisan way to work with the agency's inspector general. That investigation led us to look more broadly at the whole program and how it worked. It's obviously shrouded in secrecy, but our investigation raised important questions about how the program worked and what was going on. Was it a worthwhile program? As a result of our investigation, the agency implemented some changes with regard to personnel and processes. No hearings were held. No news stories were written. But the investigation effected real change. Within the scope of our mission, we looked at how taxpayer dollars were being spent and created some accountability within that department and agency. DHS management was very responsive to the work we were doing with them. It was a very positive experience.

I worry that under Democratic leadership, the committee will be so distracted with all things Trump that this type of oversight just simply won't happen. It's now the House Oversight and Reform Committee. Will they make any effort to reform government that does not benefit their political warfare? The ratio of Oversight staff to government employees is already pitifully small—there are some sixty or so people staffing the committee majority and another thirty in the minority. Put that up against 2.2 million federal employees. It may be the second-largest committee in the

House, but it is still minuscule compared to the breadth of the $4 trillion going out the door each year to fund the government.

If you're spending money and dedicating personnel to sift through the Trump Hotel guest list and see who spent how much on a minibar—what are you missing? This goes to the heart of a committee that takes out the word *government* because they don't think there is anything to look at there.

CHAPTER 9

REAL REFORM LOSES TO POLITICAL THEATER

If we want different results from Congress, we need people in positions of power who are willing to be part of the solution, not part of the problem. And to do that, we need to expand the definition of what it looks like to be a solutions-oriented politician. We often look to the lawmaking function to see who has solutions. But anyone can introduce a bill, or sign on as a cosponsor. In reality, most bills go nowhere. The ones that do get heard are chosen by party leadership. That's why party has come to matter so much in American elections.

A better way to evaluate the commitment to finding solutions is to look at the results of oversight. Is there a real effort to solve the problems uncovered by congressional, inspector general, or auditing oversight? Do those problems get ignored, or even denigrated? Or is there a genuine effort to make changes to the systems that produced them?

For a party invested so heavily in marketing government as the solution to every problem, the Democrats have been strangely reluctant to take advantage of opportunities to build trust in the institutions of government. Instead of demonstrating the ability to crack down on abusive behavior, they have excused it. Then they wonder why Americans might be reluctant to turn the one-sixth of the United States economy related to health care over to a federal bureaucracy that too many lawmakers pretend is exempt from oversight.

If there is one thing that became patently obvious during the Mueller investigation, it was that the bureaucracy—the Deep State, if you will—operated with very few constraints. They were virtually above oversight. We had the FBI trafficking in unsubstantiated rumors and opposition research, lying to the FISA court, entrapping administration officials, and engaging in unauthorized leaks. We saw widespread use of personal email and text messaging to conduct off-the-record government business. In response, we had Democratic leaders like Chairman Nadler falling all over themselves to excuse that behavior.

Because Congress has thus far failed to use the lessons of the Mueller investigation to demand better accountability measures within the Justice Department, it has only further undermined public trust in federal law enforcement. We will never solve problems we don't acknowledge.

The truth is, Democrats have before them historic opportunities to restore public trust in government. They could theoretically steal President Trump's thunder by solving the problems he will campaign on. In doing so, they could demonstrate competence, discretion, and the ability to enact substantive reform. So far, they have shown little interest in such a strategy. The missed opportunities are piling up.

Preserving Government Records and Accountability

The problem of government employees using off-the-record communication to bypass federal records laws, though heavily exploited by the Obama administration, is not unique to Democratic administrations. It's a proliferating problem that legitimately needs to be addressed. Yet Democrats have not only failed to address solutions, they have mocked the problem and ignored the bias that prevented the FBI from prosecuting it.

In June 2018, Justice Department watchdog Michael Horowitz released an OIG report on his review of fired FBI director James Comey's handling of the Clinton email investigation. Horowitz determined that the FBI director's actions were "extraordinary and insubordinate" in violating the department's norms.

The OIG report's overall findings were damning to the credibility of the FBI. The report documented preferential treatment of Hillary Clinton and her lawyers, widespread leaking throughout the agency, and potential bias. In particular, the report called out Peter Strzok, who would play prominently in the early Mueller investigation.

"We did not have confidence that Strzok's decision to prioritize the Russia investigation over following up on the midyear-related investigative lead discovered on the Weiner laptop was free from bias," the report said, referring to sensitive materials found on the laptop computer of disgraced congressman Anthony Weiner. Weiner was married at the time to Clinton aide Huma Abedin.

More critically, the report addressed the use of private email accounts and cell phones to conduct official government business. This problem went all the way to the top of the executive branch. Even President Obama had used Secretary Clinton's private email address to communicate with her. The revelation that even the highest level of leadership in federal law enforcement was bypassing government records laws indicated a serious accountability problem with implications far beyond one candidate or one presidential election.

Instead of using the opportunity the OIG report presented to address the widespread use of private email communication, many high-ranking Democrats actually mocked the allegations. A popular meme developed on the left to undermine any legitimate concerns about public records abuses. "But her emails" became a rallying cry by the resist crowd to minimize the significance of Deep State secrecy. Even Hillary Clinton herself, in response to the OIG report's finding that Comey had used his personal email account for government business, tweeted the finding with her own comment: "But my emails."

There was no acknowledgment of a problem—much less any attempt to find a solution. This wasn't just about Hillary Clinton's yoga emails. In her case, we were talking about information so sensitive that only a handful of people in the world were allowed to see it. Information that put lives at risk—that, if made public, could get people killed and operations compromised. Keep in mind, you can't just forward classified emails from one account to another. You use different hardware, different software, and you usually view it only in secured facilities. It is not easily transmitted.

I had this discussion over the phone with Director Comey at the time. I remember it clearly. He explained it to me like this. He said: You can go and read hundreds of pages of communiqués that are classified. You can't then simply take that information in your own words and retype it. It's still classified. The content is still classified content.

If you've never had a security clearance, you may not realize how difficult it is to expose classified material. It's not as if you're sitting at your computer and some emails are classified and others are not. The emails are on two different systems, physically separated from one another. For the ease and convenience of senior officials, it is possible to access classified information from home.

Taxpayers had to pay to refit a Sensitive Compartmented Information Facility (SCIF) in Clinton's home so she could review documents day and night. But she had to view them from that separate room in her home. The only way for classified emails to migrate from that secure setting was for Clinton to deliberately remove them from there—or ask someone on her staff to do so. She was so sloppy and cavalier that she created a real danger. The target of that investigation was not so much Clinton as it was the process by which she evaded critical national security protections.

The OIG report clearly concluded that Hillary Clinton was sloppy with how she handled classified information. She used unsecured devices in foreign settings, left the door open to her secure SCIF facility, and didn't even use a password. The bigger question I had, which has still never been answered by the State Department or Congress, is: How is it that so many people were involved in this scheme? At one point I was told by a State Department witness there were up to three hundred people involved in the trafficking of classified information in an unclassified setting.

Secretary Clinton was fortunate that the vast majority of senior officials in the Justice Department were loyal enough to her to protect her from the legal consequences of her own behavior. For example, we know the FBI failed to investigate, much less prosecute, her for lying to Congress. Director Comey drafted a letter exonerating her for mishandling classified information before she was even interviewed by the FBI. They allowed material witnesses to act as her attorneys during questioning. Ultimately Director Comey gaslighted the public to believe that he could not prosecute breaches of classified information unless he could prove intent. Even with such favorable treatment, the truth of her actions spoke for itself.

Has anyone been disciplined? Are no safeguards needed?

What's so upsetting about the cavalier approach of some House members to this investigation is the double standard. When they find a scandal that just happens to fit their political narrative, they'll reach the opposite conclusion. Already we've seen complaints that Ivanka Trump used a personal email account for government business. In that case, Democrats suddenly came to believe compliance with the law was important again. This is why so many Americans have difficulty taking Democrats seriously.

While using private email for government business is certainly inappropriate, there was no comparison between Clinton's and Trump's situations. Ivanka Trump reportedly used a private email for a limited time prior to receiving training about government records and submitted all relevant emails for storage as required by law. To suggest that Ivanka Trump's limited short-term use of a private account is in any way similar to Clinton's deliberate scheme to evade federal law and her careless exposure of classified information is a false equivalence.

More important, some of those same people accusing Ivanka Trump were the very people laughing at the Clinton email investigation. They overplayed their hand with these criticisms, revealing their hypocrisy in their feigned exasperation. These are the very people who refused to take a systemic approach to the problem. By laughing it off and mocking it as "but her emails," they sent the message that protecting classified information is not really that important.

You can't pretend to put the country's interest first when clearly the only things you're interested in are things that fit your political narrative. In the aftermath of the findings of classified information exposure, I saw no movement behind the scenes from anyone in Clinton's party to fix or address the national security failings she exploited. I saw only roadblocks to getting something done.

Supposedly the State Department itself was going to conduct an internal investigation to address the security concerns. As far as I know, no report was ever produced. The failure of Congress to ask for one is yet another missed opportunity to be part of the solution, not part of the problem. Can the State Department demonstrate to Congress what changes, alterations, improvements, or safeguards were implemented to ensure this never happens again?

In a June 2018 hearing with Deputy Attorney General Rod Rosenstein following the release of the OIG report, then–ranking member Nadler complained that the hearing was addressing Clinton's emails rather than the plethora of baseless political investigations pushed by his party. In his statement, he said:

> *And we have not held a single hearing on allegations of obstruction of justice at the White House. . . . Now, with the year coming to a close, with the leadership of the Department of Justice finally before us, what do my Republican colleagues want to discuss? Hillary Clinton's emails.*

Nadler's decision to characterize a hearing about systemic problems within the FBI as a discussion of Hillary Clinton's emails minimized the very real concerns Americans have with the nation's premier federal law enforcement agency. Furthermore, Nadler and his colleagues had just spent eight years telling those of us in Congress that we had no right to conduct oversight on any issue that was part of an ongoing investigation (often referring to the OIG investigation of Clinton). Yet with a special counsel in place expending enormous resources on an investigation that was at that time incomplete, Nadler complained that Congress wasn't duplicating that ongoing effort.

Nadler went on to make excuses for the report's findings, arguing there was nothing illegal about Comey "sitting down to draft an early statement about the Clinton investigation" and excusing Strzok's bias-filled text messages to his mistress and colleague Lisa Page by saying, "Peter Strzok did not say anything about Donald Trump that the majority of Americans weren't also thinking at the same time."

The inspector general was not so glib about the report's findings, writing:

> *The damage caused by these employees' actions extends far beyond the scope of the Midyear [Clinton] investigation and goes to the heart of the FBI's reputation for neutral factfinding and political independence.*

By failing to grasp the significance of the damage to the FBI's reputation, the party of big government has actually undermined big government. Each time a new OIG report is released, Congress should be working hand in hand with federal agencies to make government work better. Instead, they excuse poor behavior and then wonder why Americans don't trust government to single-handedly end the earth's heating and cooling cycles. They are happy to make allegations when the opposing party is in power, but when they hold power, they have shown no interest in enacting reforms that would apply equally to both parties.

This is a missed opportunity for Democrats to address the proliferating problem of government functioning off the record. That's important. But an even bigger opportunity lies ahead.

Stopping Invasive Government Surveillance

With the release of a new OIG report identifying serious abuses of the nation's FISA Court, the House will have yet another opportunity to prove government can be held accountable. Don't hold your breath, though.

The Foreign Intelligence Surveillance Act (FISA) was established in 1977 in response to concerns about President Nixon's abuse of the nation's surveillance apparatus for domestic spying. The law set up a FISA Court to determine whether probable cause exists to suggest the target of surveillance is a "foreign power" or an "agent of a foreign power." The purpose of the process is an important one. It helps us root out terror and identify foreign spies.

The FISA Court is designed to provide a check of the executive branch to prevent unauthorized surveillance of American citizens.

FISA abuses during the Obama administration were revealed in a landmark memo released by then–House Intelligence Committee chairman Devin Nunes in February 2018. The memo concluded that the FBI relied on undocumented allegations in the Steele Dossier to apply for and renew FISA applications for Trump campaign adviser Carter Page. Undisclosed to the FISA Court was the fact that the Steele Dossier was a collection of baseless allegations against Donald Trump brought by partisan opposition researchers and paid for by the Clinton presidential campaign and the Democratic National Committee.

I was on the House Judiciary Committee's Crime Subcommittee when the FISA process came up for reauthorization in 2017. As we were talking about the reauthorization, many of us did not want to agree to a long-term extension. We were worried about the potential for abuse of power, particularly in light of the court's record of almost unfailingly authorizing FISA surveillance requests. In the thirty-six years ending in 2015, the court had rejected only 12 of 38,169 applications. That's an approval rate of over 97 percent. Just how much scrutiny were these applications receiving?

I had left Congress by the time FISA was reauthorized. But as the reauthorization approached, I asked then-chairman Goodlatte if we could talk to a former or current FISA Court judge to help us get a better understanding of the process. I wondered if I could attend a FISA Court proceeding. The answer, in no uncertain terms, was no. The process is very secretive. Apparently, they don't meet very often. They come and sit in a secure facility, plow through the paperwork, and then almost 100 percent of the time, they acquiesce to whatever the government requested.

I was concerned that there is no one to argue the other side, which puts the onus on the Justice Department to give a clear and complete picture of why the request is necessary. The FISA Court operates in such secrecy that even members of Congress charged with oversight and reauthorization know little about it.

I'd like to think I would have been brave enough to vote against the reauthorization, but there is a lot of pressure. Despite the risk of abuse, surveillance of foreign spies is a critical and necessary tool for national security. But I knew at the time that the process was also ripe for abuse.

With the release of the OIG report, will Democrats rise to the occasion by looking for solutions to a well-documented problem? They should. I found my Democratic colleagues to be very helpful on privacy issues. This is an area of bipartisan agreement.

Back when attacking the FISA Court was helpful in attacking Republican president George W. Bush, Democrats were outspoken in their calls for reform. Even the liberal Brennan Center published a report in 2015 analyzing what went wrong with the FISA Court. But with the FISA Court in the crosshairs of a plot to undermine President Donald Trump, how willing will House Democrats be to acknowledge the abuse committed on their behalf? Will they be willing to provide serious oversight when doing so requires them to take a political hit?

There remain systemic executive branch problems that good oversight can positively influence. Democrats have a valuable opportunity to demonstrate their ability to make government work.

Furthermore, there is important follow-up that needs to be done on previous successful investigations to ensure that the laws we passed actually resolved the problems we sought to fix. Did our attempts to empower inspector generals in the wake of the Clinton email scandal result in better access to agency documents? Did the culture at the Secret Service improve after our bipartisan work to hold senior leaders accountable and to address the perverse incentives in the pay structure? Have our reforms of the Freedom of Information Act resulted in a more responsive document production process? Is there more that needs to be done?

Many of those investigations were bipartisan in nature, with Cummings directly engaged in the collaboration. They started with an investigation and ended with a solution. I hope he will take some time away from Trump witch hunting to continue some of that important work. The opportunities to identify and address instances of waste, fraud, and abuse are as plentiful as ever. Scrutiny of executive branch function is not a bad thing. It's critical to good government. But with so many committees consumed by the effort to get a specific outcome—to take down the president of the United States—will Democrats be part of the solution, or will they be part of the problem in Washington?

Congress must focus its limited time and effort where it can have the greatest *legislative* impact. It is a dereliction of duty when the committee abandons programmatic and effective oversight of those trillions of dollars and instead focuses on nongovernmental activity.

Headline-grabbing congressional investigations do not necessarily signify a strong and functional legislative body; to the contrary, they can be a sign of a dysfunctional and weak body. Functional legislative bodies are there to legislate. Dysfunctional ones resort to political messaging that never seems to produce actual legislation. All of this gets us further and further away from the original premise of the House Oversight Committee, which had been in place for more than two hundred years—to review government expenditures. The committee is not set up to be the truth police, nor is it meant to duplicate the prosecutorial work of the executive branch with regard to the private sector. Our focus is and always has been government.

House investigations are meant to be solutions driven, not outcome driven. For Congress to identify an individual person as a target and then use the full force of congressional oversight to destroy that person is a gross abuse of power. To do so merely to remove a political obstacle is abhorrent and likely unconstitutional. Yet that is exactly what this Congress is doing to this president. It's what Nadler has suggested doing to Justice Brett Kavanaugh.

Maintaining White House Security

If there's one current investigation that legitimately offers a chance to resolve a systemic problem, it is the oversight of the White House security clearance process. Chairman Elijah Cummings and his committee have prime jurisdiction over security clearances at the White House. It's an important issue and a legitimate investigation to pursue.

Chairman Cummings has a whistle-blower whose allegations are exactly the kind of testimony Congress should look into. But the way the committee is going about this investigation is all wrong. It doesn't seem to be about getting to the bottom of a serious problem, but instead about winning the news cycle.

Let me explain. The committee wanted to hear testimony from White House security chief Carl Kline. If Kline appears voluntarily, he is entitled to a government attorney to advise him. If the committee has to subpoena his testimony, he is required to pay for his own legal expenses. The types of attorneys who have high enough security clearances to work with a witness like Kline do not come cheap.

Instead of giving Kline the opportunity to appear voluntarily before the committee, Chairman Cummings immediately issued a subpoena, thereby stripping Kline of the opportunity to have a government attorney. In response, the White House advised Kline to follow in the footsteps of Obama administration officials and ignore the subpoena. They were willing to fight the subpoena in the courts. That would have taken time.

Given the limited number of legislative days, the White House could have simply run out the clock until the next election. You can see why that option would be tempting. It's a precedent set by previous administrations. I don't agree with it. But I can understand why we can't have one side subject to rules the other side does not have to follow. Chairman Cummings, having seen this move made by the Obama administration, responded the same way I responded to Attorney General Holder's failure to comply with a congressional subpoena. He threatened to hold Kline in contempt. Unlike Holder, Kline was not in contempt. He was willing to testify. But he wanted to do so voluntarily, taking advantage of the legal counsel to which he was entitled.

For Chairman Cummings, this was not about getting to the truth. This was about winning the news cycle. It looks better for Cummings if the witness appears uncooperative and has to be compelled to testify. It looks better for Cummings if the witness is held in contempt of Congress.

In this case, Chairman Cummings overplayed his hand. He knew from the Holder precedent that a court battle would take years to play out. Ultimately, he ended up agreeing to the voluntary transcribed interview. But not until he had enjoyed a week of negative news stories about Kline's alleged unwillingness to testify before the committee. This is how the game is played when politics trumps truth. It's all about the news cycle, not about the truth.

Cummings was wrong to jump the gun on issuing a subpoena. Government witnesses do not want to engage their own counsel. A threat of a subpoena is generally enough to elicit the commitment to comply. If I encountered resistance from the administration, I would tell them I had paper and pen in hand. I was ready to issue the subpoena. One time I even took a picture of the unsigned subpoena and texted it to a witness. When I asked if he wanted me to send this for real, he complied. In my experience, 100 percent of the time they will agree to come in voluntarily if for no other reason than that they have more rights as a voluntary witness.

"Shining a Light" or Illegal Leaking?

A sure sign of an investigation that is more part of the problem than part of the solution is one that defines "shining a light" as winning the news cycle. Perhaps it goes without saying that an investigation involving selective leaks by one party or the other is likely to generate more heat than light. When you see an investigation that seems to be working in lockstep with the media or the bureaucracy to launder selective leaks, something isn't right. Truth does not have to be selectively edited. It can be released in its full form.

We've seen an unprecedented level of selective leaking used by Deep State operatives to undermine President Trump. We will undoubtedly see it deployed to shore up political narratives coming out of the many ongoing oversight investigations as well.

According to data released by the Justice Department, referrals for leaking classified information dramatically increased when President Trump took office. In the last two years of the Obama administration, agencies transmitted just 55 leak referrals—18 in 2015 and 37 in 2016. In the first two years of the Trump Administration, the Justice Department received referrals for 120 leaks in 2017 and another 88 in 2018. Those leaks are seldom prosecuted. In fact, as recently as May 2019, the Justice Department inspector general released a report indicating his office had found a "preponderance of evidence" to show a senior FBI official—a deputy assistant director—had violated the law by disclosing to a reporter sealed court filings. That same individual had numerous documented unauthorized contacts with the media and had even accepted a $225 ticket to an event from a reporter. How did the Justice Department respond? By declining to prosecute. Leaking is both a systemic and a cultural problem within the Justice Department.

Congressional committees, too, have a well-deserved reputation for leaking. They are often the first to receive important information and get the first opportunity to release it. Being the first to put your political spin on new information can pay huge political dividends. I wish I could say this was a Democratic problem. But to be fair, both sides have been guilty of this.

The problem is not the release of information, but the release of classified, untrue, or incomplete information. Such leaks provide a short-term boost with a long-term price tag.

Although it may be hard to believe anyone would risk violating the law to divulge classified information, reporters have different expectations. I remember receiving numerous classified briefings in the bowels of the Capitol Visitors Center. Such briefings followed the Boston Marathon bombing, the Brussels airport bombing, and other major incidents. At the top of the stairs and to the south, the media would inevitably be staked out with a hundred or more cameras and reporters, hoping to get someone to talk. Often someone did—off the record, of course. To me there was no story worth divulging classified or confidential information. That was simply a line I would not cross.

Nonetheless, there is a reason Congress has a reputation for leaking. Perhaps the most relevant example is Intelligence Committee chairman Adam Schiff, whose lack of discipline and of candor as a ranking member has now compromised the reputation and efficacy of the very committee he now chairs.

The Intelligence Committee's stellar reputation has been tarnished by unprofessional, unethical, and quite unprecedented leaks of closed hearings on anything related to President Trump. After information from closed Intelligence Committee testimony by Donald Trump Jr. was leaked almost simultaneously in 2017, many pointed to the committee's then–ranking member, Representative Schiff. Although Schiff initially denied leaking Trump's testimony, he later defended the leak on CNN. "That's not a leak," he told CNN's Wolf Blitzer. "It is exposure of his noncooperation and his stonewalling of our committee."

Whatever Schiff wants to call it, the practice did lasting damage to his and his committee's credibility. Such leaks are the reason former Oversight Committee chairman Trey Gowdy believes Congress has proven itself incapable of conducting serious investigations. I wouldn't go that far, but there can be no doubt that the actions of Schiff and others who leak protected information have done lasting damage to the institution. That damage is compounded when the leaks prove to be untrue.

We saw firsthand how leaks can compromise the work of a committee when former FBI director James Comey demanded a public hearing for his testimony before the House Oversight and Judiciary Committees. He cited the fear of selective leaks as the reason to request an open hearing. The concern is a legitimate one. But it also conveniently allowed him to posture in favor of a process that would be easier for him to evade.

Public hearings are very useful for exposing conduct that is already well documented in evidence. Forcing someone to publicly answer for bad behavior within their agency is embarrassing and generates a lot of publicity. The threat of having to go before the public and explain why an incident was mishandled can be an influential deterrent and a means of providing accountability. But the public hearing setting is not the best place to get answers to highly complex questions from a hostile witness.

The leaking of nonpublic government information is a crime in itself, although rarely prosecuted. Veteran Senate Intelligence Committee staffer James Wolfe was indicted in June 2018 after leaking information to reporters. But Wolfe was only charged with lying to the FBI about the leaks and only sentenced to two months in prison. Nevertheless, there is a fair amount of irony in the fact that Chairman Schiff would leak information in an effort to get someone prosecuted for lying to Congress when in fact he himself is also violating the law by leaking nonpublic government information to the media. But in the run-up to 2020, we'll see once again that in the world of Speaker Pelosi, the rules only apply to the opposition.

Sometimes information has been withheld by executive branch agencies simply because it was embarrassing or politically inconvenient, even though it was true. In such cases, I have taken the position that the release of information should be done very publicly, with my name attached. If the information is true, complete, and not classified, the public should know about it.

That's what happened in October 2016 when news broke that the FBI had obtained the laptop of former congressman Anthony Weiner, whose wife, Huma Abedin, was an aide to Secretary Clinton. The laptop apparently contained classified information. This news surfaced at a very inconvenient time for the presidential nominee, with the election just days away.

I learned of it when legal counsel for the Oversight Committee, Liam McKenna, called me on Friday, October 28, 2016. I didn't answer the first call. Then he immediately called again, which was code for "I *really* need to speak with you." McKenna told me to check my email. We had just received a letter addressed to me from FBI director James Comey, essentially stating that the investigation of Hillary Clinton had been reopened.

I couldn't believe what I was reading. But over the course of the next thirty to forty minutes, we read and reread Comey's letter. It was addressed to multiple people. It was not classified. It had no markings suggesting the information was secret. There was no information suggesting this was even confidential. Comey did the right and necessary thing by informing Congress, given that he had assured our committee the investigation was closed. He had previously testified that no additional resources were being used in any way, shape, or form to investigate Clinton. That was no longer the case.

At this point, a week before the election, I think it's safe to say almost everybody thought Clinton was going to win. I certainly did. But that's beside the point. The election had no bearing on whether this information should be made available to the public. So in a carefully worded tweet, I wrote,

FBI Dir just informed me, "The FBI has learned of the existence of emails that appear to be pertinent to the investigation." Case reopened.

All hell broke loose. The tweet went viral, the story spreading at the speed of the internet. I later heard from some reporters that when it came out, Clinton and her top staff were all in the air. Normally the campaign airplanes have Wi-Fi access, but that afternoon it wasn't working. I was told by the reporters that the Clinton war room exploded in concern when the tweet immediately went viral, being retweeted tens of thousands of times. But they were rudderless and unable to respond. It took them hours to get something out the door.

I have no regrets about sharing this information. I didn't leak it. I attached my name to it. Had it been marked classified in any way, my decision would have been different. But the public had a right to know. The FBI was letting us know in a public way that they had reopened the investigation. Over the next few days, Democrats and their media allies tried to frame it as some sort of illegal leak. But it was absolutely 100 percent accurate and complete, it could be documented, and it in no way threatened national security. The underlying letter was a government record subject to FOIA and was to be released publicly by the FBI. CNN's Jake Tapper was one of the first journalists to run with it. He asked for the underlying letter and I provided it.

That situation is very different from taking bits of classified information or dribbling out details of a closed-door hearing as an anonymous source. I summarized a letter, put it in a tweet, later released the full letter in context, and received no pushback whatsoever from the DOJ. They knew they were giving us formal notice. I worked to expose truth. This was happening in real time.

Good, solid investigations may yet be done by Democrats. We can only hope so. We would recognize them because they will be evidence based, they will inform legislation, they will be tied to government waste, fraud, or abuse, and they won't need to rely on leaks to convey truth. The truth will tell its own story. Unfortunately, thus far the new crop of committee chairmen in the House seem so focused on discrediting the president that they have missed some key opportunities to forward their own agenda.

The political stakes in the 2020 election cycle have never been higher. With the White House up for grabs, control of the Supreme Court still within reach for both parties, redistricting on the horizon, and narrow majorities in both the House and the Senate, a wave election for either side could mean long-term control of the direction of the country. Will the nation's traditionalists and patriots manage to preserve free markets, limited government, and minority rights? Or will the pro-socialism, big-government agenda of the progressive wing of the Democratic Party carry the day?

Along with the standard campaign tactics seen in every high-stakes election cycle, bigger tactics are on the horizon. In addition to the replacement of Super PACs with nonprofits and the deployment of online small-dollar fund-raising, we may well see the use of impeachment proceedings to weaken a sitting president followed by the attempt to scrap two-hundred-year-old political institutions that stand in the way of obtaining power.

CHAPTER 10

THE IMPEACHMENT DILEMMA

To hear her talk about it, you'd think impeachment was the last thing on Speaker Pelosi's mind. She told the *Washington Post* in early 2019 that impeachment would divide the country and was just not worth it. Oversight Committee chairman Elijah Cummings also struck a conciliatory tone, arguing, "You've got to have bipartisanship. Right now, when you've got forty-something percent of the country pleased, I guess, with what the president's doing. I think Pelosi realizes this." House Majority Leader Steny Hoyer in January 2019 called impeachment talk a distraction, saying, "We're focused on substantive bills."

Yet for two years, impeachment talk has been all the rage. On the House Judiciary Committee, where impeachment hearings would likely originate, Representative Jerry Nadler, a New York Democrat, campaigned in early 2017 for the ranking-member role (what would become the chairmanship when Democrats won the majority a year later) pointing to his impeachment experience.

According to the *New York Times*, a leaflet touting Nadler's qualifications read:

> As our constitutional expert, and with his demonstrated leadership on impeachment in the 90s, Nadler is our strongest member to lead a potential impeachment.

Even as House leadership was giving lip service to the notion that impeachment was premature, Speaker Pelosi assigned two outspoken pro-impeachment Democratic freshmen to the House Judiciary Committee. Representative Joe Neguse of Colorado and Representative Veronica Escobar of Texas are both on the record saying impeachment should happen.

Demands to impeach the president began the moment he won the election—and in some cases earlier than that. An angry base predictably looked for any way to reverse what they saw as a catastrophic election result. No doubt such calls were nothing new. Many on the right were similarly devastated by the previous reelection of President Barack Obama. They, too, might have been tempted had they believed there was a means of reversing that result. But the difference this time was the response from members of Congress, who seemed certain Donald Trump was guilty of something. They just had to figure out what.

By May 2017, they would all unite around the pretext of obstruction of justice in the firing of FBI director James Comey as their justification for the outcome their bases were demanding. But even before then, congressional Democrats were citing a laundry list of shallow pretexts for impeachment, grasping incoherently for some justification to overturn the results of the election.

Democratic representative Jamie Raskin of Maryland called for Trump's impeachment before the president was even sworn in. He cited emoluments clause violations. This early criticism of the president-elect sought to equate arm's-length commercial transactions at Trump-owned businesses with foreign gifts intended to impact public policy.

I refused to open an investigation on this issue when it was first raised, as there was no evidence that President Trump had violated the Constitution. Three subsequent lawsuits filed by progressive law professors; Maryland and Washington, D.C., district attorneys; and 196 Democratic members of Congress, respectively, were unsuccessful. The courts found none of the plaintiffs had standing to sue. Had they succeeded in redefining the emoluments clause, the new definition would have put early presidents Jefferson, Madison, and Monroe in violation for the routine selling of crops from their plantations to Europe.

House Financial Services Committee ranking member Maxine Waters frequently articulated a case for impeachment, telling MSNBC in January 2017 that "we know that the Russians played an important role and they tried to support Mr. Trump and they tried to make sure that Hillary Clinton didn't get elected." There was no evidence connecting the Trump campaign to Russia's election activities—then or now. But according to Waters, "we know."

Representative Joaquin Castro of Texas added his own call for impeachment in February 2017, citing the president's travel ban. According to Castro, Trump "intentionally exceeded his constitutional authority" in preventing the entry of nationals from countries that could not provide adequate vetting. The Supreme Court begged to differ, ruling that Trump's travel restrictions fell "squarely" within the president's authority.

That same month, Representative Keith Ellison of Minnesota told CNN Trump had already done enough to raise the question of impeachment. The only evidence at that point was the fake dossier, but apparently that was enough for Ellison.

Representative Sheila Jackson Lee of Texas called for impeachment over Trump's supposedly unfounded claims that he had been wiretapped, telling the *Houston Chronicle*: "If you do not have any proof and you have been saying this for three weeks then you are clearly on the edge of the question of public trust and those actions can be associated with high crimes and misdemeanors for which articles of impeachment can be drawn." Given what we now know about the origins of the Trump dossier, do Democrats really want to be setting a standard that someone can be impeached for making a claim without evidence?

Perhaps one of the most telling calls for impeachment came from Representative Tulsi Gabbard of Hawaii. At an April 2017 town hall meeting, Gabbard told voters:

> *I am studying more about the impeachment process. I will just say I understand the calls for impeachment, but what I am being cautious about and what I give you food for thought about is that if President Trump is impeached, the problems don't go away, because then you have a Vice President Pence who becomes President Pence.*

The "problems" don't go away? What problems? Assuming the reason for impeachment was high crimes and misdemeanors, those problems would go away. What Gabbard suggested was that impeachment wouldn't make a Republican president go away. It wouldn't reverse the results of the 2016 election. It doesn't solve the problem Democrats are trying to solve. That's the giveaway—the high crime progressive voters are worried about from this president is the crime of being conservative.

With the firing of James Comey in May 2017, Democrats did what they often accuse Republicans of doing—they pounced. They seized. They came out of the woodwork to capitalize on what they hoped would be a fatal mistake by the president. By mid-May, twenty-four House members and two senators were talking about impeachment.

The Perils of Impeachment

Before embarking on any impeachment effort, lawmakers have to weigh the costs and the benefits. Impeachment is an important constitutional remedy—one that I believe should be used more often and more broadly against those who abuse their power. But there could be heavy political consequences for the party that is perceived to be using impeachment as a means to reverse an unfavorable election outcome.

More than sixty times the House, which has sole power to begin the impeachment process, has initiated impeachment proceedings. Fifteen federal judges have been impeached, but only eight successfully removed from office following impeachment. Furthermore, cabinet secretary William Belknap was impeached in 1876 and North Carolina senator William Blount in 1797. I attempted to impeach IRS commissioner John Koskinen in 2016, but the effort was derailed by House Republican leadership.

The chances that impeachment could actually remove this president are quite low. Impeachment is just the first step in the Constitution's only process to remove a president before his term of office expires. To invoke it, lawmakers in the House have to file formal charges alleging that a president has committed "treason, bribery, or other high crimes and misdemeanors." Any members of the House can introduce articles of impeachment—and indeed, they have. California representative Brad Sherman filed articles of impeachment in the House in July 2017 and again in the first week of the 116th Congress. Sherman cited as a high crime and misdemeanor the president's firing of FBI director James Comey. Freshman representative Rashida Tlaib, who made headlines when she was recorded telling an audience to "impeach the mother****er," is introducing her own articles of impeachment against the president for violating the Constitution. Filing the articles is the easy part.

If one or more articles of impeachment receive a majority vote, they are passed on to the Senate for trial with the Chief Justice of the United States presiding. With the opposition party to the president holding the majority in the House, that part may also sound easy. But consider that many of the seats Democrats won were very close races, with seven in California that involved heavy ballot harvesting to get across the finish line. Can vulnerable members in Republican districts afford to support articles of impeachment?

Assuming they do, and a simple majority votes to forward one or more articles of impeachment to the Senate, conviction requires a two-thirds majority—66 votes—in that body. That implies a need for bipartisan support. Both Andrew Johnson in 1868 and Bill Clinton in 1998–99 were impeached by the House, but neither was convicted by the Senate. Republicans now hold 53 seats to Democrats' 47. To get Republicans to vote for conviction, Democrats would need a slam-dunk case for high crimes and misdemeanors.

Even with a conviction, removal from office is still not automatic. It is just one penalty that can be invoked upon conviction. Furthermore, since the process of removing a president from office has never been invoked, questions remain. A constitutional crisis could ensue over the question of whether an appeal could be brought and to whom.

The chances of a successful impeachment that removes the president from office are slim. But if the goal of invoking the process is to weaken the president prior to the 2020 election rather than to remove him from office, some may see it as a risk worth taking. However, the opposite is also a possibility. Early 2019 polling suggests that even among Democrats, support for impeachment is falling. CNN reported in the spring of 2019 that an SSRS poll found a 7-point decline in support for impeachment among Democrats between December 2018 and March 2019.

With the president's approval rating on the rise and a strong economy driving support for his policies, the threat of a backlash to impeachment efforts cannot be ignored. A March 2019 analysis done by *Politico* titled, "How Trump Is on Track for a Landslide in 2020," concluded, "But if the election were held today, he'd likely ride to a second term in a huge landslide, according to multiple economic models with strong track records of picking presidential winners and losses."

Republican Efforts to Impeach President Obama

I wish to make one thing clear: I never called for President Obama's impeachment, nor contemplated it. But I did respond to a question about it. Ironically, if you were to do a search of Republican calls for impeachment of President Obama, my name would be one of the first to come up.

In a 2013 interview with Thomas Burr, a well-respected reporter for my hometown newspaper, the *Salt Lake Tribune*, I spoke about the lies we had uncovered from the Obama administration with regard to the Benghazi attack. Burr asked me if I would rule out the possibility of impeachment. At that point, we didn't know what we would find.

Would I rule it out? That was the question. Of course not. Why would anyone do that when you don't yet know what you're going to find? How many Democrats were ruling out impeachment before the Mueller Report was released? I responded, telling Burr:

> It's certainly a possibility. That's not the goal but given the continued lies perpetrated by this administration, I don't know where it's going to go. . . . I'm not taking it off the table. I'm not out there touting that but I think this gets to the highest levels of our government and integrity and honesty are paramount.

The *Tribune*'s story went viral, with *Politico* and many other national outlets running with headlines like: "Chaffetz: Impeachment Not Off the Table" and CNN's "Chaffetz Doesn't Rule Out Impeachment for Obama." Suddenly it had blown up into a global story. It seemed every political reporter in America was calling for a quote on a topic I hadn't even brought up.

I can say with confidence that at no point did House Republicans sit down together and strategize how we could use our investigative power to impeach the president. That never happened. Had evidence come back implicating Barack Obama, that would have been a different story. Impeachment is a constitutional remedy that exists for a reason. Why would I take it off the table? It would be irresponsible to summarily dismiss it.

The hyperbolic response from the mainstream media and the exaggeration from left-wing blogs and pundits took me by surprise. Pundits seemed to be talking impeachment more than anyone in the Republican Party. Jonathan Chait actually wrote a piece for the liberal *New Republic* in October 2010 predicting that Republicans would impeach Obama. In retrospect, his arguments were prophetic. Not with regard to Obama—they were completely off base there—but with regard to Trump.

Chait, in a piece called "Scandal TBD," predicted that Republicans would impeach Obama if he won a second term. Chait believed then–Oversight Committee chairman Darrell Issa, Republican of California, would lead the charge. None of that turned out to be true, of course. There was never a serious effort to impeach Barack Obama by Issa or anyone else. But if one reads Chait's predictions and substitutes the name Donald Trump where Chait has written Barack Obama, and Jerry Nadler where Chait has written Darrell Issa, the whole thing makes a lot more sense. Chait writes:

> *No doubt more outrages would command Issa's attention. Just as a rigorous IRS audit of a taxpayer is bound to turn up some-*

thing, an investigation by the likes of Issa will eventually produce a scandal. Once you have grasped hold of the investigative machinery, the process drives itself.

Chait went on to cite statistics showing 35 percent of Republicans already favored impeachment in 2010. Yet today, Democrat support for impeachment has bottomed out at 36 percent after hitting 43 percent in December 2018. According to Chait, "That is a large base of support to impeach Obama for literally anything at all." Chait's assessment of the opposition party's view of the president is even more applicable today than it was when he wrote it, provided you make a few changes:

> *This is the* ~~*conservative*~~ *progressive view of* ~~*Obama*~~ *Trump—a* ~~*left-wing*~~ *right-wing radical who seized power via an economic crisis, smuggled radical views into the White House, and used unfair tactics to force an unpopular transformative* ~~*left-wing*~~ *right-wing agenda upon a* ~~*conservative*~~ *liberal country.*
>
> *The history of modern Washington is a history of the social norms that once restrained political parties from no-holds-barred warfare falling by the wayside, one by one. Why would* ~~*Republicans*~~ *Democrats impeach* ~~*Obama*~~ *Trump? The better question is, why wouldn't they?*

They still might. By the spring of 2019, with the economy humming, support for the president rising, and hopes for a collusion or obstruction charge dashed, impeachment wasn't looking like such a good strategy after all. That's when a new strategy surfaced.

The Slow-Bleed Strategy

Just six weeks after Pelosi's leadership team assumed their roles in the House majority, word leaked that Democrats were planning a slow-bleed strategy against President Trump. Axios's Mike Allen described a strategy of "lengthy public hearings and scores of witnesses to methodically pick apart Trump's finances and presidency." The strategy would be coordinated with six to eight committees, essentially putting Trump on trial for the duration of the 2020 election cycle.

Allen quotes an anonymous source close to House leadership as saying, "Many in leadership believe impeachment could help Trump get re-elected," and therefore, leadership instead planned to "pivot the anger to defeating him on the campaign side next year. . . . The last thing they want to do is help Trump like it eventually helped Clinton."

Indeed, the impeachment proceedings against President Clinton were widely believed to have helped the man accused of lying under oath about his sexual escapades with an intern and obstructing justice in the effort to hide it. Polling shortly after the impeachment vote showed a drop in support for congressional Republicans and an increase in the president's support, with 67 percent of Americans telling pollsters they approved of the job Clinton was doing at the time.

Incidentally, some of the same players in today's impeachment drama had bit parts in the Clinton impeachment, this time on the other side of the argument. A young Adam Schiff announced his decision to run for Congress shortly after the conclusion of the Clinton impeachment hearings in 1999. He told the *Los Angeles Times* that incumbent representative James Rogan's role as a House manager in the Clinton impeachment hearings left Rogan out of touch with his district. "The record shows that persistent local needs have never held much interest for our local congressman," Schiff said at the time.

Today Schiff stands at the forefront of the effort to destroy Donald Trump. As chairman of the House Intelligence Committee, Schiff has taken it upon himself to be his party's narrative maker. Unfortunately for Schiff, many of those narratives he created for the media have not aligned well with the facts ultimately released. The *Federalist* analyzed the competing narratives given to the press by Schiff and Representative Trey Gowdy, a South Carolina Republican, in advance of the Intelligence Committee's FISA report release. Schiff told the media the committee's report would contain cherry-picked, misleading information that was highly classified and would compromise sources and methods.

His narrative contradicted information from Gowdy, who previewed a report that would show the FBI had presented the unverified and uncorroborated Steele Dossier as evidence to the FISA Court without divulging the Clinton campaign as the source of that material. When the report was released, Schiff's spin was exposed as false. There was nothing reckless or dangerous in the memo, as Schiff had suggested. The facts bore out Gowdy's story, not Schiff's. Schiff has repeated that performance again and again, promising evidence of collusion that a year later still has not surfaced. He pointed to the president's Twitter feed as evidence of high crimes and misdemeanors. Schiff is so busy spinning narratives to promote impeachment that he has destroyed his own credibility.

Likewise, Maxine Waters is singing a very different tune about the Trump impeachment than she did in 1999. At the debate to plan an impeachment inquiry of President Clinton, Waters spoke passionately against the proceedings. In her floor speech, she attacked the bias of Special Counsel Kenneth Starr, saying, "Mr. Starr's close relationships with groups and individuals with demonstrated hatred for the President taints the independent counsel's investigation. This Congress does not need a protracted, open-ended witch hunt of intimidation, embarrassment and harassment." Of Special Counsel Robert Mueller, Waters in December 2017 said in a press conference, "There is an organized effort by Republicans . . . to spin a false narrative and conjure up outrageous scenarios to accuse Special Counsel Mueller of being biased." Of Clinton, Waters said impeachment proceedings only tear the nation apart. "It's time to move on," she said at the time. "Reprimand the President. Condemn him. But let's move on. These grossly unfair procedures will only tear this Congress and this nation apart. . . ." Fast forward to 2019 and Waters is all in for the process she once said would tear the nation apart.

When Impeachment Is Called For

I am a big believer in the impeachment remedy for civil officers. In fact, I called for the impeachment of IRS commissioner John Koskinen after he repeatedly provided misleading testimony to Congress, failed to comply with a congressional subpoena, and failed to preserve 24,000 emails relevant to our investigation of IRS targeting of conservative nonprofits. But for the president of the United States, the ultimate check on his power is an election.

With the next presidential election already under way, voters get the ultimate say on whether allegations against President Trump represent grounds for impeachment. They get to decide whether firing James Comey—a man the FBI, the OIG, and some Democrats said was "insubordinate"—constituted obstruction of justice. Voters can decide whether they believe President Trump violated the Constitution by imposing travel bans, criticizing the media, or building a wall.

Impeachment of an elected officer should be used sparingly and with great caution simply because there is another, less intrusive check on power in the form of an election. In such cases, impeachment overturns the will of the voters, divides the country, and distracts the government from the priorities Americans care about. However, in the case of civil officers, there is no other remedy to remove someone who is nominated by the president and confirmed by the Senate. This type of impeachment should happen more frequently.

One of my great regrets about my time in Congress is that House Republican leadership refused to back my committee in the effort to hold IRS Commissioner Koskinen accountable. They didn't think protecting our subpoena authority and disincentivizing future witnesses from lying to Congress was a worthwhile endeavor. I think even the Democrats should have supported that effort. They are the ones who will now bear the consequences of the precedent they supported. The administration could not be blamed for believing they could get away with a failure to be responsive to congressional investigations, given what Republicans allowed the Obama administration to get away with. The president, who obviously wasn't very concerned about the efforts of Koskinen's agency to shut down conservative groups, refused to remove him. Impeachment was the final check and balance Congress could impose.

Nevertheless, impeachment should be a last resort, not a first resort. I do think impeachment is appropriate when administration officials overtly lie to the committee. In our battle over Koskinen, it was a last resort. The problem was, I couldn't get nearly enough other members of Congress to support it.

During the Obama presidency, we never seriously considered impeachment of the president. Had we not been asked about it by reporters, the subject would not have even come up. Democrats should not resort to impeachment without solid evidence of criminal wrongdoing.

A warning to Democrats from David Axelrod, former chief strategist to President Barack Obama, made one of the best arguments I've heard. Axelrod wrote on Twitter,

> *Dems should NOT commit to impeachment unless & until there's a demonstrable case for one. It is not just a matter of politics. It's a matter of principle. If we "normalize" impeachment as a political tool, it will be another hammer blow to our democracy.*

Axelrod is right.

Impeachment was never intended to be a do-over of an election result some voters don't like. To treat it as such undermines the most foundational components of the most successful government in human history. But this is exactly what Democrats have done. They were never interested in using impeachment as a check on government corruption. Weaponizing hysteria and hyperbolic rhetoric, they reduced an important constitutional tool to a partisan power grab.

CHAPTER II

A POSITIVE PATH FORWARD

The no-holds-barred effort to delegitimize President Trump has polarized the electorate, paralyzed the Congress, and popularized contempt for key elements of our constitutional framework. It wasn't just the contrived allegations of Russian collusion, the nonstop coverage of evidence-free allegations, or the hand-wringing over whether to "normalize" the president of the United States. It was the knee-jerk resistance to every nominee, every policy position, every human being who dared support the sitting U.S. president. In exaggerating the threat of Trump to such an extreme degree, Democrats have themselves *become* the threat. They have personified the very menace they warned us about.

Refusing to accept the results of an election undermines our whole system. This is one thing Hillary Clinton got absolutely right. In a preelection rally in 2016, she criticized candidate Trump for failing to acknowledge whether he would accept the results of the election if he lost. Doing so, she said, would pose a threat to our democracy.

We've been around 240 years and we've always had peaceful transitions no matter who won or who lost. . . . We know, in our country, the difference between leadership and dictatorship. And the peaceful transition of power is one of the things that sets us apart. It's how we hold our country together, no matter who is in charge.

Her words proved prophetic, even though they applied in reverse. Her supporters were the ones who refused to accept the results of that election, but her prediction of how that response would impact our system has proven true. Rejecting the results of the election, many instead turned to a resistance dogma that continues to undermine our most successful institutions. Ironically, even Georgia's Stacey Abrams, who has yet to concede her loss in the 2018 Georgia gubernatorial race, weighed in on the damage Trump's refusal to preemptively agree to concede would do. "Trump's refusal to concede the election if he loses proves he is a petty man uninterested in our national stability," she tweeted in October 2016.

This dogma has especially infected Congress, compromising that body's ability to perform the functions that move our country forward. Congress has always been driven by politics. But what we've seen in the last two years is truly unprecedented. The shortsighted efforts to win the news cycle are not just undermining public trust but creating long-lasting damage to foundational institutions.

Many like to give lip service to the Constitution even as they seek to eliminate its most effective innovations. Others insinuate that we have somehow outgrown the government given to us by the Founding Fathers—that some of the key structures they built have become archaic and no longer work for a large, diverse, multicultural country.

To the contrary, I think adherence to the principles in the Constitution remains the only formula that will hold us together. We need to recommit to those principles, not abandon them.

The future is and always has been a choice between freedom and force. Either we can recommit to the principles of freedom that made us great or we can double down on the move toward a socialist system that can only succeed through force. Those are the choices. There is no "Democratic socialism" that magically combines freedom and force. Socialism relies on greater and greater degrees of force to sustain itself. Ultimately, trading our proven structural foundations for ideologies with a long record of failure is a bad deal for America.

We already have the structural institutions to ensure diverse voices are represented, but we need to protect them. We have a framework of checks and balances across the federal government to withstand abuses of power, but that framework needs reinforcement. We have the ability to utilize a robust system of federalism—shared power between federal, state, and local governments—to sustain diverse communities. We must renew our trust in that system. Our Bill of Rights provides durable protection of individual liberties without which our system becomes incompatible with freedom. These principles came to be in our Constitution because the framers were looking to solve the very problems we now face. They are not new. But we as a nation have allowed our politics to damage our institutions. We don't need new institutions. We need to recommit to the ones that already form the foundation of the most successful government ever known.

Returning to the Constitution

Arguably, both sides in the 2016 election operated from a sincere belief that the future of the country was at stake and that the opposing candidate represented an existential threat to all we hold dear. However, this is hardly the first time a presidential election has been waged between two sides who firmly believe a victory by the other would ruin the nation. Polarized times like these sparked the ideas for government under which we now operate.

We can look all the way back to the election of 1800, between Democratic-Republican candidate Thomas Jefferson and Federalist candidate John Adams, to see similar polarization. The 1800 election was the first peaceful transition of power in American history and would dictate the course of the young nation's future. For them, it truly was the most important election of their lifetimes. Emotions ran high and campaigning got ugly.

The issues really weren't that different from today's, notwithstanding the different partisan divisions. The Federalists sought a strong central authority. The Democratic-Republicans wanted instead to disperse more power among the states. We're still fighting that battle today. Federalist incumbent Adams was attacked over his deficit spending. He also had to defend his position on the Alien and Sedition Acts. These four laws restricted immigration, naturalization, and speech critical of the federal government, as well as empowering the president to deport what we now call criminal aliens. Jefferson, on the other hand, was attacked for his close alliance (collusion, if you will) with an unstable France.

Even more so than our 2016 race, the presidential election of 1800 was characterized by mudslinging and personal attacks. The Federalists called Jefferson "a mean-spirited, low-lived fellow, the son of a half-breed Indian squaw, sired by a Virginia mulatto father." But that was only in response to the Democratic-Republicans calling Adams a "hideous hermaphroditical character, which has neither the force and firmness of a man, nor the gentleness and sensibility of a woman." One newspaper predicted a Jefferson victory would mean that "[m]urder, robbery, rape, adultery, and incest will be openly taught and practiced, the air will be rent with the cries of the distressed, the soil will be soaked with blood, and the nation black with crimes."

We can all imagine how disturbing Jefferson's subsequent victory must have been to anyone subscribing to such views. Our hyperbole may be slightly more sophisticated today, but our modern media was no less inclined to tar President Trump as someone too extreme to be normalized.

In the intervening years since 1800, we've had a lot of dramatic elections. Sometimes voters chose the wrong man, although we might disagree about which times those were. Sometimes our presidents overreached. Other times our judges or our lawmakers did so. More often than not, the constitutional checks and balances put in place by our founders have done the job they were designed to do. They continue to do so today. Many of those crazy predictions we heard about a Donald Trump presidency were far off the mark. Nevertheless, even when this president or this Congress or the courts have tried to overstep, checks and balances have done their job.

A positive path forward lies in the very constitutional mandates bequeathed to us generations ago. The answers that worked for the founding generation continue to work in our generation. They are founded on truths that have not changed. Human nature has not changed. The economic impact of freedom has not changed. Indeed, the formula for prosperity has not changed. We must protect the balance of power between large and small states, maintain a robust system of checks and balances, rely on federalism to address our most divisive policy differences, and preserve the freedoms granted through the Bill of Rights. This is our best hope in the face of Democrats' assault on election security, polarizing focus on politics over policy, and attempt to dismantle the guardrails protecting our republic.

More Freedom, Not Less

The temptation to restrict freedom as a means to solve problems always has been and always will be hard to resist. But freedom has been the secret of America's success for more than two hundred years.

The easy option for solving problems with the nonprofit sector, for example, is to pass legislation forcing every nonprofit to disclose donors. That's the approach taken in H.R. 1, but in my view it isn't compatible with freedom. Given the rampant targeting of political donors for expressing opinions some find unacceptable, expansion of disclosure laws will only chill free speech. We would also risk chilling contributions to charities that have not been politicized. A vibrant, healthy nonprofit sector is important in a free society and must not be jeopardized.

We could require government funding of political campaigns, as Democrats have proposed, to combat the corrosive influence of fund-raising. But policies that compel Americans to fund campaigns they do not support, and restrict them from funding campaigns they do support, are also not compatible with freedom.

Instead of taking action that curtails donations, we need more eyeballs scrutinizing what's really going on. Nonprofits receiving tax-exempt status should be required to make more information available to the public—particularly information regarding their political activities. Charities must be held accountable for using their resources to pursue the missions for which their nonprofit status was granted. This might involve greater scrutiny from the IRS or enable the rise of independent watchdogs to help hold entities accountable. Or some combination of both. Instead of focusing attention and resources on small charities with "tea party" in their names, for example, the IRS needs to be doing more to scrutinize the largest charities. If taxpayers are going to indirectly subsidize charities with tax-exempt status, they need some assurance that the charities are actually doing the charitable work they promised to do.

Admittedly, this is a problem that needs much more analysis. The pieces I have learned about are the tip of the proverbial iceberg when it comes to America's nonprofit sector. This is a problem that needs far more attention.

Preserving Our Electoral System

Our path forward must also include defensive efforts to protect what is already working in America's electoral system. Local control of elections and mechanisms that give voice to minority communities are critical. And by minority, I do not just mean protected classes. Diversity is more than just variations in skin color, gender, or sexual orientation. The founders understood that the geographic variation of individual states created very different political priorities and that those differences threatened to undermine the cohesion that held the United States of America together. The Constitution was written specifically to ensure that a diversity of voices could be heard, and not just urban city dwellers concentrated in heavily populated areas, but farmers and ranchers, miners, oil workers, and truckers living in America's heartland, fishermen on her shores, loggers in her forests, police, nurses, and teachers in her suburban neighborhoods, and first-generation immigrants along her borders. The two most prominent foundational structures supporting those voices have come under fire from those who perceive short-term political gains from the removal of long-standing foundational structures.

The Electoral College and the representation in the Senate by state were important compromises that ensured smaller communities would not be subjugated to the priorities and demands of more populated urban areas. Since those populated urban areas today tend to be dominated by one party and the rural areas by another, the topic of small-state representation has become part of the partisan divide. In the current cycle, Democrats believe they can win national elections more easily without the Electoral College. Instead of winning the battle of ideas by appealing to a more diverse audience, some in the Democratic Party prefer to simply jettison the institutions they see standing in the way of their access to power. Make no mistake. The effort to "reform" the Electoral College and the Senate is nothing more than a partisan power grab.

Over the past two hundred years, proposals to abolish the Electoral College have been put forth more than 700 times. After Hillary Clinton won the popular vote in the 2016 presidential election and still lost the presidency, calls to abolish the institution have been deafening. Democratic senator Barbara Boxer of California introduced legislation shortly after the 2016 election to do away with the two-century-old tradition, perhaps recognizing that doing so would enable her heavily populated state to more or less call the shots for everyone else in America.

Democratic presidential hopeful Senator Elizabeth Warren has been outspoken on the issue, arguing that "every vote matters. And the way we make that happen is that we can have national voting and that means getting rid of the electoral college." Fellow candidates Beto O'Rourke, Senator Kamala Harris, and Mayor Pete Buttigieg soon followed. Predictably, the Democrats' nonprofit and media allies soon amplified the calls.

But not every vote matters when you get rid of the Electoral College. Only urban centers matter, because just two or three heavily populated states can run up the vote tally and overwhelm every other state.

The process for electing a president was laid out by the framers and subsequently defended by Alexander Hamilton in Federalist 68. Then, as now, a majority of the population resided in a few urban centers. Recognizing the universal truth that the priorities of urban centers differ from those of other sectors of the country, the framers devised the Electoral College and the representation in the Senate by state as two ingenious ways to ensure that rural populations did not become perpetually subjugated to the priorities of the urban ones. The election of 1800 between Adams and Jefferson exposed some minor flaws in the process after a tie vote in the Electoral College resulted in the House choosing the president. The House quickly figured out how to game the system, necessitating thirty-six separate votes to determine a president and vice president in that election. That debacle resulted in modifications to the process that subsequently became the Twelfth Amendment to the Constitution.

Warren's argument that every vote should count in electing president is not wrong. But her conclusion that some kind of national popular vote achieves that end is simply incorrect. The 2016 election perfectly illustrates the problem. When Hillary Clinton won the national vote by a sizable 2.86 million votes, that sounded like a national consensus. But she won a single state—California—by a margin of 4.27 million votes. Remove that one state and you have a convincing popular vote win in the other direction.

In a memorable analysis for *National Review*, Dan McLaughlin pointed out that Clinton's support was geographically narrow. She won the popular vote in just 13 of the 50 states. Trump, on the other hand, won a majority in 23 states, including 7 of the 10 largest states. Clinton's support was heavily concentrated in a few geographically similar locations—primarily major coastal cities. This is exactly the result the framers were concerned about.

A popular meme on social media following the election was two maps depicting Trump Land and the Clinton Archipelago. The Trump map showed the United States as a landmass with the Clinton-supporting areas underwater. That map largely resembled the current United States, minus some strips of coastline, with enlarged Great Lakes, and what appeared to be smaller lakes in New Mexico, Colorado, Illinois, and Mississippi. By contrast, the Clinton Archipelago map depicted three islands along the California, Texas, and New York coasts, connected by a string of smaller islands along the coastlines with isolated outposts in inland urban centers. Because those small islands contain large population numbers, the framers knew their interests would always overwhelm the interests of less populated areas. That's why we have an Electoral College and why each state, large or small, has two senators—another institution the Democratic base is itching to jettison.

As a representative from a less populous state, I have no difficulty imagining what a popularly elected president and Senate would do to minority communities. I belonged to a delegation of three (later four, following redistricting in 2012) in the House. When we would sit alphabetically by delegation, our three Utah members were next to the Texas delegation of 32 (later 36). California's delegation was even bigger, with 53. This was a huge advantage for these states. But we made up for it by having access to two senators, just like every other state.

Meanwhile, back in Utah, I represented a district composed of seven counties. Two of those were urban counties and five were rural counties containing large swaths of federally owned land. It quickly became apparent that those five counties with the lowest population were the places requiring the most intervention to address invasive federal policies. Several of those counties had a larger area than some states.

San Juan County, with an area nearly as large as New Jersey, was the home of iconic rock formations, a famous national park, precious natural resources, and dangerously isolated landscapes. Yet its population of just over fifteen thousand, including many in the Navajo Nation, gave it little clout in national politics. The county was 92 percent owned by the federal government. It drew thousands of tourists every year, requiring infrastructure, public safety services, search and rescue, and other costs. Yet only 8 percent of the county's landmass generated property tax to pay for those services. The county was fully dependent on a federal landlord that paid no property taxes and had little incentive to listen to the voices of a mere fifteen thousand people.

Each year, Congress would have to vote on an appropriation to provide PILT money (payment in lieu of taxes) to such communities. In my state, that averaged $1.20 for each acre of federal land—a small fraction of what a property tax would have generated. Yet getting support in the House for that minuscule appropriation was like pulling teeth. Many western communities shared the same problem, but none of them were heavily populated. There just weren't enough representatives with a stake in that problem. None of the states east of the Mississippi River faced that problem, as none of them bear the burden of hosting large tracts of public land. But in my state, almost 70 percent of our total area is federally owned and managed. Decisions about that land were heavily influenced by deep-pocketed environmental nonprofit groups who could appeal to hundreds of representatives from the Clinton Archipelago regions of the country.

Meanwhile, the federal government was far more deeply involved in people's day-to-day lives in those rural counties than in the urban centers. In such counties, the federal government got to decide where and when livestock could graze, how water could be accessed, and whether Native Americans could use ATVs to hunt and gather or perform religious ceremonies on traditional lands. It provided health care through Indian Health Services and duplicative law enforcement services through an alphabet soup of federal agencies. It dictated whether restroom facilities could be built to accommodate the hordes of tourists being drawn to the area by environmental groups intent on "saving" previously unknown monuments. The government decided how rivers could be accessed, whether local outfitters could drive their boats to the river or would be required to carry them overhead, and where locals could ride their bikes. With so little private land, communities had difficulty even getting internet access as broadband infrastructure could not reach isolated communities without crossing restricted federal land. In a time of drought, they were denied access to needed water because federal officials were worried about the habitat of a bird not seen in that county for twenty-five years. Every time these people turned around, there was a federal agency telling them what they could not do.

While these areas have a huge federal footprint and a heavy presence of federal bureaucrats in their counties, what they don't have is influence. Their livelihoods literally depend on federal policies that impact only states with small populations. Yet we have people clamoring to create an electoral system that would completely shut these people out. Eliminating the Electoral College doesn't elevate the little guy; it *silences* him. With the Electoral College, some public land states actually are swing states. Nevada, which is 85 percent federal land, gets a lot of attention from presidential candidates because of its status as a swing state. Even that small degree of influence would come to a screeching halt if not for the Electoral College.

Fortunately, abolishing the Electoral College is not a matter of simply passing legislation. It requires a constitutional amendment. That process can only be successful if two-thirds of the states ratify it. Given the long odds of getting broad support to narrow the electorate, changing the Constitution is unlikely.

Instead, opponents of the Electoral College have created an end run around the Constitution. The National Popular Vote Interstate Compact (NPVIC) seeks to gain cooperation from states for a radical new approach to electing a president that guarantees large liberal states can control the outcome without getting rid of the Electoral College. States merely have to agree to give up their Electoral College votes to the eventual winner of the popular vote nationally.

The group's website disingenuously describes the process as a way to "guarantee the Presidency to the candidate who receives the most popular votes in all 50 states and the District of Columbia." Except that is not true. The candidate who wins the most popular votes in Colorado, for example, will receive no Electoral College votes from that state, which recently joined the compact. Instead, Colorado will by law pledge its votes to the national winner. In the last election, that winner received her entire margin of votes over her opponent from one state—California. And who will care about the needs of a Navajo voter in a less populous state when they really need to win the vote of a Silicon Valley executive?

The caveat of NPVIC is that no one has to give up those electoral votes until they manage to completely rig the election by gaining support from enough states to represent a majority of the 538 electoral votes. The needed number is 270. With the pledge from Colorado's new governor, Jared Polis, in March 2019, the total of pledged electoral votes stands at 181. Those 181 votes come largely from the Clinton Archipelago states of Vermont, Massachusetts, New York, New Jersey, Rhode Island, Maryland, the District of Columbia, California, Hawaii, and Illinois. New Mexico is on tap to join next. Nevada's Democratic governor recently vetoed that state's attempt to join the NPVIC, releasing a statement that explained, "Once effective, the National Popular Vote Interstate Compact could diminish the role of smaller states like Nevada in national electoral contests and force Nevada's electors to side with whoever wins the nationwide popular vote, rather than the candidate Nevadans choose."

Beyond the constitutional questions raised by this effort, one has to wonder if supporters have truly thought it through. Governor Polis, who some readers may recall joined me for a CNN online series called *Freshman Year* in 2009, is a very progressive Democrat running a state that is controlled by its Blue urban centers. He and I were chosen as freshmen to be featured by CNN because we represented the opposite sides of the freshman class that year.

Try to imagine what would happen if Donald Trump manages to win the popular vote in 2020. How would Polis explain to his liberal voters that NPVIC would theoretically send his state's nine electoral votes to Trump? Though NPVIC is not likely to be in place by 2020, it would be fun to watch the fireworks if voters in places like New York, the District of Columbia, Hawaii, and California were forced to consider the possibility that their states' electoral votes could all go to Donald Trump. There would be an absolute national crisis.

The idea that a state's electoral votes could be pledged to a candidate with very limited support in that state flies in the face of the whole notion of one person/one vote. The system will produce only politicians fighting to win Californian votes. If your state's votes are pledged to the winner of California, you do not have one vote. You have no vote.

The other target of Clinton Archipelago representatives is the Senate, where Democrats argue a profound small-state bias gives an inordinate power to kill legislation supported by popular majorities. In fact, one popular meme after the 2018 midterms was a misleading attempt to combine all Democrat and Republican votes in Senate races across the country to come up with a popular vote total. It went something like this: Senate popular vote—55.4 percent for Democrats, 43 percent for Republicans, but Republicans gain three seats. This messaging was used to argue that Senate representation is inherently unfair and does not represent the will of the people.

What gets lost in the popular vote messaging is the truth. Once again, the biggest state has an outsize influence. California's supermajority Democratic legislature has adopted a jungle primary system that allows the top two vote getters in the primary to face off in the general election regardless of party. This effectively eliminates Republicans from contention in statewide races where the state's densely populated urban counties outvote their rural counterparts. With that one state's massive Democrat advantage, races for U.S. Senate don't often have a Republican challenger in the general election. So the 40 percent of Republicans in California don't even have the option of voting for a Republican on election day. Furthermore, with only one-third of Senate seats up for election in any given year, there are disparities in the number of incumbents from each party. In 2018, Democrats were defending 26 seats. Republicans only had 9. Sure, each race still has two candidates, but many races involving incumbent candidates are lopsided in favor of the incumbent.

The notion that because one party lost an election, they should now eliminate all structural advantages to the other party, while maintaining their own structural advantages (such as proportional representation in the House of Representatives), is anti-American. Our system was created to protect minority voices and viewpoints and to ensure those voices are not drowned out by a large number of votes in a small number of locations.

Restoring Checks and Balances to Prevent Abuse

Even more critical than protecting our diversity of voices is the need to maintain and strengthen traditional checks and balances among the three branches of the federal government and down through the state and local levels. The good news on this front is this: checks and balances work. They do slow things down. They aren't as expedient as putting all the power in one convenient dictator, but they prevent abuse. They create accountability. And most important, they have bipartisan support. But there is a caveat to that support. That support can be conditional upon which party is in power.

Too often the party in power, seeing no immediate benefit in strengthening or protecting those checks on itself, looks the other way when abuse happens. In this case, building bipartisan support for stronger checks and balances is difficult. It's not hard to get support on this issue; it's just hard to get it from both parties simultaneously.

Reining in the power of the executive branch to make law should be the first order of business. For decades, Congress has allowed the executive branch to take on authority not granted in the Constitution. For example, in 1976 Congress passed the National Emergencies Act authorizing presidents to use broad discretion in managing and funding emergencies without congressional approval.

Since then, presidents have invoked that power fifty-eight times. I believe President Trump had the authority to designate the situation on our borders a national emergency, thus enabling him to redirect money to build the wall. I don't think presidents should have that authority. But the fact remains that previous presidents have exercised it with impunity. Therefore, President Trump can also do so. I agree with Representative Mark Meadows of the House Oversight Committee, who tweeted back in March 2019:

> *One thing lost in discussion: the President's executive action on the border is LEGAL, within the law as written. You can argue whether it should be, and if Congress wants to permanently rein in executive power, I'm in. Until then: @POTUS is right to address the border emergency.*

If Congress has a problem with a president exercising that authority, then Congress should by all means check the president's power. Pass legislation to rein in that authority for all presidents and let's strengthen that check and balance. But absent universal action, I can't support a position that suggests that the exercise of discretion over national emergencies is available to some presidents and not to others.

It was telling to me that during that whole debate, we didn't hear Democrats demanding legislation to permanently restrict a president's power to designate national emergencies. Their argument was that President Trump should not wield that power. I don't know if Democrats, who favor a strong central government and lean toward socialism's greater reliance on force to restrict freedom, could ever be persuaded to rein in the executive. But if ever that were going to happen, it would be now, during the Trump presidency. Republicans in the Senate should initiate and vote on such legislation. If it doesn't pass, let Nancy Pelosi and her House majority explain to the public why they wouldn't support strengthening their own check and balance on Donald Trump.

Now is also the best time to shore up oversight authority by passing legislation to give Congress a means of enforcing subpoenas for documents and witness testimony. Relying on the Justice Department to enforce those subpoenas is a mistake. It has not worked. Once again, President Trump's administration is in a position to follow in the footsteps of its predecessor and ignore congressional subpoenas. They can technically ignore document requests, deny access to witnesses, and basically refuse to participate in congressional oversight investigations. Again, they shouldn't have that option. But because Congress allowed other administrations to do so, they have little argument to stop the Trump administration from following suit. If they want to enforce cooperation with their investigations, they need to create laws that apply to Democratic and Republican presidents alike. Responsibility for the failure to enact such measures falls equally to the leadership of both parties. Certainly Speaker Pelosi has shown no interest in permanently recovering power her party long ago ceded to strong executives. But Republican leadership during the Obama administration was equally culpable for their unwillingness to choose this battle.

There is one area in which Congress is threatening to overstep the authority of the checks and balances granted to the body. With a Supreme Court now leaning conservative and with the very real possibility that another liberal justice could be replaced with a conservative appointee, Democrats are seeing the Supreme Court potentially move out of their reach for a generation. They themselves weakened the check on judiciary appointments during the

Obama administration when Senate Majority Leader Harry Reid got rid of the sixty-vote requirement on most nominees in 2013. This paved the way for Republicans to apply that same threshold to Supreme Court nominees.

Now, with the possibility of a third Trump appointment to the Court, Democrats are considering changing the process to favor their party in the short term.

Presidential hopefuls Kamala Harris, Elizabeth Warren, and Kirsten Gillibrand have all acknowledged they would consider sweeping changes to the Supreme Court to offset the conservative majority. Beto O'Rourke and Pete Buttigieg have also signaled possible support for expanding the court to neutralize conservative justices. Warren calls it "depoliticizing" the Supreme Court. Kamala Harris suggested, "We are on the verge of a crisis of confidence in the Supreme Court."

For their part, progressive nonprofit activist groups are all in for packing the courts. Ezra Levin, cofounder of Indivisible, told *Politico*: "Any Democratic presidential candidate who is serious about implementing a progressive agenda has to seriously consider appointing new justices to unpack the courts." Wow. How did the courts get "packed" in the first place? Apparently because the Republican Senate refused to hold a confirmation vote on an Obama appointee (Judge Merrick Garland) in 2016. Advocacy groups like to pretend that Garland was denied the seat. In reality, he was merely denied a vote. To be sure, it was a norm-breaking move for Senate majority leader Mitch McConnell, but not one that changed the balance of power on the Court. Democrats never had the votes to confirm Garland.

The fact is, every Supreme Court justice now sitting on the bench got there through a legitimate confirmation process. To imply that the courts are "packed" and that there is a "crisis of confidence" merely because conservatives hold a slight majority on the Court is a level of hyperbole even Donald Trump can appreciate.

Fortunately, not every Democrat in the Senate is on board with the court-packing plan. Senator Jon Tester told *Politico*, "It's like changing the rules of the Senate. I think it's a mistake. Probably the biggest mistake I ever made was voting on the rule change on judges." I agree with Tester. Anytime we mess with long-standing institutions, we risk undermining our own stability. Changing the process or the size of the Court to suit short-term partisan goals is a bad precedent to set. As this process has already shown, any advantage to one party can eventually be used to favor the other. Better to reach bipartisan consensus on any major structural changes that affect checks and balances between the branches of government.

A check on Congress that could use some shoring up relates to oversight responsibilities. In my book *The Deep State* I wrote extensively about the changes I believe need to be made on that front and the subversive powers that fight against them. But suffice it to say that the boundaries of congressional authority as set in Supreme Court precedent in *Watkins v. U.S.* need to be codified and enforced. The case found that oversight investigations could not have an unlimited scope, but must "be related to and in furtherance of a legitimate task of Congress." That is still a broad mandate to oversee government, but it restricts oversight from interfering in individual lives or private markets.

Congressional oversight, even partisan-driven oversight, can be effective when used to inform legislation and check executive branch expenditures. Using oversight authority in that way helps maintain credibility and improve outcomes. Unfortunately, the oversight function has lost a lot of credibility even just in the short time since I've been gone from Congress. Intelligence Committee chairman Adam Schiff arguably abused his authority by trading on the credibility of his security clearance to spread misinformation. That same Representative Schiff, upon first being appointed to the Intelligence Committee, thought differently of the committee's role.

It's the least partisan and probably the most productive of all the committees on the hill. That's in large part because the meetings are in closed session due to the classified information. There's no grandstanding because there is no one to grandstand to. We get our work done and don't use each issue to bash each other.

A return to those values would certainly help. Schiff's own efforts to politicize the committee, misrepresent classified information, and prejudge the outcome of investigations may have provided some short-term advantages for the 2018 midterms, but the long-term implications weaken his leadership and his committee's credibility. Speaker Pelosi should remove him and replace him with a chairman whom the intelligence community can trust.

I worry that the extreme left and the socialists among us are engaged in a massive power grab, not because we the people have come together to say this is the direction we're trying to go in, but because they don't think the public will defend what we have. What does that mean to people like you and me? We have to defend our rights.

Let the Rule of Law Govern

We also have to defend our laws and our standards. They are under threat—not from those who would destroy them, but from those who would selectively enforce them. We are a nation of laws. But if our laws are not equally applied, they are meaningless. As American citizens, we cannot afford to let emotion drive the enforcement of the rules or the application of our standards.

We cannot tolerate one standard for Hillary Clinton and another for Donald Trump. Too often we are being asked to condemn people for behaviors long tolerated by previous administrations. When we call it out, we hear cries of "Whataboutism"—suggesting that just because it was done by a prior administration, that doesn't make it right. That may be true, but it's important to call out double standards. We should not settle for a nation in which laws and standards apply only when we disagree with the person being accused. That's not the nation we want to live in. We can do better.

As we evaluate the work of Congress, we will get better results if we can learn to look past the narratives we are being fed and instead demand to see the factual and the evidentiary foundations of the work Congress is doing.

Protecting the Bill of Rights

There is no positive path forward without preserving the rights we sometimes take for granted. Americans have always had to vigilantly protect the God-given rights spelled out in the Constitution's Bill of Rights. Despite broad agreement that those rights are inalienable, we don't always agree on how to apply those freedoms. They were hard won, but they can be lost in a single generation.

Our First Amendment rights still come under attack in countless ways—a problem that I have seen escalate since 2016. We face blatant suppression from social media censorship, unwritten restrictions on college campus speech, prohibitions on our ability to finance campaigns, and overly broad definitions of racist, bigoted, or hate speech that encompass the expression of long-standing religious beliefs. In my observation, these attempts to restrict speech are almost always aimed at shutting down political speech. The number of news stories that have been written suggesting that engaging with Trump supporters somehow normalizes abhorrent views is a disappointing narrative coming from the fourth estate.

I have come to appreciate how strong and powerful freedom of speech is, but I'm disheartened by how quickly free speech supporters change position when they encounter someone with whom they disagree. In my experience, the people who preach tolerance the loudest are often the least tolerant. Preserving this fundamental right to free speech is not optional. It is a bulwark of our system. If that means we sometimes have to protect speech with which we disagree, that is the price we pay to live in a free country.

Our Second Amendment rights are perpetually under siege as antigun groups attempt to punish the law-abiding for the sins of criminals. This is an issue near and dear to my own heart.

I didn't grow up with guns. My family didn't hunt. We enjoyed hiking and camping in the outdoors, but my dad was not one to take us hunting. I shot a gun at camp, and I was intrigued by guns, but it wasn't until my own family became the target of a crime that I came to appreciate the right to bear arms.

I was maybe ten years old. My dad was out of town. I was home alone with my mom and brother. The weather was dark and rainy outside; flashes of lightning and rumbling thunder filled the night. It was past my bedtime but I had not yet fallen asleep when I heard the doorbell ring. All the lights in the house were off. I got up to tell my mom someone was at the door. When she saw me, she quickly grabbed me and pulled me into the closet, where we dialed the police. I remember being so scared.

She had gone to the door and had seen a suspicious stranger standing outside the window. She realized we were in a vulnerable situation. We stayed on the phone as police arrived to search our yard and the adjoining open field that dropped down into a steep canyon. The operator was telling my mom that the police were there and not to worry, but I did worry. When they told us it was safe to come out, we went to the front door where a sopping-wet policeman stood. You could see the muddy bootprints of the man prowling around our home. I remember that police officer as clear as day, just leaning down and telling me, "You know what? I'm not going anywhere tonight. I will look after you." He promised me that he would stay on our street all night.

Later in life, when I became more responsible as an adult, I got my own sidearm. I really enjoy shooting for recreation. But given some of the threats directed at my family during my time in office, I felt better knowing we could defend ourselves against an intruder. I feel safer. I sleep better. My wife and I are both concealed-carry permit holders. I know that if, heaven forbid, something like that happened to me now, I could protect myself and my family. So when I see these people up talking about how they want to take away my constitutional right to bear arms, I'm highly offended. Guns aren't for everybody. If someone doesn't want one, they shouldn't get one. But our response to criminal use of guns should not be to restrict them from law-abiding people who just want to protect themselves. I think about these young people—women and men—who want to protect themselves, too.

I also see threats to the Fourth Amendment from unreasonable searches and seizures, particularly in light of the FISA surveillance abuses, but also from standard tools like GPS surveillance. I believe people have a fundamental right to privacy. In today's electronic age, the story of our generation more and more will be about the balance and tug-of-war between security and liberty. I don't trust the federal government. If I'm a law-abiding citizen above suspicion, I have a right to privacy. I also worry about the ways in which our information can be exposed for political purposes. Such concerns were long considered fringe conspiracy theories, but we watched the Obama IRS target conservative groups, asking invasive questions, exposing their donors, singling them out for audits, and in other cases, releasing confidential tax information. These are threats we cannot afford to ignore.

Finally, we need to recognize the value of the Tenth Amendment, which delegates broad powers to states and limits the powers of the federal government. For too long, we've allowed ourselves to lose sight of this important innovation.

Never has there been a better opportunity to restore a more federalist approach to governing than right now. I was hopeful when President Trump was elected that we might see Democrats embrace one of our founders' best ideas. But after eight years of focusing on top-down solutions with President Obama, Democrats had lost a great deal of power in state legislatures. During the Obama presidency, they lost close to one thousand state legislative seats.

But today, after modest gains in statehouses during the midterms, Democrats may be ready to join with Republicans in more measures to empower states. They picked up 323 state legislative seats previously held by Republicans, losing only 100 to Republicans. According to the National Conference of State Legislatures (NCSL), Democrats picked up state control (control of the governorship plus majorities in the House and Senate) in 7 additional states, for a total of 14. In 2018 Democrats also won control of both houses of the state legislature in four additional states and picked up four attorney general seats. Republicans still have the edge, maintaining state control in 22 states and holding majorities in both bodies of eight more. These gains may not make Republicans happy, but they do increase the probability that we can get Democrats on board for greater autonomy, flexibility, and empowerment of states.

The concept of federalism was transformative when the revolutionary idea was put into practice in the earliest days of our republic. The idea that power should be divided and shared, not just horizontally across different branches of the federal government, but vertically from federal to state to local levels, is the component that sets this nation apart from every form of government that came before. It allows a liberal state like Massachusetts to pursue policies right for New England without forcing those policies on rural voters in Oklahoma, enabling each to forge an identity that is unique to the people who live there.

The one-size-fits-all, cookie-cutter approach to federal policy has created a long list of failures. From President George W. Bush's No Child Left Behind to President Barack Obama's

Affordable Care Act, the inflexibility of federal programs has created headaches for local communities. Furthermore, duplicative programs at each level create conflict and waste taxpayer dollars. Why should the EPA and the state environmental agency employ the same expertise and work on the same problems? So much of what is coming down from the federal level could easily be managed at the state level.

Following the 2016 election, we did see some small movement by Democrats at the state level. They seemed mostly focused on pushing back against immigration policies, climate policies, and challenges to the president's travel ban. Some states began pushing marijuana legalization initiatives despite federal law prohibiting the drug. Others, seeing the rightward shift of the Supreme Court, have pushed for extreme abortion policies at the state level, permitting the practice all the way up to the due date.

Notwithstanding these small moves toward federalism, the party's base has increasingly doubled down on the push toward federalism's antithesis. Socialism depends on a strong central government to force people to comply with its high taxes and restrictive mandates. It leaves little room for state-level innovation and customization as socialism's expensive cradle-to-grave social programs gobble up every available dollar. As the Democratic base and its well-funded collection of advocacy nonprofits move further and further to the left, the danger of losing one of our most revolutionary innovations grows.

Fortunately, the threat of a second term for Donald Trump, a conservative Supreme Court, and a U.S. Senate majority that is virtually out of reach for Democrats in 2020 may be enough to nudge members of Congress to try their socialist experiments at the state level. Meanwhile, giving states greater authority to experiment with reducing the costs of delivering Medicaid, embracing health-care innovations, or customizing their own environment regulations could pay huge dividends.

Can there be any question that the United States, functioning under this Constitution, has been the most successful government in recorded history? We already have the solutions. Our fathers paid a heavy price in blood and treasure to leave them for us. We need to build faith in those institutions, not invalidate them.

Our country faces problems and challenges that sometimes seem insurmountable. Sometimes what we see on television or read online makes us lose hope. But we must never forget that the United States is still the greatest country on the face of the planet. We have the right to engage in debate, to practice our faith, to assemble, and to petition our government. We still value and protect minority voices. We have the ability to use states as a laboratory of ideas that tests different approaches to problem solving. All of these innovations came to us through that miraculous document that still governs this nation—the Constitution.

When I was in Congress I had the honor of traveling around the world. No matter where I went, whether in Libya, Pakistan, Vietnam, China, even Papua New Guinea, I encountered men and women who were willing to wear the Stars and Stripes and serve our nation. In the foreign service, the National Guard, the active-duty military, or perhaps one of our intelligence agencies, people were proud to serve. I've always gotten the most hope and promise from ordinary Americans doing extraordinary things. You don't always know when your number will be called or something dramatic will happen, but collectively when those men and women serve around the world representing us, I take a deep breath and I realize that somehow, some way, things will be all right.

You look into the eyes of our kids, and for me into the eyes of my granddaughter, and I really truly am optimistic for the future. Preserving what we have been given will continue to require vigilance. It will require participation. It will require standing up for what we believe in against those who would take away our freedoms and our liberties. We can't let that happen. Politics can be a corrosive business. You can never truly separate corruption from power, but we have a system that helps minimize its impact. There will always be those willing to trade away our long-term foundational institutions in exchange for a short-term power grab. But the answers to our problems today are the same innovations that have kept us prosperous and stable for more than two hundred years.

ACKNOWLEDGMENTS

Do you ever wonder, "How did I get here?" Not the birds-and-the-bees kind of getting here, but where you are right now in life as you read this book.

It strikes me you are peculiar and different from most. You made a purchase to read or listen to a book about the problems and challenges in Washington, D.C. You are among the minority who will invest time, effort, and resources to understand the challenges we face and help to solve them. For that, we should all be thankful. I hope this book has been of value to you.

Life has a funny way of putting us in places we didn't necessarily foresee. Through its unforeseen twists, turns, and choices, life happens to us. Sometimes those twists and turns are for the best. Other times we wonder what possible purpose they could serve. In fact, the problems we face are often painful and distressing.

During the times I endured the hardest of hard, I have come to appreciate how those difficult times mold us, make us stronger, give us character, and hopefully make us more loving and caring. It is those difficult times that can knock us down and beat us up, but it is also during those times we have a choice that can lead us to being better people. Hopefully that is the case.

In my case, the toughest of personal, family, and professional times have shaped my character, perspective, and approach—generally for the better.

I was very blessed to grow up in a loving household with parents whom I adored and who doted on me. They cared for me, nurtured me, let me struggle, and let me have it when I egregiously stepped over the line. Their love for me was unconditional. The opportunities for success and failure were numerous. I am grateful for the life they gave me.

Through my travels and experiences I have increasingly come to realize how good I had it growing up in California, Arizona, and Colorado. I'm grateful for my experiences moving on to college at Brigham Young University in Utah. My dad was able to help me secure an athletic grant-in-aid, which led to a role as the starting placekicker on BYU's nationally ranked football team for two seasons.

From afar it probably appears I had it even easier than I did as a young boy awkwardly transitioning to a geeky teenager and then taking on the responsibilities of a man, a husband, and a father. Yet, no matter how affluent the zip code, divorce and cancer have a way of forcing reality into life typically unimaginable to someone who has not yet come of age.

Perhaps someday I will write a book about those hard, dark, difficult experiences. For now, suffice it to say that I, with the help of a key few and relying upon the very real power of prayer, not only survived some horrific life choices but used them to gain strength. Miraculously those tough, strenuous situations had the power to make me stronger, smarter, more compassionate, and loving. I also came to realize I couldn't do it alone—and I didn't need to.

My life has been shaped for the better by my family. My dad was tough but fair. He was competitive and helped instill that in my core. He opened doors and helped create possibilities. My mom was omnipresent, loving, and caring. Through her early and long battle with breast cancer we experienced the ultimate highs and lows of that battle. But our family grew closer together through the experience. My mom gave me confidence when I was awkward and unsure. She was a mother who loved her son and I knew it. Nothing else mattered.

Both of my parents have passed, but with any success I have, I must acknowledge their positive influence and early formation of principles in my life.

In my youngest years it was my younger brother, Alex, whom I shared life with day to day. We experienced the good and the bad together, and I count on him still today for guidance, love, and perspective. Thank you.

In my twenties Julie came into my life. She doesn't recall the first few times we met, but from day one I was mesmerized and in awe of this angelic person. She is truly the nicest, sweetest, most caring person I have ever met. She made me better in every way. I never could have been able to lead the life I have led without her as my wife, partner, and mother to our kids. As I write this book, we have been married for more than twenty-eight years. I cannot imagine life without her. She is everything to me. Thank you.

Together, Julie and I were blessed with three wonderful children. I was away from home a lot during my time in Congress, but Julie was able to always be the foundation of our home. I am thankful for my family's unwavering support of my political ventures. There is a very real cost to being in the public eye, and yet they have always taken it in stride. Thank you.

Our now adult children are thriving and successfully launching into life in their own directions full of hope and excitement for the future. It is hard to ask for more than that as parents.

Yet, candidly, it is a difficult transition for Julie and me. The reality of an empty nest is more challenging emotionally than I had anticipated. I don't like it, but I wouldn't have it any other way.

We are also blessed to be grandparents. We have one granddaughter and we eagerly await the day we have a few more. We started our family at a young age, so we have been blessed to enjoy playing the role of grandparents at a relatively young age. No way anyone seeing Julie will think she is a grandma.

As I look at our little granddaughter and daydream about the world she will grow up in, it does create cause for concern. Sure, she has wonderful, loving parents, and she is already fortunate being born in the greatest country on the planet. But the issues facing our society and the planet as a whole are deeply concerning. My hope for her future gives me drive, motivation, and inspiration to forge ahead and work to make our country the best it can possibly be.

For more than eight years I was honored to serve as the representative of Utah's 3rd Congressional District after serving as campaign manager and chief of staff to Jon Huntsman Jr., the sixteenth governor of Utah. These were amazing experiences for which I will always be grateful. Thank you.

I am very fortunate to now be affiliated as a contributor with Fox News Networks. I consider it a rare opportunity, and one I am most grateful for. I want to thank Rupert Murdoch and the whole of the Fox News family for allowing me to share my thoughts day after day with such a wide audience. When I first arrived on the scene, I asked them what they wanted from me. They said, "Just you be you. Be authentic and tell us what you really think." What a wonderful directive. Thank you.

Television was a natural fit for me, but writing a book was a new experience. David Larabell and the good folks at Creative Artists Agency (CAA) walked me through the process and bridged me with the best editor in the business, Eric Nelson at Broadside, part of the HarperCollins company.

Eric helped guide me through my first book, *The Deep State*, on its way to becoming a *New York Times* bestselling book. Wow. Not only is Eric an exceptional editor, but he has an uncanny ability to see the big picture. He has helped me focus on the most important experiences that ultimately helped build a compelling book. None of this would have happened without that team. Thank you.

Once again, I've been fortunate on this book to work with David Larabell and Eric Nelson. I enjoyed working with my team to put together the first book, but this book flowed even faster and easier. It has allowed me to share deep concerns and contribute a perspective my experiences have uniquely shaped me to see.

At my side, making it a reality, was Jennifer Scott. From day one of my venture into politics she has been at my side. I cannot even begin to express how impressed I am with her perspective, smarts, tenacity, and grounding in conservative principles. My name is on the front of this book, but Jennifer really made it all come together into something special. From the campaign to the congressional office to my time on television and writing books, Jennifer has been the most effective and critical part of our team, and to me personally. I can't thank her enough. Thank you, Jennifer!

Somehow, some way, the culmination of my experiences brought me to working with Eric, David, Jennifer, and a host of others engaged in the research and writing of this book. I look back at all the things I had to experience before this book could happen. I am grateful for the many people whose support has contributed to my ability to make a cogent case in these pages. It happened and I am most grateful. Thank you.

Whether it is in the pages of this book or in *The Deep State*, whether in the discussions on Fox News or in reflecting back on my time in Congress, the people I bump into have the same questions time and time again: "What can I do? What should I do?"

I wish I had a simple, easy answer to solve all our country's problems and challenges. There is no single, easy three-step answer to untangle our history, unify us, and fix everything.

But I do know this: the United States of America is the greatest country on the face of the planet and somehow, some way, we will

figure it. Yet it takes all of us, in our own way, in our own neighborhoods, to be involved, engaged, and educated on the facts.
This is the miracle of our Constitution. Government is not going
to solve these problems unless we the people demand the change.
Government works for us. At least it is supposed to.

It is my hope that these pages will illuminate the issues and help
you more fully understand the mess that is Washington, D.C. The
mere fact that you are reading or listening to this at the end of the
book gives me hope. Your engagement demonstrates you will be
part of the solution and not part of the problem. For that, I thank
you.

God bless,
Jason Chaffetz

INDEX

ABOUT THE AUTHOR

JASON CHAFFETZ is an American politician and Fox News contributor. He was elected as a U.S. representative from Utah in 2008 after spending sixteen years in the local business community. When he left Congress in 2017, he was the chairman of the United States House Committee on Oversight and Government Reform.